# THE POWER OF

# Soul

# Loving

## A Spiritual Guide to Love and Freedom

R E B E C C A   G A B R I E L L E

**BALBOA.**
PRESS
A DIVISION OF HAY HOUSE

Scripture quotations are taken from The Holy Bible, New International
Version®, NIV® Copyright © 1973, 1978, 1984, 2011 by Biblica,
Inc.® Used by permission. All rights reserved worldwide.

Balboa Press books may be ordered through booksellers or by contacting:

Balboa Press
A Division of Hay House
1663 Liberty Drive
Bloomington, IN 47403
www.balboapress.com.au
1 (877) 407-4847

Because of the dynamic nature of the Internet, any web addresses or links contained in
this book may have changed since publication and may no longer be valid. The views
expressed in this work are solely those of the author and do not necessarily reflect the
views of the publisher, and the publisher hereby disclaims any responsibility for them.

The author of this book does not dispense medical advice or prescribe the use of any
technique as a form of treatment for physical, emotional, or medical problems without the
advice of a physician, either directly or indirectly. The intent of the author is only to offer
information of a general nature to help you in your quest for emotional and spiritual well-
being. In the event you use any of the information in this book for yourself, which is your
constitutional right, the author and the publisher assume no responsibility for your actions.

Any people depicted in stock imagery provided by Getty Images are models,
and such images are being used for illustrative purposes only.
Certain stock imagery © Getty Images.

Print information available on the last page.

ISBN: 978-1-5043-1847-1 (sc)
ISBN: 978-1-5043-1848-8 (e)

Balboa Press rev. date: 09/28/2019

# Contents

*I dedicate this book to my children Johannes, Sasha and Nathan,*
*to my soul friends whom I call my earth angels,*
*and to the awakened and yet to be awakened souls.*
*May the power of soul loving be your inspiration*
*and your reason for being.*

# Acknowledgments

There are innumerable souls who have helped and guided me along my spiritual journey. I am grateful for their wisdom, their personal experiences, and the ways in which their own example is a shining beacon for my souls' journey.

I thank those beautiful wise forerunners of our collective spiritual awakening, who have taught me how to see, feel and sense my spiritual essence, and to recognise that Divine Love is our soul-path and our natural way of being. Thank you to the many spiritual lightworkers who pave the way and give us a language and landscape from which to learn and grow. The following people I consider to be my spiritual mentors, even if they don't know it. They have enriched my life in a way that has changed me forever, and I am eternally grateful. My heart and gratitude go to you all, though I know there are so many more people in my life that have deeply touched my soul and helped me to grow immensely.

Thank you to Louise Hay, Dr Wayne Dyer, Dr Barbara D'Angelis, Doreen Virtue, Radleigh Valentine, Robert Reeves, Robin Sharma, Don Miguel Ruiz, Don Miguel Ruiz Jr, John Holland, James Van Pragh, David Richo, Esther Hicks (Abraham Hicks), Oprah Winfrey, Colette Baron-Reid, Sonja Choquette, Jerry Braza, Paulo Coelho, Heatherash Amara, Ralph Smart, Dan Millman, Marianne Williamson, Caroline Myss, Debra Landwehr, Anoeda Judith, Lao Tzu, Eckhart Tolle, Rumi, Lissa Rankin, Dianne Parker, Linda Thompson, Jeff Olson, Gina Spriggs, and Sandy Howard. These are just a few of the amazing souls who have inspired me through their own teachings and taught me so much more about my own spirituality and the meaning of our soul-journey.

I give my gratitude and thanks to those people who have facilitated the completion of this soul-work, including Anthony Reeder of Life Stories Workshop, who provided me with his wise and useful editorial advice.

To my beautiful soul friends, whom I also call my earth angels – you know who you are. Thank you from the bottom of my heart for being in my life and supporting me, loving me, and for being your beautiful self. Each of you have been a significant part of my life in recent times, and each of you have gifted me with your own wisdom, perspectives and the example of your own life and soul journey. I love you so much. Most of the time you were probably unaware of how your own light and love has been, and continues to be, a gift and a blessing to me. Thank you. May love always be your guide.

I would not be the person I am today if it were not for my wonderful family. I love you all. I am surrounded by people in my life who, in their own way, offer their love and support. We are always gifted by people in our life-path who, by the example and contrast of their own life, can show us other perspectives and ways of being that are valuable to our soul growth.

To me, each and every person I meet is a gift. I see each persons' soul and I am blessed to know you all, to feel your presence in my life, as we travel the path of our soul journey together. The ripples of our life experiences will always have a purpose and be exactly what we need for our spiritual growth and maturity.

*"We are all on a soul journey, living and learning.*
*Even though our experiences*
*and the context of our lives may be different,*
*we share something in common in this life, we are human,*
*and we are Divinely connected."*

*Rebecca Gabrielle*

# Preface

Ever since I was a child, I dreamed of writing a book, which I sensed would be the beginning of a purposeful time in my life marked by personal and spiritual growth. In recent years the desire to write returned to me more strongly, particularly following a significant catalyst and change in my life. It is amazing how challenges in life, particularly the big ones, can stop you in your tracks to claim your attention with the purpose of delivering impactful soul lessons that cannot be ignored.

When life feels tough there is a reason, and there is usually an opportunity to reflect on our choices that have brought us thus far on our soul-journey. How many of us have felt the uprising swell of heart-felt questions that compel us to ask, 'What am I doing here?', 'Why am I experiencing this?', 'What do I want in life?', and 'What is my purpose?' They are significant questions deserving our attention and reflection, however most of us hesitate to stop and look more deeply within for the answers. Why is that? Are we afraid of what we will hear deep within our soul? Are we playing the game of avoidance and denial by allowing the distractions of our life to dominate? Are we afraid of what we will be compelled to do or experience as a result of listening to the truth of our Soul? We can spend a lifetime ducking and weaving if we choose to, however our Soul is persistent and determined that we listen to the call of the Divine that urges us towards greater love.

Life is not about perfection or waiting to have all of our 'ducks lined up in a row'. It's about saying *yes* and embracing those opportunities when they present. I always tell myself, *'every day is a new day'*. Every day brings new opportunities, new possibilities to feel great and do what I love. I don't need the answers to everything. Life is not certain and there are always risks, but in the unknown are beautiful gems waiting to be revealed to us. Life is abundant, and there are innumerable resources and opportunities always within reach. What is available to one person is available to everyone.

So many of us wait for the right timing, the right moment or conditions, or enough money or notoriety before we take action. This is mostly a stalling tactic because we feel nervous or fearful of things not working out. We fear failure, looking stupid, getting hurt, or being rejected. As a result, we often resist the opportunities for love and growth, and we turn them into obstacles of fear that we must suffer and endure. Our life can become a long-term strategy of avoidance that constricts who we are and diminishes our energy. When we say *yes* to life, we expand our energy and attract opportunities that are in alignment with who we are being in that moment.

Prior to writing my book I recognised it was time to give up being fearful and start building the muscle of saying *yes* to life. Life is too short to say 'no'. It will be over before we know it. The key is to be our true self. I realised, *don't try to be like other people; be the real me and do what makes my heart sing.*

The pages in between reflect my inner and outer journey, the soul-calling that I could not ignore, and the enriching experiences that I came to know are my soul lessons and spiritual growth during a time of significant personal transformation. Through these experiences I crawled, cried, walked and ran towards what I learned was the path to greater love. I have opened my heart and my life, and allowed myself to be honest and vulnerable, so I can share with you what I learned about myself on this magnificent spiritual journey we are all living, and yet many of us are hesitant to notice and embrace.

For those of you who have the courage to dive deeper and step into the unknown, join me and see what you can discover for yourself. Perhaps we share something in common. Through my self-discovery and the challenges of mid-life change, I experienced deep heart-felt pain and an unmistakable metamorphosis that transformed me from the inside out. This is the soul growth and wisdom I was ready to embrace. My story is not unique nor is it special. All of us experience life as a valuable testimony to the soul lessons of our physical existence.

I have learned to see the beauty and love within people's soul, which many do not yet see for themselves. I feel people's energy, their life stories, their joy and their sorrows. I also see how so many people are dying a slow spiritual death through fear, a lack of self-love, and a life that is lived unconsciously as they internally suffer from the torment of their mind. What I have come to see is that they have not yet had the experience of Divine Love, and so there is a gap in their soul-growth. The soul knows True Love, and we are all created and seeded by this infinite love and universal connection.

Through my life experiences, I have realised there is no quick fix or fast path to our soul's growth and spiritual maturity. It requires us to do the inner work and to experience the duality of our physical life, so we can have the soul lessons we need to recognise that Divine Love exists within each of us.

Soul transformation is undeniable, though many of us are fearful to let go and allow this natural process to occur. A caterpillar cannot bypass the metamorphosis process to become the beautiful butterfly. We know what happens if we interfere with that process. If we intend to speed up the process of transformation to skip the effort and discomfort that's required for the change, then the butterfly's growth is stunted, and it dies! However, when we trust and let go, we can embrace our soul's growth and be transformed in a way that allows the light and power of the Divine to lift us to greater love.

Many of us may recognise the inner promptings of Spirit, and the urgings of our Soul to awaken from our unconsciousness, and to live as our authentic self. However, fear tends to step in and drown out the call to dive deeper, to discover our own truth and the essence of who we really are. Facing the truth can be very challenging. As we try to protect ourself from inner pain, we can easily ignore the truth, that we have been living a lie. We have buried ourself beneath the pain of past experiences, limiting self-beliefs, and the obligations of our job or family life so that we no longer see our true self. Perhaps we have spent years focusing on the routine and daily distractions of life and indulged in the drama of our family and friends, and the problems of the world, all of which may have led to the neglect of our emotional, mental, spiritual and physical well-being. It's interesting and sad that so many of us choose to stay with the pain and the un-resourceful habits we know because we believe it is easier to do this, rather than face making an uncomfortable change that could lead to amazing creativity, growth and the joy of living a life we love.

It's human nature to fear the unknown and what feels uncertain. What will happen if we discover that our real authentic self is different to the person and life we have been living? Then what? Knowing the truth about ourself means we are faced with the choice of either making a change (which can be frightening in itself) or continue to stay on the same path and get the same results in life. Facing the truth brings us front and centre with our true self and demands our attention and our immediate response.

In the pages of this book, it is in my heart to share with you what I discovered through my own soul-journey. Hopefully this will give light and inspiration for others through their own soul's transformation. It's important to acknowledge that every person is as unique as are the choices we make in our life. We cannot be compared to each other. Every person's journey is exactly as it needs to be for their own soul growth. There are no two people who are the same and therefore no two people with exactly the same life purpose.

As spiritual beings our very essence is always connected with each other and the Universe. There is a powerful pool of knowledge and collective soul experiences from our past lives from which we can draw wisdom, support and nourishment for our soul. Unfortunately, many people live with the illusion that we are alone or separate from each other and this is what causes us to live in fear and pain, and eventually decays our mind, our body and our loving spiritual essence. Living as our authentic self means to be true to our Soul. In spirit we are pure love, and yet most people have forgotten this in their earthly lives.

Living as my true self is living my life with 'spice', with vitality, joy and gratitude. I'm the first to admit that I am a work-in-progress, with many soul lessons I am yet to master. We are all a work-in-progress. Are we willing to embrace the challenges in life, knowing that there are infinite opportunities to learn something wonderful about ourself and how we can grow in Divine Love?

I was given the gift to see and feel into the soul of others. This has enabled me to sense and psychically know where people are on their soul-journey. Since I was a young child, I knew that in some way I wanted to help others see the magnificence I can see in their soul. Our Soul knows Divine Love. My life purpose is to help others reconnect with their Soul, to help them heal so they can see their own truth and come to love who they are, knowing they are unique, and they are perfect as they are. It's my desire to help others to use the power of soul-loving to learn more about how they can live in a way that is the truest version of their self.

When we embrace the Divine Love within, we can create joy that is not dependent upon others or our circumstances. It is Divine Love that radiates from the core of our soul and is expressed through our spiritual connection with Source and with other soul-beings. When we choose to respond to the call of our Soul, and tap into our Divine essence, we can draw on the power of soul-loving to live a life that is a reflection of our true and authentic self.

May the *Power of Soul Loving* ignite within you a desire to live your life with greatness, with spice, and with never-ending love.

Namaste.

Rebecca Gabrielle
Sydney, Australia

www.livingwithspice.com.au
rebecca@livingwithspice.com
PO Box 600, Mosman NSW 2088, Australia

# Introduction

At mid-life I experienced a compelling awakening of my soul that was at last undeniable and led to an irreversible personal transformation. For a long time, I felt plagued by a lot of confusion, inner conflict and guilt for what I was thinking and feeling. I couldn't make sense of the pain and anguish I felt, living as if I was happy and in control on the outside, when on the inside I was depressed and frustrated for not being true to myself. I felt ashamed of my feelings, and I often told myself that I should feel grateful for all that I had in my life and that I should not expect anything more or anything different. I spent a great number of years suppressing my feelings, denying they were important or relevant, and believing that I was not capable of fulfilling any of my dreams.

Marrying at a young age and raising three children were my priority and during these family years I silently put my dreams on hold. However, those inspired dreams and feelings did not leave me. There was a strong pulsing urge in my heart, a calling from deep within my soul that had been there since I was young child. I had always felt a deep knowing and awareness of a higher power and presence far greater than myself. A power that was all-knowing and everywhere at the same time, watching over me, guiding me and protecting me. With this heightened awareness I began to feel a soul-purpose to my life, and I believed that one day this would be revealed to me.

At the age of 16 years, this calling was brought forward to my consciousness during a very personal spiritual encounter. It was an experience that I can only describe as surreal and very intense. I felt a complete disconnect from all time and space, and all physical matter. It was a very different sensory experience I had not felt before. I received messages, or communication, that seemed to completely embrace me or fill my entire being with such intense love that it did not feel humanly possible. There were no words exchanged, and yet the experience left me with this deep inner knowing that I can only describe as a touch from the Divine. From that moment on, I knew my purpose was to help others discover the meaning of Divine Love and how each one of us can make changes to our life that brings us ever closer to this experience.

For many years I ignored this spiritual experience and the soul-sense that I had a purpose to achieve. I had dreams for my life and yet I was accustomed to believing they were unachievable, and I was incapable and unworthy of such dreams. I had settled into telling myself this was as good as it was going to be for the rest of my life.

However, the inner urge became irresistible, calling me to be true to my Soul and honour the person I was meant to be. The feelings grew stronger with each passing year. I knew I was reaching the time in my life to make a change for a new direction; the path that would lead to my transformation and transition toward fulfilling my soul's purpose.

Over time the promptings from Spirit became more urgent and more pronounced. It had been increasing in tempo over a period of a few years, and eventually it led to the frightening and courageous decision to leave all I had known (my marriage and the life I had created up to this time); to step out into the unknown and in some way reconnect with my Soul to reveal my soul- purpose. I had spent years feeling as if I lost my identity and my sense of who I was. It was now time to listen to the calling of my Soul, and to uncover the real me and my reason for being.

There were no guarantees of success, only my huge fear of failure, of rejection by those I loved, and isolation. I was confronted by a whole new landscape that was completely unknown to me. I stepped into an abyss, with my Higher Self telling me it was time to listen and take action; to trust and have faith in the spiritual guidance I was receiving. I was afraid and yet I also felt a calm and the presence of the Divine guiding my steps. It was not until much later that I realised I was being called to follow my Soul's path toward True Love.

In the pages of "The Power of Soul Loving" I share my personal experiences of what happened when I acknowledged and accepted the call of my Soul to change the course of my life. If I had chosen to ignore it, I knew I would be destined to remain disconnected from my real self and miss the opportunity of living my soul's true purpose. I realised it was time to make a choice to live a life for love.

As human beings we are driven by the deep innate desire to experience greater love in our life, whether it is to *feel* more love, *give* more love or recognise we are worthy to *receive* more love. So often we look in all the wrong places to find this experience of love and acceptance, and so it continues to elude us as if some malicious game is being played by the Universe to keep love from our reach. Our ego mind feeds us with ideas that distract and separates us from the path to Divine Love, a love that already exists within our soul-being.

When I stepped on to an unknown path, I began an enriching journey deep within my soul, that stretched me at times beyond any previous pain barrier. My heart felt deeply worked over, and my mind fought hard to keep me in the same place of doubt and fear, with a consistently limited concept of myself. It was the most scary and challenging time of my life, and yet when I connected to my Soul and noticed the spiritual support around me, I discovered an inner strength to keep going and to stay committed to my Soul's journey.

This has been my spiritual pilgrimage; my Soul's journey back home to True Love; a journey that will continue beyond the death of my physical body. During these transformative mid-life years, I felt like I was going through an emotional meat grinder and that all of my previous beliefs and habits were being pulled apart and ground down into digestible pieces. It occurred to me that this is what it feels like to be fully conscious and awake, when we feel the raw pain of being exercised as we grow and spiritually mature.

We are all on a soul-journey, yet not all of us heed the call of our Soul to step out into the unknown and take the risk to experience the most amazing spiritual growth and upliftment in our life. It's not a journey for the faint-hearted. It takes determination and courage, even after you have cried all the tears you thought you had left in you. It takes a willingness to feel heart-felt pain, fear that threatens to suck the life out of you, and debilitating doubts that linger in your heart and mind for days when you long for them to leave you in peace.

Despite the worst days and the miserable challenges, the rewards eventually sprout forth from the self-imposed darkness. Following the growing pains of transformation and a new birth, the most amazing feelings of enlightenment, freedom, grounded certainty and a deep connection with my Soul began to settle within me. I felt connected with Source (the Divine, God, the Universe), as if I was returning home to something that felt so familiar and peaceful. I had a new level of spiritual knowing and ease in my soul-being. I began to unfurl, to release my anger, my pain, my fear and my desire to control all the circumstances and people in my life. There was a new calm and a willingness to trust and allow the Divine to guide and support me, like a soft gentle breeze. Today, my old ways of thinking and believing are occasionally triggered and come back to visit me; however, they remind me of how far I have come. My renewed commitment for Love in my life has helped me to grow and become spiritually mature. Once we embark on a spiritual journey, it cannot be undone. What we learn along the way, we cannot unlearn.

Our Soul's path toward greater love is an experience of inner spiritual expansion, beyond our physical confines. The unconditional love that we are capable of experiencing every day is more than enough to brighten our darkest days and longest nights. It envelopes our being in a way that deeply nourishes our Soul and expands our sense of connectedness to the Universe. If we are willing to respond to the call of our Soul, we can be certain we are on the path to True Love in our life. This Love brings a deep soulful joy, peace in our heart and mind, and a connection to our soul-purpose.

Many people trudge through their life feeling defeated and unconscious of their spiritual nature and Divine power. They become disconnected and out of tune with their Soul (or Higher Self), and so they don't hear the voice of their inner being. For some, it may take a significant event in life to shake them up and get their attention. For others the call is like a constant drip that taps at their heart and mind until the tapping can no longer be ignored or tolerated. No matter how our soul seeks to get our attention, our Divine nature is urging each one of us to listen and to accept the call to transform our spiritual self and follow the path to True Love. The call for transformation towards Love is always our choice.

Our Soul is a part of, and at one, with Source (Divine Love) and is therefore connected with all other souls and the spiritual realm. When we refer to someone as being an 'old soul', it is usually because we recognise they have a deeper wisdom that seems to reveal itself with ease and demonstrates a greater sense of knowing. Over many lifetimes we gather more wisdom as our soul matures, and with each life we have more opportunities to learn spiritual lessons we have not yet mastered. Our spiritual self knows that home is where True Love is, and is always drawing us closer to that experience. We have only to tune in to our heart and soul and recognise that Divine Love has always been there, always within our reach.

Each person's soul-journey is unique, and we all respond to our circumstances and inner challenges differently. The choices we make along the way determine our soul growth and our measure of personal transformation. When we are willing to step out of our comfort zone, trust our Higher Self and let go of our fears, we can experience the transformative power of Divine Love within. As we are willing to go deeper, our energy uplifts and reveals more of this Love in our life.

There is no doubt that for true transformation to take place in our life, we must be willing to fight the good fight. To stand up and face our fears, and to take action in ways we have not done before. It took me a long time to live in a way that was not just surviving but moving towards thriving. I needed to learn how to nurture, nourish and give myself love. I have always been very adept at giving love to others, but it was an unfamiliar concept to give love to myself. I didn't even know what that meant or how to even start. I could *think* about it and *talk* about it, but I didn't know how to *do* it or know how to *feel* it in the depth of my being.

Living with love for myself every day is an ongoing process and practice in my life, and one that I invite everyone to live consciously every day. For all the men and women who live with self-doubt and a lack of self-love, please know that it is possible; it's our Divine nature. Every day I keep reminding myself, especially when I stumble, that walking the path to True Love happens one step at a time, and through the actions we take and the willingness to live from the heart. Have no other expectations other than the knowledge that Love is always there and always possible. You are never separate from Divine Love.

"The Power of Soul Loving" is not a mandate about how to live, or a documentary on what is right or wrong, because this is irrelevant on our spiritual journey. All of our experiences are valid and necessary for our soul's growth. They are there to teach us and assist us as we journey towards True Love. As human beings we are as similar to each other as we are different. The landscape of our lives may vastly differ, yet our spiritual nature remains common to all human beings. Everyone experiences soul lessons, despite our lifetime differences, and regardless of how we manifest them. The choice is always our own to make. "The Power of Soul Loving" invites you to walk with me along the path to True Love.

# *Living a Soulful Life*

When I responded to the call to live a soulful-life I knew I was stepping onto a path of new beginnings that would open a world to me that I had not yet discovered. I welcomed the opportunity to explore and go deeper within, however I was at the same time fearful and ignorant of what would be revealed to me. The soul's journey is one that moves us toward greater Love, Divine Love. However, to experience the rewards of greater love and wisdom, we must pass through challenges and soul lessons that enable us to strip away what is blocking the truth of our authentic spiritual being.

When we believe in the truth of what our heart and soul reveals, we are ready for this spiritual journey. We can sense a strong pull in our soul to release mental, emotional and physical restraints and move towards what feels lighter. We are driven by curiosity as well as a desire for something more. There is an intense excitement and trepidation, as we realise there is much we don't know or understand, and so our need for certainty can awaken our fears. We begin the journey with the opposing tension of desiring fulfilment and growth, and fearing change and being exposed at our core.

Our experience of 'love' is usually tainted by the world's conditions and expectations, clouding and limiting our view of a vast spiritual landscape that can open vistas of the Divine realm should we choose to see and experience more. It's a spiritual journey of soul growth and expansion, of being willing to live beyond our fears and the walls we build around our heart and soul. When we experience enough pain or isolation in our life, we often come to a point of desperation to let go of all that holds us as a prisoner within. In that moment of release, the spark of the Divine touches our soul and we experience the truth of Divine love.

Many of us may not have experienced True love and yet, seeded within every soul, is this longing and desire to want more love, to feel and experience a love that has no bounds or conditions. A love that knows the depth of our soul and the truth of our being. We are designed to innately move towards this truth and return to our spiritual home of Divine Love.

## What is True Love?

True Love is not something we attain, it is how we are 'being'. Regardless of our experiences, culture, society, the landscape and context in which we are living, every person has an innate desire to experience 'True Love' and 'be' one with Divine Love. When we are able to live with love and compassion for ourself and for others, we recognise we are all connected. True Love has no room for competition, comparison, fear or the concept that we are separate from others. Yet, to learn this we must experience the contrasts of our physical life through the joyful experiences, pain and sorrow, fear, self-doubt, disappointments, and our achievements.

The soul-growth we experience is a result of the life lessons we choose to embrace. We enter this world having already experienced previous soul lessons from earlier lifetimes. With each lifetime we are gifted with different landscapes (people, places, circumstances) to continue our soul-growth. Through each life we encounter various challenges and experiences that provide us with further opportunities to learn and grow in areas we are yet to master and integrate into our soul-being. Our physical life is the vehicle and landscape for our growth, and our soul-path is the journey, as we move from separation to communion with Divine Love.

To grasp a fuller meaning of what True Love is, it's helpful to understand the different kinds of love we experience as human beings. These are known as *Eros, Philos* and *Agape* love. Eros is the love we experience and share with another person. Our focus is on experiencing this loving connection with another soul-being. *Philos* is an expansion of this and includes a more general unconditional love of the people we encounter in our soul-life, such as the love of our family and friends.

*Agape* is the fullness of Divine Love and a combination of both *eros* and *philos*. It is more expanded and includes the complete and unconditional love of oneself and the Universe (all living beings and nature). It is a love that permeates the way we see, hear, feel, sense and experience our life, both in the spiritual and physical manifestation. As we experience *Agape* love, the more we can live our life with unconditional love for ourself and others.

Life offers us a multitude of opportunities to learn about love, including the difference between conditional and unconditional love. Deep down we want to experience great love in our life, and yet often we struggle to know what great love looks and feels like. Unhappy experiences in love can leave us feeling pain and hurt, which can leave us feeling vulnerable and confused about what *is* 'great' love and whether that is possible to achieve.

## Great Love leads to Awesome Loving

Great love is when you can first love yourself with compassion, acceptance, and a sense of humour. It's when you can embrace your quirkiness and your imperfections, as well as your strengths, talents and abilities. Great love is when you choose to nurture and nourish your body, so that it can provide you with health and longevity, and a means of giving and receiving love with others. Great love is when you speak and think kindly about yourself, without judgment or self-doubt. It's when you honour your truth, values and your own measure of worth. It's when you forgive yourself with gratitude, knowing that life experiences provide you with golden feedback for your soul's growth and wisdom.

Great love is living your dreams, giving power and a voice to your Soul so that it inspires and moves you toward spiritual growth. Great love is loving so deeply and completely that your heart, mind and body are in synergy. Then, one day you understand that great love for yourself transcends the idea that you are separate from others and leads you towards experiencing awesome loving for another. The fullness of Divine Love within you expands so intensely that your soul radiates love to others, nature and all sentient beings. From this experience you realise you have so much love for yourself that you are ready to share that love with another. To experience awesome love in your life, you must start with great love for yourself. Then, as if by magic, through the Law of Attraction, you will see, feel and know the wonder of True Love that always surrounds you.

The path to great love is paved by experiences that are joyous, spiritually uplifting and satisfying to the soul. However, we also need the contrasts of what is challenging, painful and stretching. It's about diving deeper to understand our true essence, how we are unique, and at the same time universally connected to all other beings and to Source.

Our lived experience in the physical realm helps us to understand love and our spirituality. When we ground ourself and become connected and rooted to Mother Nature, we connect with Spirit in a way that facilitates our understanding of love through our physical senses and our corporeal being. Through nature we connect with Divine Love that gives life to all living things and permeates all aspects of our physical and spiritual senses. Our physical life has huge value in helping us to understand the full expression of Divine Love, and thus becomes an expression of our soul's spirituality.

The contrasts of our physical life assist us to understand what experiences feed our soul and which ones drain our vital spiritual energy. Through the diversity of our life's experiences we can choose to rise up to see a broader view and higher perspective, as if standing on the top of a mountain looking down on a rich landscape that is deep, varied, beautiful and treacherous. When we are able to see beyond ourself, we can recognise our connection to *all that is*, and that separation never truly exists.

In life we can experience a myriad of physical trials, and discover the multitude of inner landscapes of our soul, all of which form the growth and diversity of our spirituality. On our soul journey we experience life through our physical senses of the mind, emotions and our body. Our physicality helps us to connect with our spirituality and is a path that enables us to move towards Divine Love.

Our Soul's maturity is reliant upon our choice to make changes that will nurture our growth. It cannot occur by thinking about it or wishing for better circumstances. We must be willing to make changes and do things differently, to be open to the idea that we can experience even greater joy, happiness, wisdom and love in our life. The choice is always ours, to transform to a new way of being, thinking and believing, or to stay where we find ourself today. Certainly, we believe there is a risk to change, and we can fear that the actions we take will not work out as we hope or imagine. There is the risk of rejection, and fear of losing something we value. Yet, often the risk is what we make up in our mind, and what we tell ourself to be true, rather than what we know to be true from our Higher Self.

There have been many times I have progressed through cycles of pain and growth in my life. When I fall to a low point with feelings of self-doubt, despondency and low worth, I notice I have once again allowed myself to make others my focus and to be distracted from my soul-path. I have repeated an old pattern of seeking happiness and a sense of love and purpose from other people. Each time my spirit guides show me this will only create more pain and is not a path that will sustain me or take me to where my soul can grow and thrive.

Allowing ourself to be imprisoned by our fear creates pain and illusion that colours our perspective and causes us to make assumptions that are deceptive and destructive. As a result, we can unconsciously live in a way that is the opposite of our heart and soul's intention. Habitual patterns of fear-based thinking resists love and joy in our life. Love and fear cannot co-exist. Where there is fear, there can be little or no room for love. If we focus on obtaining love from outside of ourself, fear can only grow from the belief that True (Divine) Love does not already exist within. However, if we learn to accept the existence of fear, we can learn to recognise and appreciate the experience of True Love and joy. The dualities and contrasts are the valuable lessons that enable us to learn and grow in spiritual wisdom.

To experience True Love means we must first give love to ourself and have respect for our being, so that we can know what it is to live authentically as our true self and be aligned with the love and energy of the Divine. Only then can we 'be' that love. Our loving energy enables us to give and receive with wisdom, clarity and a deeper awareness of our connection with the Divine (God, Source, the Universe).

## The Soul's Journey

How many of us see life as a time-line that starts at birth and ends at death? All that is between is seen as a series of events, joys and sorrows, milestones of achievement as well as those memorable points along the way where we have fallen short of hitting the mark. Life can be perceived as nothing more than a linear timeline counting down the years, spanning across the phases of our physical growth. Yet there is so much more to our being than just our physical existence from birth to death.

In some of those significant moments in our life we remember that perhaps there is more to our sense of who we are in the physical realm. It may be when we have experienced a triumphant moment and our spirit or soul feels lifted high, inspired by our own potential and beauty. Or we may be compelled to question our purpose when we have experienced deep sorrow, change that rocks our sense of certainty and what we believe to be true from our experience of reality. It's when we have that moment of realization that perhaps there is more to our routine life, a depth we are yet to discover, meaning that lies within what we have yet to tap into. When life experiences touch us in a way that snaps us out of our unconscious living, a chord is struck in our heart to awaken our Soul and remind us that there is a reason why we are here.

The moment of awakening can feel like a whisper in our Soul or a thunderous storm that comes crashing into our life. Either way, it's the call of our Soul, beckoning us to come home, to draw closer to our true self and our Divine nature. Since many of us live noisy and complicated lives we can often miss that beautiful call, like a sparrow's early morning song that is soft, gentle and yet unmistakably speaking to our heart.

As human beings, we are accustomed to experiencing our world and our reality from a very physical and tangible perspective, structured and ordered by space and time, large and demanding of our attention. We can see the world as a logical sequence of events where one experience or event leads to the next, and to the next, until we have the outcome we want, or not. We come to expect certain results or situations based on our analysis and deductions and when they don't come forth in the way we hope, we can easily feel disappointed with the realization that our efforts are thwarted. It's a painful and limiting way to live and experience our version of reality.

Soul-living goes beyond what we immediately see and experience in our physical world. When we realise that the very essence of our being is not defined by our earthly reality of time and the experience of our five senses of sight, smell, hearing, taste, and touch, we begin to move towards living a soul-life that is more reflective of our true nature and potential.

Our soul-journey is a reflection of our spiritual growth in love and wisdom, across the ages. Through different lifetime experiences we are provided opportunities to learn how to grow in understanding and wisdom, always leading us closer to what it is to *be* True Love and *give* love. This is our soul-purpose, and through our life experiences, our personalities, our circumstances, and the people that cross our path, we are given lessons to stretch and grow us. The choice is ours as to how we respond. The purpose of our life is not to count the years away and measure our experiences in terms of time, but rather in lessons learned and the wisdom we have attained. As we progress through our life our soul evolves and takes shape, growing and expanding in awareness and in love. There are times the lessons need to be repeated, with different people and circumstances, presented to us in different ways and at different moments during our life on earth.

If we see life only through the eyes of time, it can be easy to feel frustrated, since we tend to measure our progress and success in terms of how long it takes to achieve our goals and our dreams. Our soul-life is more than a measure of time. It is a combination of our experiences and growth, and of the essence within us that is seeking to understand, to be and know more of love that is waiting to be expressed. The challenge for anyone is to actually see our true Divine nature and realise how we are not limited in any way. In this earthly life our physical body and existence provides us structure and context in which to learn and grow, but it is not a reflection of our true spiritual being. We are expansive universal beings that are both past, present and future essences of ourself in the same moment.

The key to living a soul-life is realizing our enormous potential. Our true limitless self is not out of reach, though many people are still yet to see their own Divine magnificence. There are moments when we may recognise sparks of our own Divine magnificence, or we may notice the unmistakable glow of someone else's soul beauty shining from within. Or there may have been moments where we feel we have witnessed the intervention of the angels, sensing something amazing and almost indescribable, as it deeply touches our heart and soul.

Do you remember a moment when you have seen something simply so beautiful it has taken your breath away? Such an experience does not need to be large scale. It may simply be noticing the beauty of a child's imagination and innocence at play, or it can be the awareness of the beauty of rain, the unconditional love of your pet, the pleasure of tasting nature's incredible food, or something in nature's beauty that has filled you with love and you don't even know how or why. Immersing into a well of gratitude for what exists within our reality is how we experience the Divine both within and all around us.

The Divine love within connects us to the Divine love in others, nature and the Universe; souls connecting with souls; pure love reaching out and touching us all. Words are limiting, but we know what it *feels* like when we experience those special moments, no matter how insignificant they may seem at the time. When it happens there is a knowing that resonates deep inside and quite simply, makes us feel so good. If you have felt like this before, and the moments are occasional or fleeting, don't you want more of these moments? Is there not something there that sparks our human curiosity to want to know and experience more of this Divine wonder?

To consciously live from our soul-being, we need to become the observer of our life, aware and in tune with our internal radar or intuition. As we release and relax into 'being' rather than thinking or rationalizing our experiences, we become more sensitive to the deeper meaning of what we sense at a soul level. When we connect or resonate at the same vibration or frequency of another person (including animals), we understand where they are coming from. There is an inner knowing or awareness that helps us to understand the person's energy or intention. When we are open to connecting energetically with others, we are in the space to love from our heart and soul and accept all that is. From here the seeds of self-love and compassion are planted in good soil and wait to be nurtured so they can grow into the full magnificence of our soul-potential.

When we choose to live a 'soul-life', we are choosing to be open and learn to live in a way that is not dominated by fear, but instead is inspired by a loving purpose that is connected to God (Source) and reflective of Divine love. With increasing awareness of our own soul and how we are living in our current lifetime, there is an opportunity to tap into how we can become our greatest version. The *way* is always through love, and acceptance of our true self. Love is not about reaching perfection nor is it about our misguided intentions to receive love for our own gain. True love is birthed from a deeper recognition that we are all created from the one Divine Source, so we are never missing or lacking in anything other than what we believe and perceive as our own truth. As we recognise we are not separate from others, and we water the seeds of love and kindness within, those seeds of love grow and mature, and in time our soul shines more brightly and is ready to bear fruit through contribution to others.

*"Watering the seed of loving-kindness in ourselves and others is a way to cultivate love and peace in our lives". (Jerry Braza)*

True Love is always expanding. Living a life with deeper awareness of your soul-journey will lead you to the question of 'what is my purpose in life'? Or more poignantly, 'what is my soul-purpose in this lifetime?' Before we enter each lifetime we make a contract with ourself and our spiritual guides to agree on what people and experiences we will need that will most serve our soul-journey and provide us with the landscape, context and lessons to facilitate our growth in love, wisdom and understanding. As we enter each lifetime we bring with us the accumulation of what we have learned in previous lives, shaped by our experiences, pleasant and unpleasant, and the energy of unresolved lessons. Our soul-purpose is to work through those lessons we have yet to master, and move toward spiritual growth, understanding and freedom. In essence, during our lifetime we learn to love more deeply so that we become more aligned with our true Divine and spiritual nature.

However, as we move along the path of the soul-journey we discover it is not all a bed of roses. Our energy and vibration fluctuate as we slip in and out of alignment with the experience of living and being True Love. As human beings we are prone to the dualities and contrasts of living a physical life. There are many times we forget our soul-purpose and we sink to a level of disconnection and separation where we feel and believe we are alone. How many times can you remember feeling very low and believing that no-one else is experiencing what you are experiencing, or having the same thoughts and feelings as you? We can be very adept at berating our own sense of self-worth and value. It can be easy to veer from the path of True Love and become disoriented. When we become confused, we lose sight of our true self, and we fall into the mental trap of isolating ourself and believing we are not good enough or worthy of love.

The truth is, you are never alone, unless of course you believe that. As we grow in love, wisdom and understanding, our very sense of self and connection with others expands. It is not possible to grow in love and be separated from other souls or the Source of pure love.

*When you turn on the light in a darkened room, the dark ceases to exist.*

We are all souls experiencing similar soul lessons for the purpose of ultimately growing in love, wisdom and understanding. As you become more consciously aware in your life, you will notice that the people who surround you are exactly who you need at the time. If you choose to see your life through the eyes and heart of love, you will see them as your mentors, helpers, and guides to light your way. It may not always feel comfortable, and at times the challenges and inner struggles we experience are there to stretch us and reflect our shadow side to mirror where we need to work on ourself. All of our experiences are brought into our reality as a result of our energetic vibration. What we believe to be true, where we choose to focus our attention and how much effort we apply in our life, will create an energy that will attract a certain outcome. The beauty is knowing that our results, or what we experience, is the feedback to help us see more clearly what we are yet to learn and understand about ourself and about Divine love. Everything is there to help us become more aligned with the path to Divine love, if we choose to let go of control and be open to the soul- journey.

Our soul-journey is simply all that we experience mentally, physically, emotionally, and spiritually. What we learn along the way becomes the lessons of our soul-journey. Once lessons have been learned and integrated, and we experience a soul-transformation, we do not need to repeat them. We may be tested to see if our understanding and commitment to the path of love is for real, and that transformation is actually completed. When the learning is done, we can move on.

As we move through our soul-journey, the key is to embrace the challenges, the learning and growth opportunities, and to discover our own soul-purpose in this life. What's important to realise is that we are not here to live another person's soul-journey or life purpose. We are here firstly for our own soul growth, and this is the number one priority.

We can recognise when we have veered from our own soul-path when we have become attached to another person or situation in our life. Whenever we make our purpose about someone else and we find that our sense of joy and meaning is tied to another person's actions, thoughts or intentions, then we have become misaligned with our own spiritual path. Adopting someone else or something else as our complete point of focus is actually indicating we are attempting to fulfil a need of our own, to fill a void, to feel needed, or to feel approved of in life. You are not fulfilling your soul-purpose if you are piggy-backing the life-path of someone else. If you are feeling regular bouts of anxiety, dis-ease, anxiety, doubt and confusion, then these are indicators that you are off track. It's always a good measure to check in with your emotions, and to listen to what your body is telling you. Signs of stress, tension or poor health when you are focused on someone or something else other than your own soul-journey is a red flag for your attention.

Along the way, there will be times when people enter our life and we experience the immediate benefit of their presence. It can be for a short time or it may be for the long duration. They will likely match our vibration in an unmistakable way, as we sense their energy resonate with our own, and so there is a feeling of alignment. It may be that we share the same values, or that we connect mentally, emotionally, physically and spiritually. The magic of the meeting is that we can sense an ability to 'read' each other or speak each other's language with ease. The purpose of the meeting is to mutually assist each other with soul growth, whether it's for a moment, a few days, weeks or years. When we connect with someone for the longer term it's often for the purpose of long-term soul growth. These relationships are often termed soul-mate relationships and can be between any gender, regardless of age, race, background, religion etc. They are relationships with a spiritual connection to facilitate soul-learning. Some soul-mates become partners due to the close intimate communication and connection, but this is not always the case, nor is it necessary. The purpose of a soul-mate, is to assist and support the other person's soul growth.

Unlike popular belief, soul-mates are not limited to an intimate heterosexual relationship. A soul-mate relationship can occur between a parent and child, between two same-sex friends, or between a male and female in a partnership. When soul-mates show up in a male-female partnership the connection is often a very intimate and expressed as a strong physical bond. The important thing to remember is that this kind of relationship exists to firstly assist each other's soul growth and the path towards greater Love.

It's a blessing when we recognise our soul friends and the mutual gift of supporting each other's soul journey. However, it's important to remember we are only ever responsible for our own soul growth and our soul-purpose in this life. We cannot live for someone else or do the growing that they require on their soul journey. To attempt to do so is a selfish act, as it robs them of the opportunity to learn and grow from their own initiative. As any teacher will advise, you can guide, support, and shine a light, but we cannot do the learning or make the choices for someone else. Through our own life experiences, with the challenges, struggles, joys and soul connections we encounter, we can come to know ourself more deeply and the more direct way to Divine Love.

Learning to raise our vibration and conscious awareness will help us to be more in tune with our spiritual essence and the truth of our spiritual nature. As we learn the lessons of Love, we feel drawn more closely to the Divine and the experience of 'coming home'. Our journey towards True Love is greatly assisted when we master deep listening, stillness of the mind, a healthy body, and an open heart. When we are tuned into the present moment of being, then we may more aptly hear the call of our Soul.

# 2

## The Call of My Soul

Our soul is the spiritual essence of our being (our Higher Self) that knows the depth and expansion of Divine love and our oneness with all that is. On this physical plane our soul is constantly communicating with us, guiding us through our physical experiences, towards the path of True Love. However, we are so attuned to the physical realm that we are often not listening at a deeper spiritual level. Our constant state of busyness and mind chatter keeps us distracted and energetically focused at a lower level of vibration, so we miss hearing our soul whisper to us the guidance and wisdom we seek.

The moment we hear the call of our soul is the moment we awaken from our unconscious slumber. The call may be recognizable as the whisper of our inner voice, the nudging of our conscience or the unmistakable gut feeling that persists and won't go away. Sometimes the call of our soul will sound like a background noise that reminds us to pay attention to something important, or it could feel like a familiar friend who has just slipped into the party unannounced. Over the longer period of time, it's likely the call of your soul has been subtle, like the drip feed of a slow and steady percolator brewing with intensity.

Unfortunately, we don't often notice the subtle calls of our soul, because we are so focused on the egoic mind that demands our immediate attention to meet its need to be heard. The chattering mind fills the spaces of our heart and soul so that we become numb, deaf, unconscious. If we have been paying attention, we will have that sense of knowing there is something important to which we need to give our time and energy. Thankfully Spirit has a way of persisting to ensure we are listening. If we refuse to heed the call with our acts of denial, avoidance, and fear-based habits, then our Soul will begin to increase the intensity of the call.

How often have you felt an unease about a decision, and yet you have taken action against your own gut feelings or intuition? Hindsight is a wonderful thing however it cannot change what is done. We often recognise in hindsight that paying attention to our intuition would have better served us. If we have not been paying attention to the subtle signs, we may experience a more confronting event or wake-up call, which can manifest as illness, an accident, recurring poor health or any other unresolved conflicts in our relationships, finances, and in our career. When we hear ourselves complaining, then we have slipped into unconsciousness and our mind has us believing we are a victim to the world's harmful intentions.

The call of our Soul seeks to gain our attention so that we remain on the path of True Love. The intention is always to shine a light to help us get back on track, or to encourage, support and guide us as we continue to grow in love, wisdom and understanding. We are all experiencing a physical life for the purpose of soul-growth, so we can fulfil our soul-purpose in this lifetime.

Throughout my life I felt the presence of God and of Spirit, and it was always an experience of loving guidance and support. I remember as a child feeling the loving presence of God's angels. We all have guardian angels and they serve us by providing the spiritual nudges that we may experience as gut feelings, a knowing or an intuition. I can recall countless times I sensed God's presence (or the Holy Spirit). Sometimes it was more feeling or sense about a person, a situation or a choice I needed to make. At other times the angels would provide a bigger nudge to get my attention, either through an experience or an earthly sign that I could understand. I have experienced their whispers in my ears, signs through animals and nature, and different incidents such as the time when they prevented our family car from sliding over a cliff.

God, our angels and spirit guides are always with us, and yet we may not be consciously aware of their presence in our life. Our willingness and openness to acknowledge our spirituality is a positive step towards being receptive to God's communication with us. As spiritual beings living a physical experience we can often disconnect from our spiritual essence. Our physical life draws us into experiencing our world and our life through our physical senses, and so it feels familiar to relate to our life in a physical, tangible and measured way. When we become so focused on this part of our being, we can easily close off our conscious awareness of our spiritual nature. This is why we can become stuck in habits that don't serve us in our life. When we relate to our life and sense of purpose only through our physical world, we cut ourselves off from the spiritual guidance we regularly receive that is the true path to love.

Our soul is that very core part of our being that connects us to our true spirituality. This is our connection to the Divine. It's perhaps not the best way to even describe our true nature, because referring to a 'connection' also implies we are separate. However, we are truly not separate from the Divine. As humans we have a tendency to believe we are separate from each other, from nature and from God, and so we create the experience of feeling dis-connected. This is an illusion, nevertheless it is how we perceive our reality.

Divine nudges can occur daily however we may only notice these signs if we are open and receptive to receiving the spiritual guidance being offered to us. The easiest way to be in-tune with our Soul and the spiritual realm is to firstly create inner stillness. Consciously making the choice to tune into this higher frequency will certainly enable us to hear the call of our Soul, as well as open the channels of communication with God, our Angels and our Spiritual Guides. Many of us are not in-tune with this higher frequency because of our intense focus on the physical realm, our lack of conscious awareness, and the attention we give to our mind chatter.

If we have become so accustomed to living this way over a longer period of time our numbness or unconscious awareness can lead to a more abrupt wake-up call. This can occur at any time in our life. It may be more noticeable when we reach certain milestones during our life, such as when our children leave home, when we achieve some success in our career or with a personal project, when we approach mid-life, or perhaps when we experience a loss of a relationship, illness or a significant financial challenge.

Mid-life can be a natural time to question our choices from our younger years and to review the path we have been travelling. Entering mid-life was my wake-up call. It has been, and still is, an incredible time of spiritual and emotional growth.

As we enter mid-life, or experience some form of transformation, we may be consciously aware of the transition approaching, or it can come upon us suddenly. At any moment we can choose to embrace it with curiosity or with trepidation. The onset of change may feel exciting and liberating, or it may feel incredibly challenging and even frightening. When it does happen, we can choose to either notice the change and pay attention to the signs that a new season is approaching; or we may choose to ignore the onset of change for fear of having to wake up from our unconsciousness and accept the possibility of being uncomfortable at the very least.

The call of my Soul began as a whisper many years ago. I heard the calling, felt the nudges and for a long time I squirmed and struggled to understand what it meant. It began as a feeling of discomfort and feeling out of alignment with myself. I noticed that I was increasingly becoming unhappy and there was a growing sense of unfulfillment and disconnection from my true self over several years. The more I resisted listening to my inner truth and justifying my discomfort with rationalizations and externalizing the causes, the more I sank into depression and I began to manifest dis-ease in my life. I felt incredible conflict within which I struggled to understand. I noticed that my inner light was dimming rapidly. I began to put on weight and my usually sunny disposition became dull.

Coming out of my state of unconsciousness was actually very painful at times, as much as it was liberating, exciting, and strengthening. I have often noticed that human beings are creatures of habit and quite predictable. It's when the pain inside increases so much and we feel like we are drowning, that we finally make the decision that we don't want to put up with the discomfort any longer. Curious, isn't it? That we wait until we are feeling so bad, or that circumstances become personally unbearable, before we decide to take action. It's in these moments that we choose to either sink or swim. We either listen to the call of our Soul to pick ourselves up and do things differently, or we decide to give up. This period of darkness and reflection, of inner conflict and confusion, is often referred to as the *dark night of the soul*.

It's usually in our darkest moments or most troubling times, when we feel like we have hit rock bottom, that we take notice of our inner voice. In those moments when we feel most helpless, confused, and overwhelmed, we are potentially at our most open and vulnerable. Spirit knows this. This is why our choice to either pick ourself up or give up, can have a most powerful influence on our life and soul-path. It's important to understand at this point, that we do not need to know the answers. We very rarely have the clarity at this moment to know what to do next. However, what matters is that decision in your heart. Are you prepared to listen to your Soul or your Higher Self? Are you prepared to look at other possibilities and to consider that you are the creator of your life?

It's quite natural to feel lost, disillusioned or to feel disappointment. We've all experienced these feelings at some point in our lives when what we have hoped for has not been delivered or we have got something other than what we expected, despite our efforts. It can feel like we have had the life sucked out of us and there is nothing left to give. There's a temptation to throw our hands in the air and declare that life is not fair. You have done everything you knew how, and yet it was still not good enough. You come to the conclusion yet again, that you have failed. You are convinced that the world really has been conspiring to work against your every effort and it's chewing you up and spitting you back out. All you want to do is scream about the injustice of it all. You are a good person, so why does this keep happening to you? Sound familiar?

It's human nature to want to give up, when you feel emotionally and physically exhausted, however this moment is crucial. It's now, when we feel our hands are tied, that we are encouraged to listen and realise that we always have a choice, even if we don't always see our options. We can either use this challenging situation to say 'no' in the face of fear and hopelessness, and succumb to the pressure, or we can choose to turn it around by doing something different.

Our mind loves to complicate things by telling us why we can't possibly do this or that, and we give ourself all the reasons why our life and circumstances can't change. Be aware. This is FEAR talking (False Evidence Appearing Real). The mind or ego is so frightened of change that it will always seek to avoid it and stay in the pain and discomfort it already knows or run far away from what we perceive is causing the pain. It is a false sense of security to want to avoid change. We think we will avoid more pain and hurt if we stay with what we have been doing all this time. However, we cannot expect transformation or movement towards True Love, happiness and authenticity if we continue to think, believe and do the same things.

When we recognise that change in our life is approaching, it can feel risky to step away from what is familiar. However, think of the positive possibilities. It's helpful to know that the Universe is working 'for' us and not against us. Taking a leap of faith requires us to trust, to trust in our Higher Self, in God, and in Divine Love. It's trusting that our Soul knows what is best. Love is always our Soul's compass and guide.

Fear is what stops us from letting go and creating change in our life. Fear of being hurt, of feeling vulnerable, and fear of not feeling loved, significant or of value. Fear is not the enemy it is an emotion that is giving us information about what we need to notice and understand about ourself. What if everything that we fear or tell ourselves is better and not worse than we imagine? When we have love and compassion for ourself, fear disappears. When we live in a realm of positive possibilities, and the belief that we can create what we desire, then we become powerful manifestors in our life.

When we are at a crossroad it can feel challenging and conflicting. We can feel overwhelmed by the different voices in our head that represent our fears about which choice to make. There is the voice of reason that wants us to stay where we are, because we perceive it to be safer and less risky to stay with what we know. There is the voice of fear that reminds us how last time we took a risk to step out into the unknown, it resulted in pain and rejection. Then there is the inner voice of our Soul, that whispers over the top of the noise of our chattering mind, providing guidance for the better way forward.

Listening to our doubts and fears will cause us to go in circles, creating mental and emotional anxiety that eventually affects our health. I have learned, from painful experience, that when the doubt creeps in, it is better for me to pause and check how I feel in my heart and in my body. I reflect on whether I am feeling at peace or whether there still lingers some anxiety and fear.

Our Soul (or Higher Self) will always speak lovingly, with clear and consistent guidance that is aligned with our life purpose. Each time we listen, we can expect to feel an inner peace because our Soul is our authentic spiritual essence and knows what lights us up and what it takes to feel joyful. Any time we are doing what we love, it will never make us feel burdened or anxious. When we are aligned with our true self, we feel light, inspired, and on-purpose. We become connected with our spiritual essence which then connects us with the Universe in a more spiritual and enlightened way.

Life is actually much simpler than we realise. Simple doesn't mean life is without growing pains. It means there is a path that will guarantee more love and wisdom without the chains of our complicated mind chatter and the drama we ultimately create for ourself. Simplicity in life is a form of intelligence and sophistication. It's only our mind and our sense of pride and ego that wants to make our choices (or the appearance of no choice) appear too complicated and beyond our comprehension or our ability to take action. It's in these moments that our mind will remind us of the rules and conditions we must live by, whether they are societal, cultural, familial, or work rules that we use to constrict our perspective and limit our choices. In truth, these rules and conditions are an illusion.

The illusion is that we believe there are limited choices in life, and if we can't see the alternatives or the options, then they don't exist. The Universe doesn't work that way. There are infinite choices and paths. We are only limited by our imagination and our willingness to see and be open to the possibilities.

Contrary to most people's belief, the Universe (God, Source) is there to support, guide and work with us to create, using the energy of pure love and infinite possibilities. The key is to surrender and let go of resistance. Surrender does not mean to give up or become submissive in the face of adversity. It means to open the heart and to truly listen at a deeper level.

## Soul Sandwich

Our mind will convince us we have no choice in life, and that it is safer to give up, or to minimise the risks to avoid pain and discomfort.

The key is to surrender and let go of control and resistance. When we open our heart and listen to our inner truth, our Soul will guide us toward greater possibilities, and ultimately greater love.

## Pause. Ponder. Reflect

Acknowledge the pain or discomfort you feel.
Reflect on why you may be getting the same or similar outcomes.
Review other possibilities.

**Next Steps**

Describe what it means to you to be more open and receptive?

Describe a time when you believed you had no choice and later realised there were other options.

How did it feel when you chose to surrender and let go of a thought, belief, person or situation?

How can you do or see things differently going forward?

# Opening the Door

Your Soul is your Higher Self. It is not separate from you. It is your spiritual essence that is not limited to time or what we know as our 3D physical reality. We are gifted by our Soul, as its purpose is to guide us with love so we can learn and grow. We are reminded of our connection with our Soul in moments of complete vulnerability, when our mind has relaxed and we can let go of wanting to control our thoughts, other people, and our circumstances. It's when we are open to the Divine guidance that is within our very being and expressed through our spiritual essence.

*Our vulnerability can be our greatest gift.*

God and the angels are waiting on stand-by for us to let go and hand over what we cannot yet manage ourselves. If life has given you lemons, then see this as an opportune time to listen, learn and grow. Take your hands off the wheel for just a moment and observe. Take some time to *pause, ponder* and *reflect*.

When we are out of alignment with our Soul or Higher Self, we become deaf, dumb and blind. We are closed off and no longer able to receive the subtle signs from above that are being presented to guide us along the better path. There are many paths we can take, but wouldn't it be preferable to take the path of least resistance, the one that will nurture and grow us in a more palatable way?

Life is a choice. It is what we make of it, and what we choose to create. Rather than force our life to 'be' a particular way (which is a form of control), we are best served by learning to listen to the flow of the Universe and work with this energy to achieve our Soul's purpose. Surrendering is about going deeper to listen to our inner voice and what resonates with our very being and essence.

We notice we are out of sync with our Soul when things appear to no longer work, or we are out of flow. This is the Universe knocking loudly on our door to get our attention, to let us know we need to turn around and take an alternative path. It may be incredibly frustrating at the time to continually notice things not working or when we experience disappointment, however it's not a disaster. We have an opportunity to turn it around.

When I've been in the position of disappointment and things have not turned out the way I expected, I have felt utterly deflated and miserable. Unfortunately, my own response to the disappointment became a form of self-torture. Eventually I decided I didn't want to feel that way anymore. It was too painful feeling sorry for myself. So, over time I began to change my response when life delivered an unexpected turn.

It takes time to change our behaviour and to do so successfully means being prepared to make mistakes despite our best efforts. With practice we can choose a better way of responding so that we learn from the experience and feel inspired with more positive results.

Developing a heart and mind of gratitude also makes the way forward so much easier. As we choose to feel gratitude following disappointment, we have the opportunity to reflect on how we can do things differently so we can change the outcome. Our thoughts are very powerful and can influence how we feel in the moment, and what we choose to do in response.

When I am confronted by disappointment, I now say to myself, *"Thank you. I hear you. Help me to see more clearly the better path for me to take. Please give me the strength and the faith to trust and keep going, to follow my heart and what brings me joy".*

This gives me the opportunity to review, reflect and take a different approach. It also helps me to be open to Spirit's guidance and the inner nudges of my Soul. I know from personal experience that at times I have been completely unaware, closed off to my intuition and soul guidance. I have also been plain stubborn, refusing to listen to my inner voice that is telling me to consider a different way rather than hang on to what I desperately wanted. Other times I've been too scared to make a change, and what I really wanted was to feel safe and to have all the answers before stepping out into unknown territory. In those moments of feeling the fear, my trust and faith in my own ability dwindled. I doubted Spirit and I refused to listen, because I was scared.

There are times we want what we know is not good for us. What I've learned along the way is that it's better to pay attention to the flow in my life (or lack thereof). If circumstances are flowing with ease and I am living in alignment with my values, this brings me joy and matches my overall intention and life purpose. However, when things are not in flow and out of sync, problems arise and solutions are not easily worked out. Circumstances tend to present as recurring issues with loads of agitation around the situation. When this happens, I know the Universe is giving me feedback and that it's best for me to stop and review what is happening. There is often a good reason as to why there is no flow. When I've taken time to reflect, I usually see what was previously hidden to me. In moments like this I have discovered the best option is to pause and reconsider my options.

There have been many times when I've not read the signs and I've jumped in too fast, or I've listened to my ego (which wants what it wants, when it wants it). In the end I've caused myself more grief than was necessary. I may have got what I initially wanted, but later it usually backfired in some way. Stubbornness or coming from a 'push energy' does not lead to peace within.

The best avenue for achieving success in life is to listen to your intuition, which is the opposite of choosing to resist. This is what our Soul is guiding us to do. When we listen to our intuition it feels more peaceful and harmonious. To be in a state of harmony doesn't mean to submit to something that is not good for us, it means to be in a state of calm, preparedness, and reflection. In this way we are open to hearing our Soul speak words of wisdom. When we heed the warning or spiritual guidance, we can make better choices.

It's human nature to want to have the answers up front, with everything figured out before we make the next move. When we are in a state of flux, feeling the pressure of confusion and the inner conflict that comes from indecision, it's a temptation to listen to our impulsive desires rather than our intuition or our Higher Self. Temptation is recognised when we get caught up in that inner dialogue of bargaining and convincing ourself that 'x' is better than 'y', and then we oscillate between the two.

When we compare ourself with others (which can lead to believing you are not good enough), or when we become so focused on making a list of the possible 'what if' scenarios that could happen, we end up veering off course, away from our true authentic self. Allowing the voice of fear to dominate will always lead us away from love and from connecting with our true self. Fear breeds self-doubt, confusion, indecision, anxiety and feelings of hopelessness and helplessness.

When we are caught up with this inner chatter, it's a great time to step back and take a breather, so we have the space and clarity to reflect. If you are finding it difficult to get into a place of inner stillness, do something else to distract yourself from your monkey-mind until the dust settles. When you are in a state of confusion and emotional turmoil, it's not the time to make life changing decisions. A lack of patience and fear will usually lead you to draw conclusions or make decisions that are not in your best interest, as they have not come from a state of peace or clarity. When I'm feeling fearful, I often find myself pulling away from a commitment. I doubt my ability and I tend to fill-in the gaps where information is missing. In other words, I make stuff up (assumptions) and inevitably this is not the real truth.

When we are calm, we can more easily discern the difference between our monkey-mind (fear) and when our Soul is speaking to us. We can hear our inner voice more clearly when we are in tune with who we are, and we are being true to ourself. That means, doing what we love to do, honouring what we value most in our life, and coming from a place of self-love.

I have found it is easier to reconnect with my true self when I raise my energetic vibration to a higher level. As living-beings we are constantly generating energy from our physical body as well as through our emotions and spiritual intentions. This creates an energetic frequency and vibration that is unique to ourself in any given moment. When we are in a state of fear, doubt and anxiety, our energetic frequency and vibration operates at a lower level. Our energy can be described as feeling dense or heavy, and this can make it difficult to feel clear in the mind and be open to receiving spiritual guidance. Our mind and our body may feel sluggish and lethargic, and we may feel drawn to eating foods that are dense, such as starches and sugars, in an attempt to gain more energy.

When our energy is low, we tend to make decisions that are more focused on meeting our needs to survive. We may become overly focused on our finances, where we are going to get our next job or meal, and we may feel the need to constantly seek out the company of others to feel more secure. When there is a high focus on 'surviving' it can quickly develop into behaviours that indicate high levels of dependency, a mindset of lack, and feelings of being a victim of life's circumstances.

When we learn the skills to raise our energetic vibration, we can live in a way that enables us to be the best we can be. This means we will find it much easier to follow our intuition, be open to spiritual guidance, and have clarity of mind and body.

**Suggestions on How to Raise Your Energetic Vibration**

- Spend time outdoors in nature, connect with animals who have a natural ability to be aligned with the creative life force.
- Swim in the ocean, meditate for 10 minutes by being still in the body and mind, or have a good sleep.
- Eat more fresh fruits and vegetables and avoid alcohol and caffeine.

**Pause. Ponder. Reflect**

What are some ways you can lift your energy?
For more tips on raising your energetic vibration, see Chapter 8 – The Shift Towards Self-Love

When we detox the body from harmful chemicals, processed foods and hormones like cortisol (which we produce more of when we are in a state of anxiety), we are better able to improve our energetic vibration. As a result, we can create a state of calm and clarity, so we can be more receptive to tuning in to our authentic self and hear the voice of our Soul whispering from our heart.

You may have heard that people who are interested in growing their intuition and spiritual knowledge will often make the choice to become a vegetarian or vegan. This is because naturally produced plant-based foods are high in living energy. Meat is generally denser in vibration and carries the energy of the traumatized animal that was slaughtered. Since moving to a more plant-based diet I have discovered that I have more energy, I feel lighter, less sluggish in my body and I am definitely clearer in my thinking. My overall health has improved, and I've noticed how mentally and emotionally I feel lighter and more positive. All of this has contributed to increasing my intuition and my ability to receive insights and spiritual guidance. Doreen Virtue and Robert Reeves co-authored a book on *'Nutrition for Intuition'* which has some wonderful tips on how to raise your vibration through eating natural and organic foods.

Sometimes a great way to get out of my head is to do something physical, like going for a walk or for a swim in the ocean. Other times I may listen to soothing music or my favourite podcast, take a long shower followed by a good sleep, or I may journal my plethora of thoughts so I can process them and clear my mind. What works for you to stop the mind-chatter?

Whatever you choose, steer clear of sharing your woes over and over with a friend so that it becomes draining. It is also helpful to avoid mulling over problems in your mind while you are all stirred up. Over-thinking and analysing the situation will have you going around and around in circles.

Insights and true wisdom come when we are in a state of peace. For this reason, many people find meditation (creating stillness) as a great way to bring calm to the mind and create a state of receptivity. Giving yourself 5-10 minutes to relax and be still can make a huge difference. What works for me is a slow morning walk by the beach, feeling the sun on my face and the sand under my feet, or I may sit for a while under the trees and listen to the birds. Nature's energy has a way of being able to ground us and clear away any toxicity that affects us on an energetic level, physically, mentally, emotionally and spiritually.

# 3

## Sink or Swim

In the moments when you move from being unconsciously competent to consciously competent (ie self-aware), you realise the difference between where you have been and where you are now. You recognise how much you don't know and that there is so much more to learn. The progression can feel very humbling, and lead to new feelings of vulnerability and insecurity. For some of us, there is an instinctive urge to retreat under the nearest rock as we become aware of our glaring infallibility.

During the years of raising my family I was too busy going through the motions of running around and looking after the children to be in tune with my own needs or to feel connected to my soul-being. I was very diligent at ensuring their physical, emotional, social, spiritual and intellectual needs were being met. Both my husband and I were always aligned when it came to our love and dedication for our children. However, over the years we became rather insulated in our life. When the business of establishing a career or raising a family takes precedence, it is easy to tune out from your own emotional needs or spiritual growth.

How many of us can relate to living a life that feels like we are on a treadmill, going through the motions, repeating the same routines each day, week, month and year? We watch our children grow, and gasp in unison with our friends when we recognise that the years have flown by. This is what I began to recognise as my own state of unconscious slumber. Where had the time gone? Where had I disappeared to? I didn't even know who I was anymore. I felt lost and disconnected from my true self. There was a deeper part of myself that I conveniently covered up every day as I tended to the needs of my husband and children. At the time I told myself they were more important. I believed that my role as a wife and mother was to solely support their growth and provide for their needs. A very large part of me was happy and willing to do this. I loved my family deeply and I was committed to giving them all that was within my capacity.

However, over a longer period of time I began to feel a void growing within. I sought ways to learn more about my spirituality and for many years I engaged in pastoral pursuits and formal spiritual education. However, there were aspects of my true self that remained hidden or untapped. It felt as though the real me had disappeared and this shrouded my true feelings, disrupting the connection between myself and my husband. I was longing to go deeper in my spiritual connection with him, but I was struggling to find a way to make it work between us. We seemed to be on different planets, speaking a different language, and the lines of deeper connection were difficult to find. What I had not realised at the time was that my desire for a deeper spiritual connection needed to happen within me first before I could experience that in my relationship with him.

When I believed I could no longer manage the void and the disconnect within myself, and I was keenly aware of how our relationship was suffering as a result, I knew I needed to step away to work on myself. I wanted to learn more and discover how I could respond to this deep inner longing to connect with my soul and my spirituality.

Eventually I found it impossible to ignore this spiritual calling. The veil had been lifted and light was streaming into my darkness, showing me a new path and a different view. I was drawn to the energy of Divine light and the sense there was much more for me to learn and experience. With this invitation, however, came the understanding that I would need to move away from the comfort of what I had known, to accept the call to follow my Soul's path and move towards greater love for myself. This deep inner love was my connection to the Divine.

I had reached the tipping point, the moment of realisation that I needed to make a decision to either stay on the path I had been travelling or change direction. At first, I felt curious, fascinated and drawn to the idea of exploring something new. I wanted to go deeper and follow what felt natural and more closely aligned to my inner spiritual world. Yet my new interest and fascination began to recede as I became increasingly anxious, unsettled and full of doubt. The more I listened to the call of my Soul, the more I could feel myself being drawn away from the path that was comfortable and familiar. I felt a mixture of curiosity and doubt as I pondered what may happen if I was to choose to change. Fear set in.

My heart knew it was time to follow my passion, the things that made me feel more alive, expanded and fulfilled. However, my mind began to resist and struggle with the concept of stepping into the unknown, filling me with fear and all the reasons and justifications why it would be too radical and dangerous for my well-being. It was the battle of my mind versus the call of my soul. I was on the edge, at a significant crossroad in my life and soul journey.

The realization I could no longer tolerate the pain in my heart, was the catalyst for breaking free from all that was burying me deeper into my demise. It was exhausting, and I knew that if I didn't listen to my Higher Self and make a significant shift, I would not experience the life or spiritual awakening that I dreamed was possible.

Acknowledging where we are in this moment of our life, is the first step towards our spiritual awakening. Once we decide to listen to our Soul's call it's more difficult to return to our previous state of unconsciousness. The door is opened, and the first small steps toward our inner transformation begin to take place. I felt both excited and terrified.

I was aware that I had finally made a decision to commit to myself, and yet I had no idea what to do next. I believed it would require immense courage and I would likely experience the pain of rejection and disapproval from others. I had a great deal of fear around a lack of finances and being on my own. Yet deep inside I felt a strong desire to listen to my Soul, to connect with my true self and find a way to reveal what I was feeling on the inside. I didn't want to listen to myself complain, to feel defeated or be consumed by my depressing thoughts. I had been living in a state of dependency for a long time, and this became an emotional addiction that kept me bound and victimised.

At the time the only way I knew how to respond was to separate myself from my husband and family and be in my own space to begin the work on my inner self. It was the most difficult and excruciating experience. It took me to deep dark places in my soul, and I felt incredible sadness. It was at least 3 years of working through the mess, going deeper within, making mistakes, reflecting on my past and present, all the while trying to keep my head above water and maintain some sense of dignity and self-compassion.

In the early days I was very hard on myself, believing I should have the skills to snap out of my negativity, to be up-beat, grateful and to look at the bright side of my situation. I had put so much energy into surviving that it caused me a great deal of emotional and mental suffering. However, I was determined to go deeper, to understand the real me, and to know my purpose for being. It was a time of real soul-searching in what seemed like the eternal darkness. However, I didn't want to give up on myself. I had gone through so many challenges and heart-ache that I didn't want it to be all for nothing. I knew this was all part of my soul-growth and soul-journey.

After several years of continuous cycles of reflection, healing, and growth, I reached a point where I wanted to move on from the painful state I kept subjecting myself to, and create a better way of living and being. Eventually I realised all I wanted was to be happy and to feel greater love for myself. It was not about getting it perfect or making the 'right' decisions. I knew I didn't have the answers, and it was futile trying to force this to happen. I just wanted to feel better, think better, and do better.

During this growth period I put enormous pressure on myself. Having trained as a life coach, with previous qualifications in psychology and counselling, I felt obliged to get up and get moving and to have all the answers. I told myself that I should know better and that I should have my act together. I was very impatient with my slow progress in getting over this dreadful experience. For some reason I believed I was failing miserably and that I was losing my ability to function and feel happy. I wondered for such a long time if I would ever feel good again, and if the pain, guilt and despair would ever leave me.

When I was growing up, children were told to 'pull up their socks' and to get up and get going if they were feeling down in the dumps. Feeling sad or depressed was an uncomfortable topic for most people and generally not spoken about. In my youth I believe many people suppressed their true feelings as they didn't know how to talk about them, nor did they feel safe to do so. At the time a popular way to deal with significant challenges was to drink away your problems, become addicted to something or someone, or get medicated to numb the emotional pain. For me, none of these choices were a good option. I had seen how dependency and addiction destroys the mind, deteriorates the body and diminishes the soul, causing a slow death to one's spirit.

I knew that dwelling in self-pity served no healthy purpose. There were times a dear friend of mine would remind me "to put on my big girl pants", and to stop complaining about what wasn't working or what I didn't want in my life. I was grateful for the tough love when I could not get out of my own way. I needed that kind of support from my trusted friends. I also knew that any real change or personal transformation in my life meant I needed to do something different - anything, as long as it was something. For a long time, this felt too hard. I was scared, I felt disempowered, I lacked self-belief, and I didn't really know what to do.

I wanted someone to tell me what to do, anything, just so that I could stop feeling the pain. I was searching for something that would help me to feel less alone and miserable, and more valued as a human being. Looking back, I can see that this was simply a case of not taking responsibility for my own life. I had not yet learned that my happiness, my sense of fulfillment, self-love, and self-esteem were my responsibility.

I thank God for my amazing friends. They were my earth angels who gave me incredible support, and yet they never indulged me with pity. They knew this would only feed my misery, my helplessness and my belief that I was a victim. When we adopt a 'victim mentality' it's so much harder to climb out of our own despair. We may tell ourself, 'I am not good enough', 'I'll always be a failure', 'I'm always messing up and getting it wrong'. Or we may turn to externalising and blaming others for our situation and how we feel. Either way, we are not taking responsibility for our happiness or how we choose to respond to our circumstances. We cannot possibly expect to be self-empowered and improve our life whilst being a victim at the same time.

For a long time, I searched outside of myself for comfort. I had not felt compassion for myself and my body and Soul was aching for love. It's a basic human desire to experience love, and it's not necessary for us to deny ourselves the love and comfort that our friends or family want to provide in difficult times. However, there comes a time when you know it's better to let go of always expecting this from others, and to learn to love and value yourself. What I didn't know was that unconditional love, peace and freedom from self-judgment were already possible for me. I had been so conditioned to focus on giving to others that I was not skilled or accustomed to loving myself.

During this time in my life I spent a lot of time in self-reflection and I noticed I had been very dependent and emotionally immature for most of my life due to limited experience in getting to know my true self outside of a full-time relationship. I had not seen this before as I was buried deep in my own life circumstances. I had always considered myself to be an intelligent and emotionally aware person; however, what I did not see in myself was a co-dependent 'addict'. When I realised this truth, it was difficult to say *that* word - 'addict'.

I was married at a very young age, with no life experience or any notion of who I really was. Unlike my own children, I had not spent my youth developing my identity or learning from life experiences about what the world could teach me about myself. I had no concept of what it was to be in my own skin. I had no framework or idea of what I wanted to do in my life, or any notion of my natural strengths, gifts and talents.

I had not explored other relationships or gained any worldly perspective. The concept I had of me was limited to being a good daughter, wife and mother, but I did not know who Rebecca was or what she could do, think or feel on her own.

At 21 years of age I stepped into an exclusive relationship with my husband, who was equally young and emotionally naïve. At an early age we developed a life that was defined by each other's personal view and our limited experience of the world and ourself. We became dependent upon each other for everything - for company, for love and friendship, for entertainment, for our social outings, and for emotional and mental support. I also became financially dependent on my husband. In hindsight I realised we behaved more like Siamese twins joined at the hip.

Some people would say, 'what's wrong with that?' That's what happens in a committed and loving relationship. You share everything, and you support each other. It's true, this was amazing on so many levels. However, we were mostly ignorant. In those days, we modelled the example of our parents and society, which translated to the husband being the Provider (i.e breadwinner), and the wife (or homemaker) was the one who took care of the needs of the children and provided a loving home. This dynamic is a healthy environment for being a family and raising children. It's wonderful to share and support one another in a committed relationship. However, when it becomes an unhealthy dependency that limits your own growth and maturity as an individual, then the relationship with yourself and others is no longer healthy.

Eventually I realised I needed to grow-up and break free from my dependency. I can best describe it like being in a boat in the middle of the ocean. I could see water all around me, as far as the eyes could see. I felt alone, drowning in my sorrow, feeling constant anxiety of not knowing what to expect in the future. Yet, despite the huge discomfort, there was the familiarity of what I had always known and experienced. This 'boat' was my home, my life. In some ways it felt safe to be in what I knew. My life revolved around the very insular world of my family and my children, and the extensions of that life. It was closely knitted with our pastoral community of church and school life, and shaped by my husband's corporate career, and the usual conventional and societal expectations of married life.

When you are playing by the rules and not questioning whether those conditions are helpful or aligned with your true self, you are destined to live unconsciously, never quite realizing your true potential. It becomes a life of restricted thinking that is largely reactive to the external world, rather than one that is intuitively connected to the Divine and our higher spiritual self.

I was used to not making time for myself, nor did I make time to nurture what was important to me. As a result, my relationship with my husband and my friends waned considerably, and I had become disconnected from the real me. For such a long time I was deluded in thinking that I knew who I was. Looking back on the person I had become I could see I was only scratching at the surface of being my authentic self.

There is comfort in what we think we know, the unconscious numbness that becomes our measure of comfort and normality. I now realise that I rarely stepped outside of my own demographic, social circles, school activities, kids sporting clubs or the ongoing cycle of work and financial commitments that directed our family life. It was my world, which was not bad in itself, however my energy and my focus was out of sync with my Higher Self.

I was living like a robot, without the courage to question or break the pattern that kept me stuck in a life that did not feel authentic to me. I lacked self-belief and the courage to live a life that I loved. I saw only what wasn't working or what didn't feel satisfying. As a result, my life became a reflection of this negative outlook, and the self-doubt and lack of love I had for myself. The external landscape of my life was not the cause of my unhappiness or lack of fulfillment. It was how I was thinking and what I chose to believe. One day it occurred to me that I was unhappy because I wasn't tapping into the deeper part of myself, my Soul. I was completely disconnected from my heart, and I felt like I was not living as my true self.

Author Dan Millman describes how each individual is made up of three 'selves', and this influences how we think, feel and relate to our external world. He is not saying we are made up of three separate entities, however it is useful in understanding the level at which we are perceiving and relating to our experiences. There is the Basic Self, Conscious Self and our Higher Self. From our Basic Self we are aware of the importance of meeting our physical and social needs to live and function each day. However, as we become more spiritually awakened, we are able to live with greater awareness, from our Conscious Self. That is, we are more mindful of our thoughts, our beliefs and our choices.

From this new level of conscious awareness, we can hear the voice of our Higher Self, or our soul. It is though listening to our soul (or our inner voice) that we can access the wisdom we have learned through many lifetimes and receive spiritual guidance to assist us in moving closer to the experience of Divine love.

Up to this moment, the conflict I was feeling in my heart and in my life, was a heavy burden I was accustomed to living with for many years. However, with time it became more painful to live in a stupor of sameness that was a mismatch with my values and a disconnection from my heart and Soul.

Many of us choose to avoid change because it feels too hard or too painful. How often do we choose to retreat when we are faced with something new and unfamiliar? It can feel scary, threatening, and uncomfortable. Can you remember offering up justification as to why it is better, safer, and easier to remain exactly where you are? Change moves us away from our comfort zone, which means we can feel vulnerable, unprepared or unskilled to cope with what we believe could be a threat to our personal security and emotional or physical safety. Avoidance of pain or discomfort is a strong motivator for people to resist change. Fear usually keeps us stuck in a perpetual state of procrastination or mediocrity. If you take the example of a depressed person, you can observe how strong the desire is to avoid change, even when they know that continuing with the same behaviour is causing them harm or preventing them from healing and experiencing emotional well-being.

For many years I avoided change. I dreamed about how my life could be different all the time. However, I didn't have the courage to do things differently or the self-love to see the light within my Soul. I was frightened of disturbing the equilibrium and scared about the potential negative consequences that could change my life forever. The thought of altering my direction frightened me. I was worried about experiencing massive rejection and losing love in my life. I was deeply concerned about the impact on my children, my family, as well as myself. There were a host of reasons why I was fearful of change.

Over a long period of time the pain of not being true to myself and feeling constantly discontent was intensifying to the point that it was becoming unbearable. Every day the stress in my chest grew tighter. At night I went to bed full of dread, not knowing how I was going to break the chains that were binding me to self-misery. I felt trapped and very dependent upon my husband. This was not freedom; it was a form of self-torture and self-imposed slavery.

I was a slave to my mind, which had me going around in endless circles. My lungs felt constricted so I could not breathe with ease. My emotional pain and the spiritual distancing from my soul-self was transmuting into physical pain, weight gain, depression, increased stress, regular headaches and a heavy burden in my heart. At the time I blamed everything and everyone else around me for my unhappiness. It was easier for me to assert the responsibility of my circumstances onto others rather than recognise that I had created these results in my life because of what I consistently believed.

I shifted the blame onto my workplace, my dissatisfying marriage, and our desperately failing financial circumstances. My self-esteem was extremely low and despite my confident exterior, underneath I believed that I was not good enough. Everywhere I turned I could find reasons why my life was not measuring up to my expectations. Every day I lived with a dream in my heart of being the person I truly wanted to be; to feel loved, spiritually connected, and fulfilled within my soul.

When you are balancing on the thin edge of fear and deliberation, it is easy to convince yourself that staying still is the best option. Fear is paralysing. It can feel unsafe to move even an inch for fear of creating more pain. I believed I was stuck and without options. I didn't know what else to do or how to think. I tried desperately to find a solution.

I changed jobs, moved houses a couple of times, and when we went on an overseas holiday, I even hoped to find a new perspective for my life. I made attempts to escape from the discomfort and disconnection I felt within, and I sought multiple ways to satiate the thirst in my soul. Beneath the distractions of my life, I could sense my soul calling me to acknowledge and face my personal truth, to go deeper and uncover the real essence of who I was. I felt the Divine, pulling at my heart, and lifting me up out of my dark ocean.

Writing about my experiences became my prayers to God and a way for me to express my soul's deepest desires. I put pen to paper in the desperate attempt to draw out what was buried inside. Slowly I found I was able to open my heart and peel back the layers so that I could hear the wisdom of my Higher Self. In time the fluidity of writing became a portal through which I was able to translate the loving messages of the angels that poured onto the pages. In the years that followed I knew I was travelling along a soul-path to more fully understand my true self. I wrote, I felt intense emotions, I cried, I explored the depths of my mind and my heart.

There were days, weeks and months that I would retreat, with the fear of being alone, of having no money, and feeling the guilt and pain of what my children and husband were going through. It took time before I could recognise the familiar pattern of my thoughts and behaviours. I knew I had a deeply ingrained habit of making choices to suit the happiness and the wishes of other people to the detriment of my own well-being. It was an avoidance strategy that seemed to be serving me very well. I was afraid of facing my truth. It took several years to shift this mental and behavioural conditioning. Even today I am conscious of checking in with myself to ensure I am honouring my own health and well-being first, before I reach out to support the needs of others.

I regularly experienced fear and uncertainty, reminding myself about what I did not have, what I was not doing, and who I was not being. It was a scarcity mentality fuelled by years of conditioning and a habitual focus of lack in my life. I was so used to believing I was not good enough, that there was never enough money, and that taking a different path would be too risky. My beliefs greatly influenced my choices and whatever action or non-action I decided to take.

It took a lot of courage to resist the urge to collapse in the hope that someone would rescue me. I was in a space of constant tension, wanting to move away from the pain and discomfort. I felt utterly fed up with it all and heavy in my spirit. All I wanted to do was find a way to set myself free. Underneath it all, I knew I was more than what I was allowing myself to believe.

## The Choice

At mid-life I realised I was experiencing my own version of spiritual transformation. It's human nature to avoid pain at all costs, which is why so many people make the choice to pull back and pass on the opportunity for personal and spiritual growth. However, the pain of being in an emotional and spiritual void was the final clincher. My happiness, my health and the choice to live as my true self, was more valuable to me than continuing a life of personal self-torture. I knew I needed to do something different to create change and to respond to the call of my Soul.

In each earthly lifetime we are given opportunities to grow, to increase our understanding, to develop wisdom, and to move closer towards our natural spiritual and Divine self. However, we can change the course of our life path and the outcomes with each decision we make. We don't realise that every thought, every small action, what we tell ourself each day and what we believe to be true, is exactly what creates our version of reality. We have a choice to eat healthfully, to sleep well, to see the opportunities in life, to love our family and friends, and to welcome the challenges as vital learning experiences.

We don't get to control the external circumstances of our life. Sometimes disappointment happens and life is not always fair. We have bosses that don't care, illnesses that catch us by surprise, challenging relationships and friends that disappear when the chips are down. On the other end of the spectrum there are also people who *do* care about us. There are sunny days and joyful moments shared with friends and even strangers that we meet.

Whatever our external circumstances, sometimes they are unpredictable and beyond our influence. That's the contrast we experience in our physical life. The tangible nature of this world gives us grit and context, so we can live, breathe, feel the comparisons, the joys and sorrows, and the opportunity to choose what we want to think, what we want to feel and what we want to create in our life. We can embrace life's gifts and receive them with gratitude for their richness and their teaching, or we can resist them and choose to see life as working against us.

I believed for a long time there would be no benefit to leave my comfort zone and venture into unchartered waters. The more I focused on the idea of change, the more fearful I became and the longer I procrastinated. Eventually experience showed me that focusing on what I didn't want, and deliberating way too long about my next steps, only created more pain and no change. Why do we wait for the pain to build up so much before we realise the power of our thoughts and the choice we can make to move towards soul growth and greater love?

Following one of my jobs, I learned a valuable lesson about the importance of managing my thoughts and my energy, and how negative thinking can become toxic poison. Many of my colleagues were collectively complaining about their work circumstances, which left everyone in a state of low energy. The atmosphere became heavy, and even though individuals were well meaning, collectively there was a growing air of pessimism, dissatisfaction, and a lack of personal responsibility. The ongoing disgruntled attitude and mindset of the staff created a depressing environment in which to work. People began to get sick, depressed, and some even chose to leave the organisation. Collectively we had all influenced and affected each other, as we externalized our dissatisfaction about our work situation. In hindsight it became evident that the power of our thoughts and a lack of individual leadership contributed to creating a negative energy and circumstances for everyone.

It took me 3-4 years to shift my thinking from self-doubt to self-appreciation. I am now much better at consciously choosing what I think and what to focus on. It's a work in progress and there are still some days I slip back into old habits. However, with practice we can learn to redirect our attention to what will help us learn and grow. An effective way to dispel any fear and quieten the doubtful mind, is to adopt an attitude of feeling grateful, and viewing life and others through eyes of love. When unsure of how to respond to difficult times, we can always ask 'What would Love do'? Life and people are not perfect however this approach will bring us closer to the wisdom and insights of our Higher Self.

The change in my life and my personal transformation was incredibly overwhelming, particularly as I had no idea of what lay ahead. I knew I needed to let go of past ways of thinking and it would take courage to venture into unknown territory. I remember a hymn we used to sing at the boarding school where I worked, about 'leaving our boats behind, beyond familiar shores'. This was me. It was time to leave what was no longer serving me or helping me to grow.

I was definitely scared, and as I cycled through feelings of anger, self-pity and grief, I felt like my world was slowing down to a painful crawl. It was a huge effort to pretend everything was okay when in reality I felt like I was dying on the inside. Underneath the anger and grief, I knew I couldn't continue to blame my circumstances and other people for the misery I was feeling.

I procrastinated about what to do as my thoughts and feelings swung from one extreme to another. I was worried about what could happen if I was to make such a radical change, and the difficulties of 'how' to make it work. I felt lost and disconnected from my inner being. It was a lonely experience. I ached to be free and to do what made me happy. I wasn't sure that I even knew what happiness felt like, or what shape my life would take, what I would do with myself or how I might even feel.

Remaining in that place of limbo, on the edge of what was so familiar, not committing to stay or go, was self-torture. Procrastination is living in perpetual fear and trepidation of what we imagine might happen. It only prolongs the pain and delays any kind of progress or change. I was gripped by the fear of the unknown, of failing myself, of being alone and not managing. I was afraid that stepping out would mean there was no way back should I discover it was all a mistake.

I didn't have the answers, but I knew that it came down to choosing to sink or swim. If I stayed in my current life situation, I would be repeating the same patterns of behaviour and thinking, which was keeping me stuck and preventing me from further spiritual and emotional growth. I was not living a life that was authentic to me, which felt painful on a daily basis. I couldn't live like this anymore. It was time to find the courage and inner strength to move forward one step at a time.

Finding the courage to change means to accept what is, and who we are in any given moment, even when we feel overwhelmed and over-challenged to do something different. I was willing to go through the challenges that come from deep inner growth, because I knew from experience that the rewards in the long term far outweigh the immediate discomfort. I jumped into what felt like an abyss, in a huge ocean, fully committed with no option of turning back. Now I was up to my neck, in a sea of unknown depth, where I had never been before.

## Self-Reflection and Soul Lessons

- When we consciously hold onto our comfortable habits, to other people with whom we believe we cannot do without, and to those things that we form attachments to in life; we do it because we think we will lose what we believe is ours to keep. This only intensifies our anxiety and dependency, delivering more fear and pain, rather than insight, growth and peace.

- Why stew over negative thoughts when it makes us feel so bad? Sounds simple, however it doesn't always feel so simple. One of my friends always says to me, "Life is simple. We just make it complicated". It's a great pearl of wisdom. In truth, we are all a work-in-progress. It's not about overnight solutions or perfection, however I know my life is a gift to enable me to learn, transform and enjoy the beauty and love of simplicity. With every pearl of wisdom I receive, there is an opportunity for me to appreciate it, value the message and incorporate the wisdom into my thinking, into my being, and into my living. It's not a matter of convincing myself to not feel pain, or not see what is not good for me, but rather to see through eyes of love and what is the path towards True Love rather than away from love.

- When we experience fear, self-doubt and a lack of certainty, we can easily blame others for our circumstances. It's a temptation to compare, and to make assumptions about the intentions of other people. What I learned is that we cannot control what other people say, think or do. It is also none of our business. What someone else thinks is a reflection of their soul journey, not mine. What matters is that we 'mind' our own thinking. Managing our own thoughts is the first step towards managing our focus, our intentions and our energy.

- When we are in the space to more readily focus on a heart of love and compassion for ourself, we can more easily recognise that we are not separate from others. Energetically and spiritually we are all one and made from Divine Love, however most of us are still learning to understand what that means and how to raise our vibration of love so that we are experiencing this in our soul all the time.

- The most important soul lesson has been learning to love myself, to have self-compassion and to appreciate all of me, the light and the darker shadows. It's easy to say that we should love ourself, however it takes daily practice. My starting point was to pay more attention to the small things in my life, such as what I tell myself, and to enjoy each present moment. We have only 'now'. There is no past, and there is no future; there is only the experience of right 'now'. We are not so much looking for the path to take us to True Love and happiness as if it can be found outside of ourself. Our life *is* the way. Each moment we experience - our focus, our choices, and our actions, *is* a reflection of our current experience of joy, wisdom and Divine Love.

# 4

## Facing my Fear

How many times in our life have we been faced with our own fear? It can feel particularly intense when we are confronted with a significant life change that gives us reason to re-check our values and what is important in our life. For many people, the thought of change can be frightening, challenging and unsettling. However, we have a choice as to how we approach change. We can embrace it with fear and trepidation, or we can embrace change with a sense of excitement, adventure and wonder.

It's the human condition to want to avoid what we perceive as uncomfortable, painful and risky. Many people interpret change as taking away something that they know and is therefore secure, rather than seeing the possibility that what they are doing or believing is no longer working in their best interests or helping them to grow. For this reason, many people resist change.

When I initially made the decision to step away from my familiar life, and change my focus and direction, it was a scary choice. When we feel we have experienced too much pain, it's often the powerful catalyst that drives us toward change. For me, the emotional pain level had reached a point where I desperately wanted and needed to take action, to do something, anything, to change the path I was travelling. I was emotionally and physically drained, tired of feeling disconnected, and not moving in any direction that was lighting me up on the inside. I wasn't able to articulate how I felt, nor did I have clarity on what it all meant. I was drifting from my soul-path. I was ready to embrace the way forward, even if it meant accepting my fear so that I could transform myself and my life. It was a significant moment when I was able to acknowledge my uniqueness and my value. I was finding my way back towards love for myself.

> *Change is not possible unless we are willing to*
> *think, believe and do things differently.*

For many years I had I wrestled with the idea of making a radical change, which meant leaving my marriage. There was a lot at stake, and I was desperately worried about the impact on my children and family. I knew I would face rejection, anger, emotional pain, and my own fear of how I was going to survive. I was sad at the idea of loss in my marriage, disappointed in myself at how my life was not working the way I had hoped. I was scared about my future on so many levels. Yet I was also scared about what would happen to me if I stayed the same and did nothing. I knew that I wanted to be really happy at a soul level, and to feel emotionally, physically and spiritually fulfilled. For this to happen I needed to explore my soul-calling to live more deeply and more authentically. If I did not, then I would never be a true example of what I believe, which is to do what I love and live to my true potential.

I sensed the moment of personal change in my life was approaching. I knew I needed to step away and have time to think about what I wanted and needed in my life. At this stage I had no idea of what lay ahead for me, only that I was stepping into the unknown, full of fear and with a small measure of courage at the same time. My decision to follow my own path morphed into a period that became my *dark night of the soul,* a time of deep introspection and self-examination that lasted several years and became a new level of my soul's deeper transformation. During the first several months my nights felt lonely and I longed for the comfort of human company during the daylight hours. There were many times I felt completely overwhelmed. My mind taunted me with more fearful and anxious-ridden thoughts about whether I had done the right thing and I questioned myself about how I was going to survive. I had never felt like this before. I had moved away from my home, my family, my financial security, and everything that I knew. I felt vulnerable, scared and numb at the same time.

After a while I began to feel accustomed to my fears, and this slowly changed to feeling solace and hope in the idea of new beginnings. I had a few dear friends who were there to support me and provide the comfort, security, and reassurance I needed. I was relieved when I finally made the decision to focus on my own soul-path for a while. I think for a long time I was in a state of shock after I moved away. I was doing my best to keep my head up, because I was so frightened of succumbing to depression.

Eventually I found my comfort zone in my new environment. It was the first time in my life that I needed to think about how I was going to take care of myself. For a grown woman this may sound a little ridiculous, as I had spent all of my life taking care of everyone else. I knew from a mental and practical perspective how to take care of my needs, but I never stopped to appreciate that my heart needed taking care of too. In this new space and new life there were aspects of me that I had not yet explored. I felt alive and yet at the same time I felt vulnerable. My heart was in a great deal of pain and I knew I needed comfort and self-compassion.

I knew I needed to ensure I was physically and mentally healthy. I have witnessed what depression does to the soul, and how a stagnant life can negatively influence an individual's emotional and spiritual well-being. Once you travel down this spiral, it is so hard to come back up again.

When it comes to feeling healthy in my body, I have always loved walking and being outside. I realised that to manage my emotions it is important to move my body and get physical. It's also very helpful to be in nature where the energy is clear and grounding. In periods of stress or depression our body produces more stress-hormone (cortisol). When we move the body and increase our physical activity it helps to reduce the effects of cortisol and the build-up of toxins. A lack of movement creates dullness and lethargy, exacerbating the feelings of depression, confusion and a lack of motivation.

My fear of being enveloped by negativity, feelings of hopelessness and low energy were big motivators to get me up in the morning and out of bed. Many people marvelled at my determination and dedication to my early morning walks along the beach. I have always been drawn to nature and to the sea, and now it was a place of healing for me. The best motivator for my new regime was not avoiding what I was afraid of, it was looking forward to what I really loved doing.

Walks along the beach with the promise of a beautiful sunrise on most days was key to keeping myself emotionally and physically in a better place. The healing energy of the ocean, the new light of the rising sun, the trees, the birdlife, the visiting dogs with their owners; it all meant that I was feeding myself with good energy and I had a fresh start every day. It renewed me, inspired me, healed me and enabled me to reconnect with my Soul. Slowly I was transforming with small changes in my life, and over time I noticed healing taking place in my body and in my heart. I had a strong desire to help myself, to learn whatever I could to make a new life and grow stronger in love for myself.

I increased my reading on personal development and spirituality and I learned more about improving my health with the support of my health-conscious friends. I focused on making better choices around my thinking, my sleeping habits, managing my energy, and being more careful with my choices for what I was eating and drinking. Connection with my friends was also vitally important. It helped me to feel I belonged, and that I was not alone. I also began a program of self-discovery through spiritual development classes. Step by step, my new choices became food for my soul's growth.

I have always had a thirst for learning, communicating and connecting with people. In the past I enjoyed studying psychology, counselling, pastoral ministry, and life coaching. During those years of study I learned better ways to think, how to manage my beliefs, how to connect my body with my heart and mind, and the importance of taking care of my well-being. However, there was little direction on how to develop my intuition so that I could hear, notice and sense the spiritual Divine guidance that is available to us all. I was still relatively naïve about my psychic abilities and my intuitive awareness was still in its sleepy infancy. Most of what I had been taught was to relate to the Divine through someone or something else.

As my knowledge and spiritual awareness grew, I began to notice more of the contrasts in my life, the difference between negative self-defeating behaviour and inspired (spirit-in-action) living. I was developing my curiosity, my level of conscious awareness, and my ability to sense on a deeper level. I was slowly being prepared for a personal and spiritual transformation in my mid-life, which brought about significant change on an unchartered path toward greater love.

## Daring to Trust

Slowly the wounds of my heart and soul began to feel less raw. It was an essential time that enabled me to gently contemplate my life and create stillness and peace through a new practice of meditation. It was a healing balm to my soul that breathed life-energy back into my being.

As human beings there are moments when we need to feel security, comfort, compassion and certainty, particularly when we have experienced such a radical change in our life. It's the period of rest and recuperation that many of us do not allow ourselves to experience. For some reason we hold onto the belief that we don't have time for rest, and that pausing in life means we miss out on opportunities. There is a time and a place for rest, and a time for action. I recognised it was important for me to become more consciously aware of my well-being. I had become very adept at taking a logical and practical approach to my life, however I had not yet learned how to tend to the needs of my own heart and soul. I was unfamiliar with giving myself love and compassion.

For a while I was too scared to move or change anything more in my life, for fear of feeling out of my depth, and the potential for more emotional pain that I could not cope with. I still felt raw, vulnerable and lost. I had financial pressures that meant I had little room to move. I was without work for 3-4 months at one stage, and this was devasting and lonely. I was plunged into survival mode on all levels which left me feeling frozen and a victim of my circumstances. Trying to muster up more energy and courage to help myself, was not something I felt I was ready to take on.

Transformation is all about ongoing change, and this level of regular change was new and challenging for me. I was becoming familiar with fear, what it felt like and the impact it was having on me. I noticed that whenever I was falling back into a state of fear, I would feel myself freezing emotionally, mentally and physically. My energy would slowly stagnate until I felt drained and unable to move again.

In those moments of wanting to protect myself from what I perceived as more pain, I would sink into complacency and avoidance, preferring the comfort and security of my daily routines rather than pushing the boundaries of more change. I was starting to feel dependent and needy, and in some ways like a child who couldn't let go of the safety of an adult's hand. The cycle of change, growth, rest and healing became a familiar pattern for me.

At times I wasn't very compassionate with myself. Whilst I felt desperately sad, I also chastised myself for not feeling more positive, for not pulling myself together faster, and I blamed myself for so many things I had not done very well in the past. I was incredibly judgmental, believing I was not good enough, and feeling low in self-esteem and energy. I realised I had not learned to love myself or see the beauty in me that I was able to see in others.

I knew I was going through layers of growth and transformation. Each layer was uncovering a new level of awareness, and a new kind of consciousness I had not yet experienced. The inner process of transformation was beautiful and painful at the same time.

*The landscape of our life is the classroom for our soul's lessons.*

When we hold onto what is familiar, what we know and what feels safe, we can prevent ourself from entering new doors and discovering our potential. We are so conditioned to believe that choosing what feels like a 'safe' option is good for us, when often the safe option is more about our avoidance of what we fear the most. Fear closes the door to our heart, which prevents us from truly seeing the love in ourself and in others. When we close our heart, we disconnect from our Higher Self and from the life-force energy of Divine Love. As a result, we can never know our true self or respond to our Soul's calling. We end up hiding from our own light and developing personas that serve to protect and limit personal risk, or we choose to go down a path that is meant for others.

I have learned that trust and self-love is empowering, and it places me in the space of the Divine, of my spiritual home of infinite possibilities. When I was clasping at familiarity, I was not able to move any closer to my dreams. I was stuck. No amount of wishing, wanting or lamenting was going to propel me forward. What I needed was determined focus, to fix my gaze, trust my heart, and let go of resistance. It was not about having more will-power. We can muster up determination to do something, but unless we have our heart in it and we are prepared to take action, then nothing truly changes. What lay ahead for me was the promise of more love and joy in my life, but it was going to require love for myself, courage, and the desire to go the distance. Spiritual endurance became the muscle I needed to strengthen.

Later I realised that it was not effort alone that was required. The key was to trust myself and to trust in Divine timing to deliver what was necessary for my soul growth. It was important for me to know God was supporting me whilst bringing all the pieces together to provide exactly what I needed in those moments. I was to do my part and trust this was enough.

There have been many moments through the tough times that I felt so grateful for the special people in my life who were like angels to me. They never judged me, or told me what to do, they loved me.

They encouraged me, travelled with me on the journey and stood by me when I felt overwhelmed. They championed me when I took steps to inch forward, and they were there in the silence too. I will always be grateful for their love and support.

Every time I reach the next level of learning in my life, I embrace it, though sometimes hesitantly, knowing I will be bathed in more love and more enlightenment in my soul. It takes courage, but when I move forward knowing I have choice and that the Universe is there to love and support me, I know there is no need to fear, only to trust. With every lesson I integrate into my life I experience a new level of growth and wisdom. The results become the evidence that shows me time after time, that the inner path to True Love is through trust, courage and letting go of the need to control my destiny.

There have been many moments along the way that I've reminded myself of this truth. There is only Love in our Universe, but we forget this. We become fearful, doubtful, cynical, and the lens through which we see life reflects this back to us. It is our fear that creates the opposite of Love. Life is never smooth. Perhaps the experience of our life can feel like a series of waves that rhythmically rise up and fall down. That's a part of our physical and emotional experience. If we can learn to ride the waves rather than struggle to push through them, then we can more easily flow with the momentum of life and allow it to assist us on our soul-journey.

I now embrace the challenges, even when my basic self feels scared and doubtful at times. I have my off days, but I know they pass. In the moments when I prefer to hang on to what is known and familiar, I am still willing to step out of my comfort zone and remain committed to my souls' purpose, which is to move toward greater love. However, it took me a long time to learn to trust and let go.

In those days when I felt particularly vulnerable and insecure, I found it difficult to muster up the strength to be self-sufficient, independent and without fear. I would cling to my old habit of depending upon others for my happiness, sense of security and certainty. The more I hung on, the more I fell out of sync with my true self and my soul-purpose. I was out of balance in all aspects of my life, and I sank to a lower level of sadness, anxiety, loneliness and separation. I was not listening to or trusting my Higher Self to guide me along the path of True Love. I didn't realise that I always have exactly what I need in terms of my soul's growth.

There were moments in my grief and growth that I felt more desperate and disempowered. When I allowed myself to go into self-pity, my energy seemed to repel the very things I craved for – more love and security. When I felt the need for company, I often found that it was not there. Unknowingly I was pushing away the good vibes by dwelling in my pain and negativity. The more I focused on what I didn't have in my life, the more the Universe kept giving me the same in return. When my energy was low, and I craved company, somehow my friends were either busy, unavailable or out of reach. It was not a conscious decision on their part, it was the Universe reflecting back to me the energy I was projecting. When we are feeling particularly resistant to change or self-love, and focused on what isn't working for us, we tend to attract more of the same. When we perceive our world as unfair, we are likely to experience more evidence of this because this is all we believe, see and feel.

When we seek to have our needs met outside of ourself, or to be validated by others, our energy has a low vibration, and this is repelling rather than attracting. Whenever I focused too much on how things were not working - that I didn't have the job I needed, that I had too many bills, that my kids were disconnected from me, or when I believed my life would never amount to anything other than perpetual struggles and loneliness, I would simply just get more of this experience; more of the same mindset, more of the depressed feelings and more of the same outcome. It was a destructive and perpetual cycle.

When we get in our own way and see only closed doors, we block the path to our happiness. Our belief in ourself and what is possible either empowers us to take action or blocks our energy so that we are unable to think and see clearly. The path ahead becomes foggy and confusing. The longer we stay in that fog, the more quickly we lose our energy and our motivation to move forward. Our spirit grows weary and our body becomes sick. Life takes on a new level of heaviness.

I was experiencing a full range of soul lessons that showed me the power of the mind and our belief system. One winter I attracted a terrible bout of influenza that took three weeks for me to recover. I had not felt that sick in so many years. I was very run down. My low mental and emotional state was being reflected in my physical body through this illness. Lying in bed for a couple of weeks was frustrating, but it was all I could do. However, during that time my angels helped me to see that our physical health is directly influenced by our mental and emotional well-being.

It was also an opportunity for me to reflect and realise I needed to let go of my concerns, and my intense need to control every outcome in my life. I was trying so hard to make things work and to solve what I perceived as all of my problems. I had developed an energy of resistance, unable to receive or to have compassion for myself. There were many times I asked my angels to slow down with the lessons. Whilst my soul chose this path willingly, my human self was exhausted. I was pushing too hard. What I needed to learn was how to surrender to receive love and compassion, and to see that I was worthy of being loved. More importantly I needed to love who I was, and to forgive myself for all that had been and what I perceived I was not.

Forgiveness is an act of love for oneself that doesn't include judgment or self-criticism. It is self-compassion that comes from the heart and is a full acceptance of who we are. When we forgive ourself we release the bonds of judgment, enabling us to surrender to the healing peace of self-love. With gratitude for all that is, our challenges can become the soul lessons of True Love.

*Forgiveness is an act of love for oneself*

I cried many tears over the next couple of years as I moved slowly through this process of letting go, reaching a deeper understanding of myself, and feeling love and value for myself for the first time. When we try to hold on to what makes us feel secure, it's because we believe it will be taken away from us; whether it is a significant person in our life, our home, the things we think we possess, our job, our health and so on. It's having a scarcity mentality that only serves to take you deeper into an emotional and spiritual abyss. It's the belief that you are separate from all other entities in the Universe and that there is not enough love or resources for you.

Nothing could be further from the truth. With every challenge I experienced during this period of my life I was being shown spiritual truths that can set us free. My role was to hear, notice, practice and grow from these experiences. It was no overnight transformation. Each time I experienced the pain of my circumstances, and I willingly embraced the fear I felt inside, I knew it was an opportunity to acknowledge my inner truth and notice how I was responding to my life. It gave me a chance to examine my thoughts and what I was choosing to believe in that moment. Was I blaming someone else or was I taking responsibility for my own energy, thoughts and actions that resulted in a particular outcome?

It's not possible to live our life without fear, it's a part of our human existence. If we don't learn to manage it, fear can dominate our life. Rather than avoid what makes us fearful, we can learn to live with it, and even better still, we can learn to trust. Fear can be an amazing tool of revelation, to help us go deeper so we can examine, reflect, and come to a greater understanding of our Soul and of Divine Love. All of our life experiences have the potential to show us the path to greater love, not to punish us. When we embrace what we fear with a heart and mind to learn, we open the doors to infinite possibilities of experiencing expanded awareness, greater love, and spiritual wisdom.

# 5
## Living on the Edge

When we feel we are at our lowest point in life, it's common for all of our deepest fears to be triggered and to feel we are being propelled into survival mode. There is nothing worse than feeling desperate. Desperate thinking leads to desperate actions, which later can lead to unplanned and undesirable consequences.

When we become trapped by the chaos in our mind, it can be easy to succumb to a victim-mentality that can create anxiety and panic. Dwelling in fear creates the experience of more fear, and as the fear compounds, our ability to listen and respond to our Higher Self rapidly declines. Our ability to trust in our intuition and inner guidance subsides only to be replaced by overwhelming thoughts that cloud our ability to discern illusion from loving truth. Fear inevitably moves us into a state of either 'flight', 'fight' or 'freeze' mode as we respond to what feels threatening or dangerous. It's a way of protecting ourself from what we perceive as potential physical or emotional harm.

When I first made the decision to embrace a new life, I felt a sense of relief and freedom. However, I was frightened by the idea of leaving what was familiar, even though my old ways were not serving me well. I prepared to face the unknown, and what I imagined would be challenging times ahead. I was already experiencing feelings of loss and rejection from those closest to me as I stepped away from their world.

Making a radical choice to move away from the conventions and expectations of my marriage gave me enormous relief from the pain I was feeling in my soul. For a long time, I had felt conflicted and anxious about not living as my true self. On some level I told myself it was wrong to feel this way, and to desire a new life. However, as time passed, the weight of these expectations disappeared into the background, with the return of a deeper desire to seek relief from what felt like a soul-prison.

I needed time to think, breathe and to process so many thoughts, feelings and beliefs. With more time and space, I believed I would be able to adjust to a new environment away from the busyness of my life. I was going through incredible grief and I knew I needed to conserve my energy for my own healing. It was the beginning of a new phase of my spiritual transformation.

What I learned was the importance of trusting myself and to trust the process of my own personal transformation and soul growth. This is probably one of the most challenging things we face when go through significant change and growth. We are regularly tested mentally, emotionally and physically on our soul journey, as the Universe offers up contrasts in our life to help us develop our self-awareness and spiritual connection.

We are better off loving the journey and the experiences, even when we feel incredible discomfort. This is love in motion, as we witness our soul maturing as a result of our experiences. 'Love' and 'trust' are key to our joy, happiness and soul growth. Divine Love will always find a way to lift us up. It will always move around and through what we perceive to be the obstacles in our life. If we notice it's powerful and yet subtle embrace, allowing it to nourish us, the obstacles we've been focused on will subside from our attention.

## Self-Reflection

When our circumstances feel overwhelming and painful, it's a natural human response to take measures to avoid that pain. When this happens it's important not to condemn or judge ourself. There may be very valid and healthy reasons for avoiding more pain. However, it's important to take some time to reflect before making life-impacting decisions. When we are in a state of overwhelm and confusion, we can feel compelled to act impulsively in order to reduce the pain or to force a resolution too quickly.

Having awareness is the first step towards gaining clarity. Give yourself physical and emotional space to acknowledge how you are feeling without over-analysing what comes to the surface. The present moment may not be the time to immediately 'problem solve' your way out of how you are feeling or your situation.

If we suppress our feelings then they will only find a way to be heard or felt in the future, either in relationships, in our body's health, or in other areas of our life. When we acknowledge how we truly feel we can see more clearly what is not serving us.

Aim to be in a place of stillness so that your mind and body can slow down, and this will help to bring you closer towards feeling peace within. It may take some time before you manage to feel calm, especially if you are still engulfed in the pain or anxiety of grief.

Recognise that as you enter the metamorphosis of your soul, you may initially experience waves of denial, bargaining, guilt, anger, depression, and feelings of being unlovable and unworthy. These emotions are the egos' resistance to change. However, when you surrender to the process and allow the feelings to move through you without resistance or judgment, you will in your own time, come to a stage of self-acceptance and renewed hope for a new way of being.

If you are having extreme feelings of not coping or you have persistent thoughts of wanting to cause yourself or anyone else harm, then please tell someone as soon as possible. Do not wait until you reach a point of being unable to help yourself. In this situation it is best to seek professional advice and assistance immediately.

## The Healing Journey

Developing patience and self-compassion is a healthy place to begin and will help the healing process. When we are calm it is much easier to think clearly and discern what is healthy and in alignment with our well-being – physically, mentally, emotionally and spiritually.

When I first took steps to create change, I felt as if each day I was trying to survive physically and emotionally. I was on my own and the reality of my situation had begun to sink in. I was going through so many new experiences, and I felt anxious about my decision to embrace such radical change. There was a battle going on between my mind and my soul. My thoughts terrified me, taunting me about the prospects of failure. Yet, at the same time, I was receiving peaceful and reassuring guidance from my Higher Self to rise above the lower energies of my fear and experience the power of Soul Love, a deep knowing and love of who I am and the resources within me.

It was an important realization that this was *my* journey of self-discovery, and that I was travelling on my soul path. Most of the time I felt like I was groping in the dark on my hands and knees, however I sensed that if I kept inching forward, eventually I would find my way. My Soul and my spiritual guides were leading me toward greater peace and True Love.

These initial steps of change were tentative and yet they were a commitment to myself and an acknowledgment that I was worth standing up for. It felt good to take care of my own needs. My stand for independence was part of my soul's journey, and it required me to go through all of the struggles and stages of someone suffering from dependency and attachments, as I transitioned toward spiritual maturity and a true sense of my own individuality. It was a process of re-birth to new life. In my mid to late forties, I was now experiencing life on my own terms. It was strange, unfamiliar and stressful, and yet I was also feeling incredible relief and liberation about my new life and the possibilities that lay ahead.

In the early phase of my spiritual pilgrimage, the feeling of being alone tended to dominate, though it was not all bad. Living on my own gave me freedom in the form of time, quietness, minimal distractions, and the physical and emotional space I needed to get to know myself and reconnect with my inner being. It was the first time that it was just 'me' in the room in the morning when I awoke, when I came home from work, and in the evening as I finally drifted off to sleep. It was the first time that I had only myself to listen to, to think about, and tend to. I was learning to live with all aspects of myself, including my fears, my deepest longings, my shadow side and the love and wisdom that I was discovering within.

*We must know the darkness before we can see the light.*

I entered my cocoon to be alone with myself and begin an inner journey. I sensed this was needed, and although there were many times I cried, and I was frightened of my own feelings and sadness, I also found comfort in my solace. I needed to know how to nurture myself through my own grief. There were days of huge despair and what felt like an eternal emptiness within. I longed for those days and moments to pass. Eventually they did. With each new day the sun rose again, giving me fresh hope and a renewed appreciation of myself and life's opportunities. I didn't yet understand that there were true blessings in these moments that really stretched me.

We long to avoid feeling pain and discomfort, but in these moments, there are soul treasures that strengthen us and lift us to greater heights of self-love and gratitude.

The transformative process of our soul's growth is an inner pilgrimage. For some of us, changing our environment helps the process. For others, the physical surrounds may be less of a focus for what's needed on the journey within. Whatever way it unfolds, it is a time where we have the opportunity to reflect on what is personally of value, and what is and is not healthy for our well-being. The inner journey requires stillness and reflection, self-love and a willingness to embrace all that is happening in our soul's growth.

*A period of reflection, away from what is distracting and unhealthy, is one way to gain clarity and ensure your next steps are discerned with love and compassion for yourself.*

When I reflect on years that have passed, I now realise the call of our Soul is with us from birth. As young children we have not developed filters to block out our natural connection with Spirit and our Soul. We readily embrace our intuition and connection with the Universe without hesitation. As we grow older, we are taught how to think and how *not* to feel, and so we slowly disconnect from our spiritual essence and our Higher Self. Our focus becomes fixed on our external environment. In our adult years it takes a more conscious effort to be open and receptive to hear our Soul whisper to us. It's as if we need to experience a 're-birth' to reconnect with our spiritual self. In our soul-journey we are constantly receiving the call from the Divine to move closer to True Love.

## Managing the Discomfort of Change

Change is inevitable in life. It's why we are here, to experience opportunities for soul growth. When we resist change and we put more effort into staying the same, we become like blocked up drains that prevent the natural flow of love and living energy in our life. One thing is for sure, growth does not happen when we choose to permanently stay in our comfort zone. Growth stretches us and is uncomfortable, and if we have been stuck or blocked for a long time, clearing the heart, mind and body could be a more painful process than if we listen and act when we first feel the call.

It's natural to experience feeling uncertain and unstable during transformation. We may feel like we are teetering on the edge of the unknown when we move away from our comfort zone. In many ways, feeling uncertain is the assurance we are on the path of growth. Unfamiliarity can create uncertainty, and this one of the basic human needs. Certainty helps us to feel safe, protected and grounded. For this reason, when people are faced with change, they often avoid it or ignore it.

However, there are times when feeling unsafe is an indication that we need to re-assess whether we are in a good place or not, and whether we are experiencing emotional, mental or physical harm. It's important to listen to what our inner guidance is telling us. It doesn't feel good to feel unsafe, particularly if you have felt emotionally vulnerable for a long time. Feeling this way on a regular basis is a sign to stop and listen. Continuing can have profound negative effects.

When we feel unsafe physically or emotionally it can affect our ability to trust ourself and others. Our survival instinct will urge us to move away from what feels dangerous or unhealthy, whether it's a toxic environment or the kind of relationships in which we are engaged. For this reason, it's important we take the necessary action for the sake of our well-being. It may seem like a simple concept, however, when we are in a state of emotional or physical confusion, we often lose our ability to discern and think clearly. Simple things will elude our attention.

The path to True Love begins with being able to increase our level of self-awareness for our physical, mental, emotional and spiritual health. If we have been de-sensitized to our own well-being, it may take some time to strengthen this awareness or self-perception. When we are living with pain or discomfort, we often shut down or limit our sensory perception in order to focus our attention on what is hurting, or what we want to avoid feeling. This can be quite an unconscious habit that we have practiced over a long period of time. As a result, we can end up becoming numb to our inner guidance system and confusion will reign as we enter into a period of grieving what was, in the face of an unknown future.

# Passageway of Transformation

When we are first confronted by significant change in our life, whether it was planned, anticipated, initiated by another person or external circumstances, we are likely to experience the discomfort of being in unknown territory. Such a dramatic shift offers the opportunity to let go of what was, so we can move towards a new way of living and being. This is no overnight process! It's the passageway of personal transformation that requires our willing participation if we are to successfully and healthfully make it through to the other side.

There is no going around this stage, no avoiding or denying. The transformational process is happening, just as the sun rises every morning and sets every evening. Regardless of what we do, what we think or how we feel, once we begin, we are on the journey of no return. It is better to surrender to the process than resist what is inevitable.

The process of transformation requires us to let go of what has always provided us the comfort and security we have come to know. This may bring on intense feelings of fear, overwhelm, grief and loss. Elisabeth Kubler-Ross defined the five stages of grief as denial and isolation, anger, bargaining, depression and acceptance. It's not necessary to experience all these emotions during transformation, or in the same order. Emotional, physical and spiritual transformation is a holistic process that is part of our soul's journey and includes a shedding of what is no longer serving us, so that acceptance, healing, and new growth can occur.

If we are willing to embrace the change, despite our deepest fears of failure, abandonment or rejection, the process can be immensely fruitful. We may not be consciously aware that we have the inner tools and resources to assist ourself, however our Higher Self is there to guide us and knows we have all we need for the journey. If we trust and listen to the inner promptings in our heart and soul, the transformative process will heal and lift us to a new level of spiritual maturity.

Often when we feel unsettled and out of our depth, we may notice a desire to retreat from the world. We may feel overwhelm and unready to face anything new. Men may want to retreat to their 'man-cave' to process and chill out; women may desire the comfort of physical connection, to be with their friends, or spend time under the comfort of the doona. It's natural to feel this way, as we all have our own method for dealing with the unfamiliar and the uncomfortable.

During change we need the experience of self-care and working through the process in our own way and in our own time. However, if we notice that retreating is our preferred option most of the time, and it is our most common response to change and growth, then it may be a sign that we are putting on the brakes and avoiding the opportunity for true healing and transformation. It's important to do a self-check to see if our method of coping is helping us or is a hindrance. Trust what you are feeling and be honest about your fears.

Denying that we are experiencing significant change or that we may need to let go what feels so familiar and secure, is a way of protecting ourself from feeling more pain than we believe we can bear. During this phase of transformation, we may experience fear that stems from childhood memories of pain and humiliation that is now resurfacing in our adult life. Often this fear is unrealistic and yet it returns as an unconscious pattern we run in response to our belief we are in danger of being hurt or rejected. Denial or retreat can become our habitual way of avoiding pain, even if we know in reality that the fear stems from our past rather than from our present experiences.

Denial is an expression of our shadow-self and the opposite of feeling trust, love and self-acceptance. Signs of denial may be evident when we choose to fill our time with busyness, expending all of our energy on tasks to maintain control of our emotions and our circumstances. We may bury ourself in our work, or become overly attentive to our children's needs. A by-product of denial may be to manifest an addiction (obsessive behaviour) to avoid feeling pain. We may divert our attention to unhealthy relationships, or become focused on the dramas in the life of our friends. Either way, our busyness becomes a distraction to avoid feeling strong emotions and what we fear the most, whether it is the pain of humiliation, rejection, isolation, or failure. When left untended, the darker emotions of our shadow-self will continue to brew inside and cause us to delay our healing by drawing us away from our inner truth, Divine love and the experience of being our authentic self.

Working through denial is part of the process of letting go what is no longer serving us in our life. It's the first stage of processing our deepest fears. It may feel confronting and overwhelming to face our real truth and to acknowledge the changes in our life. It may also take some time before we are prepared to accept our past choices have created our current reality. Denial is a way of protecting ourself from what we perceive to be more pain, a way to avoid facing a truth that feels too difficult to bear. Accepting our own truth may mean we are willing to admit we are imperfect. To some, this may be liberating, to others it may be like hearing the same message we heard throughout our childhood, that we are not good enough.

If we are trapped in denial for too long, we miss the opportunity to see how our thinking or our choices have not served us well. We may be suffering on the inside and living in a way that feels in conflict with our authentic truth. It's not until we begin to feel safe to let go of our wall of defences that we can begin to step out of the shadows and reveal our true self. It's not until we find the inner courage to face our reality that we can make a conscious choice to see the self-harm, and the need for self-care as part of our healing process. For many of us, admitting that perhaps we have missed the mark can be humiliating, conjuring up deep fears of rejection or not measuring up to our own expectations or the expectations of others.

## My Personal Pilgrimage

For a long time during this period of transformation, I avoided being at home by myself for too long. From the moment I woke up in the morning I would pack my bag for the day and head for the beach or engage in some other activity that would keep me busy whilst in the company of others. It was my way of creating comfort and nurturing myself. I found solace in the fresh air and the revitalizing energy of the beach and the ocean breeze. I soaked up the life of the trees and the outdoors. It was very healing for me. My work was also a helpful way of maintaining some level of focus and control over my emotions, since it required me to act professionally and be in a more logical headspace for a period of time.

I knew that my preference to be away from home was because I was afraid of my deep sadness and being alone, and the guilt I felt over the pain I knew my husband and children were going through. I was very conscious of the fact they did not understand my choices or what I was experiencing. I was desperately trying to avoid falling into a pit of depression. I didn't want to go to a place of darkness that would threaten my health, healing and happiness. It was my way of protecting myself from spiralling down into an abyss that would have dire consequences for me. I knew I could not avoid the challenges that were ahead, and the necessary path of transformation for my souls' growth. Yet, even in knowing that ultimately all of what I was going through was going to prepare me for greater joy, love and fulfillment, I still experienced anger and resistance.

There were many times I tried to reason and grapple with the past, which affected me deeply. I felt anger for the pain I was going through. It felt unfair and unjust to experience such incredible loss. Though it was my choice to embrace my Soul's call for transformation, I still endured the physical separation from my family and home environment. Emotionally and socially I was initially disapproved of and rejected. There was also the experience of significant financial loss which terrified me and threw me into the fear of surviving. On all levels my world had changed and my energy and self-love tank was empty.

I was deeply wounded and despite working to keep relations calm and civil, I somehow needed to deal with the anger that welled up inside of me. For the most part I attempted to bury my feelings rather than infect others with my grief. However, it was difficult to suppress the strong emotions. I felt neglected, unloved, and my hopes and dreams for true happiness were gone. Instead I felt the pain of disconnection and isolation.

Responding to the call of my Soul was a willing choice, and I embraced the change despite the pain. I knew that with the right kind of support and perseverance, I would somehow find a way to go the distance and give birth to a new and more improved version of myself.

At this very early stage, I saw my real self for the first time. It was confronting, scary and totally unfamiliar. I began to uncover all parts of my being, the light and the dark. I didn't realise how much I had suppressed, and that I had lived this way for most of my adult life. I had always believed I was living as the real me, and yet now I was aware I was living only a small version of my greater potential. Most of us are living only a fraction of our true and amazing self. We live our life with incredible limitations, self-imposed rules, unhealthy self-sabotaging beliefs, and filtered perceptions that create the illusions of our life.

I sensed the road ahead was going to be a pilgrimage of significant personal and spiritual transformation, and like most pilgrimages, I was ignorant of what was yet to cross my path and enter my new life. I had a deep knowing it would be life changing, and I was willing to face the risks, take the leap of faith, and trust in the process of spiritual growth and renewal.

# 6
## The Courage to Love

Everyone wants to feel and experience love, and for many, it is the greatest desire as a human being. So, it's strange to think that we would need courage to love ourself, assuming we have been comfortable so far, not loving ourself. In the years leading up to my awakening I was unaware that for most of my life I was believing, thinking and behaving in a way that was reflective of my lack of self-belief and self-love. It wasn't that I had consciously made a decision to choose not to love myself. I had built layers and layers of limiting beliefs about who I saw myself to be, and years of self-deprecating habits. Over many years this led me down a path of self-judgment, poor thinking and a lack of esteem for my true self.

In time I had become well practiced in giving my love and personal power away, denying the value of myself, my uniqueness, gifts, talents, interests and well-being. My beliefs and behaviours had become a mix of unconscious strategies and habits that were designed to deflect attention and responsibility from myself, for fear that I would somehow be in the limelight and judged as the person who was not good enough, not smart enough, misunderstood and not deserving of love.

Living with this kind of self-perception was so normal that I believed this was the real me. I believed that this was all that I could expect from myself and that I should just accept it. With this kind of limiting belief, I was closing doors of opportunities, pulling down the shades, and essentially telling myself I was prepared to live each day with this heavy yoke over my shoulders. I was travelling down the road away from true love. With this mindset I could also see what was not whole and complete in me. As a result, everything in my world reflected these beliefs and perceptions. When we are unaware of the truth and we live unconsciously, we resort to deflecting personal responsibility for our choices and we attribute blame to others for our circumstances.

I am so grateful today that through a number of timely experiences, seeds of light and love were being planted within to awaken my soul consciousness. I began to hear the voice of God calling out to me, urging me back toward the path of Divine Love. In those moments when I could sense my Higher Self reminding me of my true value, there was a wonderful recognition of my connection to the Divine and at the same time, fear that a great transformation was imminent.

It seems to be in our human nature or perhaps our conditioning, that we easily allow our thoughts to drift towards the limits of fear rather than the freedom of Divine Love. We frequently experience contrasts in life to give us the opportunity to see what's possible. This became apparent as I became more conscious of my lack of self-love. Noticing the void within I began to feel the desire to move closer towards greater love in my life. My mind and my body ached, and my soul was thirsty. It didn't take long before the dark recesses of my soul were being exposed, and I was faced with my raw truth and the wounds that needed healing. It was enlightening and frightening at the same time.

Once you begin to awaken and you learn the truth, you cannot unlearn it. The more I realised what I wanted, the more I came to understand that inner change was necessary if I wanted to live with more love. For most people, the onset of significant change is often terrifying, even if we won't admit it to ourselves. I knew that staying unconscious and accepting a life of self-imposed unhappiness was no longer the path I wanted to walk. I desired more in my life. I desired to live as my true and complete self. I realised it was going to take a lot of inner work to overcome the years of mental and emotional conditioning of un-love that I had created. This is when I knew I needed to bring forth all the courage I could muster to fight the good fight, and commit to my transformation with faith, determination and trust.

Developing courage to love myself meant being willing to accept possible pain that may come with exposing everything, visible in the light of unconditional love. It meant being stretched and challenged in order to grow in wisdom, and to develop trust and love for myself.

Saying 'yes' was not a trip down easy street where living a good life would simply be a matter of everything going my way. The choice to love myself completely and unreservedly meant being stretched beyond my comfort zone. In the early stages I felt like I was constantly wading through sticky pools of mud that pulled me down into the depths where my wounds lay buried. It was seriously challenging, and yet Divine Love was my inspiration. Somehow, I needed to find my way out, towards freedom and greater love. I had been told the clue was self-compassion, and whilst I understood this intellectually, it was so difficult to believe this was possible for me, and to feel this in my heart.

*"It takes courage ... to endure the sharp pains of self-discovery rather than choose to take the dull pain of unconsciousness that would last the rest of our lives." – Marianne Williamson*

Having courage is often described as *taking action in the face of fear*, persevering in the face of adversity, standing up for what is right, following your heart and intuition, expanding your horizons, letting go of the familiar, and facing suffering with dignity and faith. However, this sounds all neatly packaged and easy to achieve, but in reality, it didn't feel this way at all. I cried many tears and at times all my doubts and confusion threatened to cripple me. I needed to accept that transformation and this ideal of loving myself was going to take some unlearning of past beliefs and behaviours, and a willingness to face my fears on my own. There is no-one who can do the work for you when it comes to choosing the path of transformation towards True Love.

Accepting my whole self and embracing the choice for change meant letting go of what I was used to doing and allowing Spirit to guide me and show me the way. It meant surrendering my limiting self-beliefs and the negative things I chose to tell myself every day. It also meant releasing the pent-up pain and anger, and allowing myself to feel it all, rather than deny or suppress it.

Without acknowledging my past choices and where I needed to grow, I could not begin the journey forward. I realised that having courage to step into the unknown required me to trust – trust in myself and trust in the power of Divine Love. It was not a matter of saying 'yep, I'm up for it, let's go', and then expect everything to change for the better. Keeping love as my inspiration and focus enabled me to manage the huge swings between resisting and allowing, failure and success.

Developing courage is a process of self-love and trust. It doesn't happen overnight, and it is an ongoing process and way of being, every day. My friends have been, and continue to be, incredible support. In the past there were many times I longed for them to take away the pain or give me the answers I was seeking. I experienced waves of emotions, from feeling weak and vulnerable, to feeling empowered and determined to forge on. I needed to feel both extremes because this was part of the evolution and transformational process that was necessary if I truly wanted to live a life that was authentic to my soul-being.

It's a wonder to me, that even when we feel we are at our lowest point, with our back against the wall and no more options, our heart and soul can still show us the way to rise above our circumstances. What we see as the last avenue becomes a doorway to more options, the catalyst that propels us into action to keep moving forward even when we don't know what we are doing or where we are going. Truly, all of us have the Divine spark of Love within that cannot be extinguished, no matter how much we try to ignore or suppress it in favour of our fear.

Over the past several years I've fallen down many times, and each time I found some inner strength and determination to get myself up and going again. I learned that every time I felt thwarted there was an opportunity to reflect on what wasn't working, and how I could take small steps to do things differently next time. I was learning to trust myself that I could find a way to improve my situation and grow from the experience. Every challenge gave me evidence that I could make a difference for myself, even if it was infinitesimal. I also realised I was not alone. God, my spirit guides and the new friends in my life, were supporting me along the way. My greatest inspiration was realising that all things are possible when we see our world through the eyes of Divine Love.

Sometimes fear can work as an effective motivator to turn our focus away from what is actually holding us back. Human beings are strongly driven by the desire to avoid pain and what we fear most in life. Most people assume that fear is something we need to remove from our experience of being, since we perceive it to be a nasty negative emotion. This can be true if we let it diminish and deplete our energy and our sense of well-being. However, fear can also be a healthy emotion when we leverage it in a way that drives us towards change and transformation.

When we embrace our fear and use it to better understand the shadow aspects of ourself, it can serve to inform us on how we can make alternative choices that are more loving. Instead of denying the existence of our fears, we are best to acknowledge our fear and use its energy to leverage our spiritual transformation. In a world of contrast, we accept the existence of fear and love. Unconditional love then becomes our true inspiration and the power for change.

In the early stages of my mid-life transformation I used my fear of not coping and my fear of depression, as a motivator to keep my head above water. I had a choice to survive, or not. I was in a state of overwhelm. With so much changing in my life it felt like my world was crumbling before me. At first, I told myself it was my instinct to survive that kept me going. I now realise that beneath the confusion and the pain, somewhere deep down I felt love for my soul-being. The call of my Soul reminded me of my Divine nature. Though it may be difficult for us to see that Divine Love exists within us, there still lies a seed, waiting for the spark of our life to bring it forth into our vision and into our experience.

Courage is not something someone can give us. It is a spiritual resource we *all* have that sprouts from the seed of Divine Love. When we are open to the process of transformation, we have vast resources we can draw on for our soul's growth. Like developing strength in our muscles, it takes consistent effort, time and patience. Most importantly, it takes a willingness and a belief to see that all we imagine is possible. Courage comes from loving who we are and knowing we are worth the effort it takes to achieve what is most important to us. As we achieve the small milestones each day, we provide evidence to ourself of what works and what doesn't work, according to what we believe.

As I managed to achieve small pebbles of progress, I knew I was capable of helping myself. Each time I picked myself up to face a new day or a new challenge, I felt my sensitivity and awareness of Spirit grow stronger and clearer. As I listened more intently to the guidance and loving messages being revealed to me, I became more attuned to Spirit. The key was to trust in myself, in God, and in Divine timing. My soul was calling me to step up and to live my Divine life-purpose.

*When we allow ourself to be guided by Spirit and*
*take action that is aligned with Divine Love,*
*this becomes our powerful in-spir-ation (spirit-*
*in-action) for facing our fears*
*and experiencing soul growth.*

Developing courage is learning how to love ourself. It takes time and practice, and there is no perfection. However, it does require us to act even in the face of fear. A great warrior always experiences fear, but it's the determination to press on with clarity and purpose that gives rise to developing love and inner strength of character.

It took incredible courage, alongside immense fear, to leave my marriage and all that was familiar to me. I knew I needed the time to process why I was feeling so deflated and out of alignment in my soul. For a long time, I struggled emotionally and spiritually, knowing I was not living as my authentic self. Inside I felt like a bird trapped in a cage.

Yes, I had what I needed materially to live, but I was not living fully as the real me, and the mal-alignment felt painful.

In the months prior to leaving my old world, I felt an increasing burning desire to stretch my wings and fly. I wasn't at all sure where I was going or what I was moving towards. I only knew that I felt a strong desire to go and find out. I wanted to learn more about myself, connect with my inner truth and discover more about my spirituality. I recognised that it was time to make a deeper spiritual pilgrimage that only I could make on my own. I was the thirsty student in search of the master.

I struggled with feelings of guilt and confusion for a long time. My love for the family was strong and so I resisted the urge to change for fear of hurting them. I believed I could manage this inner tension between what I believed the family expected of me and making the choice to follow my heart. From all appearances it seemed as though I was ticking the boxes for personal growth and fulfillment. However, as Caroline Myss says, my level of spiritual growth was at the *Eau de Toilette* stage where my ego was fulfilling the needs of my physical self. I was yet to progress to a deeper level of *'Cologne'*, which is the precursor for a deeper experience of the concentrated perfume of spiritual maturity and enlightenment.

I knew that if I didn't follow my Soul's guidance I would stagnate and the light inside me would grow dim. My Higher Self reminded me how important it is to live authentically, and that in time it would make a difference to the spiritual growth of my children. I realised that it's important to live my truth and discern what is right for me. No matter our age or stage in life, our choices and actions have an impact on others. So, it's important to listen to the Divine guidance, as it will always lead us to be a greater version of ourself and to live a life with greater love.

The more I resisted the call to go deeper, the more I could feel myself enter into a darkness within. I sank to a terrible low where everything in my life was falling away. My relationship with my husband was out of sync and I felt disconnected from my true self. I was miserable and without a sense of purpose. Around this time, I made the decision to leave my job. The joy and sense of fulfillment had long gone, and I felt undervalued. The truth is, I did not value myself. At the time I was unaware that I had lowered my energy and my poor self-esteem was creating a vibration that was not matching the truth of my authentic self.

Shortly after leaving my job I completed post-graduate studies in Christian Spirituality, and this re-ignited the light inside, like a small fire getting ready to burn brighter. Making the decision to step out into the unknown was frightening. I knew that I would be confronted with all of my fears of being alone, having no money, disconnection from my children, and judgment and rejection by my family. What I also feared was not being understood. I knew all of this was an inevitable consequence, and I felt incredibly anxious at the thought of it. However, the pain of not being my true self, and the thought of continuing for another 25 years without honouring my true path, was not a palatable option either. Deep down in my inner core, I knew there was more to being me, and I felt compelled to discover that person and dive deeper to live my true purpose.

Each time I've made the decision to take a leap of faith, I've been terrified. Yet at the same time I have been excited at the opportunities before me, and what I may learn. Over time I have become accustomed to embracing my fear, knowing that hidden in the discomfort and the challenges, are golden gems that brighten my path and light me up internally. I know that each time I have the courage and wisdom to say 'yes' to life's opportunities, I learn something new that helps me to become a better person. More importantly, it teaches me how to love myself unconditionally, and how to '*be*' love.

As I learn and grow in wisdom, I see more choices before me. The experience of my world and my reality expands to a whole new level where I feel incredible gratitude and awareness of all that is. The clarity, peace, joy and love for myself continue to increase. It's not easy. No growth happens without being stretched however I prefer to focus on how I am creating my life and to live as authentically as possible.

When we face challenges in our life, well-meaning family and friends may be quick to remind us of the pain, as some take solace in re-hashing the details of each unsavoury event. Offers of sympathy may be their way of showing love, but it's more often about meeting their need to share common feelings and circumstances. Unfortunately, this is a big energy drainer. Focusing on what is not working is exactly what has kept me stuck in the same pattern of thinking and doing in the past. It's destructive and un-resourceful, and only serves to keep me in a cycle of feeling depressed and hopeless. This kind of focus means I am not recognising the possibilities for growth and change. In this state of mind, I am only seeing the immediate discomfort and the obstacles that appear to be in the way of removing the pain.

Have you ever noticed that when you engage in negative talk with friends, complaining about how other people or circumstances are unjust and unfair, it leaves you feeling drained and exhausted? You are no further ahead towards a solution or taking responsibility for your life, other than feeling justified for being in your own mess.

*So, what does it take to stop pulling the plug on your own love energy tank?*

Developing courage to live with more love in my life means reassessing my values in terms of my health and well-being. Poor physical health, cloudy thinking, depressed emotions and a disconnection from my Soul means I am not truly loving myself.

## Pause. Ponder. Reflect

You may wish to answer some or all of the questions below to help you gain more clarity on how you have experienced love in the past, and how you love yourself today. Take time to journal and process your thoughts and feelings.

- What do you believe are your barriers to loving yourself more?
- What do you tell yourself that is not loving?
- What has stopped you from showing love to others in the past?
- How have you blocked others from giving and showing love to you?
- What was your experience of love as a child? Did it feel good, unloving or stressful?
- As an adult, do you notice any regular strategies (or behaviours) you run to protect yourself from 'un-loving' situations?
- How has this affected your openness to receive or give love today?
- What are some recent experiences of safe and unconditional love you have experienced (eg: from friends, family or partner)?
- How has this helped you to give and receive love?
- What helps you to fill your love energy tank? (ie: to feel more love within).
- What can you do each day to be more loving towards yourself?

# 7
## The Energy Shift

It's common for all of us to experience struggles in different areas of our life, whether it's in our job, relationships, our health or our finances. However, if we are regularly exposing ourself to toxic relationships, poor health, poor financial habits, and a lack of self-love, then we are likely to be living a life that will considerably lower our energy and draw more of the same kind of challenging experiences into our life.

As our energy plummets, so does our ability to have clarity and vision for our life. We are unlikely to see our true value or the opportunities that exist before us when we are focused on what's not working in our life, rather than looking for the opportunities. The downward spiral toward an unhealthy and unloving life will tend to get stronger if we don't do anything to change our focus and our energy.

When we are living at a low vibration, we will attract more experiences that match that same vibration. This is the universal Law of Attraction. We are living pure energy, vibrating at a certain frequency, and we attract what matches that same frequency, including our thoughts and beliefs about any aspect of our life.

*Being aware of our energy and managing this*
*in a healthy way leads to a life*
*that is in flow, attracting more love and abundance.*

**Reflection:** *Your mental well-being*

For optimal mental well-being it's important to recognise our habitual ways of thinking, believing and behaving.

- What do you notice about your own patterns of thinking?
- Do you regularly self-sabotage, engage in fear-based thinking, or regularly doubt your own value and abilities?
- In what ways do you limit yourself by the way you are thinking and believing?
- Do you always look for the flaws in yourself and the obstacles on your path? Or do you embrace challenges in your life with the view that life is providing opportunities to grow and to feel abundant as a result?
- Do you see with eyes of love and then notice the light in others and your surroundings and how love is reflected back to you?

Every thought we have and every belief we hold creates our experiences in life. Even our daily patterns of self-talk or conversation with our peers is powerful enough to either open doors to more love and light in our life or close them with limited thinking that draws lower vibrational energy. Our thoughts and beliefs can support our personal growth and happiness, or they can hold us back and delay our progress towards love and happiness.

Self-awareness is key to your own growth. When you can honestly accept the areas of your life that you know need improvement, it's a matter of then choosing to do things differently. It's not a matter of aiming for perfection, however if you want to live a life that's fulfilling, then taking action in the direction of self-empowerment and self-love is vital. All it takes is practice and a willingness to persevere.

Our body is a miracle and a true reflection of our mental, emotional and spiritual growth. Our *physical well-being* is a vital aspect of who we are and necessary for us to live powerfully and grounded. The concept of physical health is no stranger to us, as we are regularly flooded by the media with messages of the importance of our physical well-being, whether it's our fitness, our nutrition, or the health of our structural body. Then, there is our energetic body or our subtle body, which is less known and often a neglected aspect of our well-being.

**Reflection:** *Your physical well-being*

Take note of what your body and what your energy levels tell you about yourself.

- Do you regularly feel sluggish and lethargic, or do you feel vital and alive in your energy?
- Do you experience regularly recurring injuries or health concerns in certain areas of your body? Ask yourself why this may be happening.

Our bodies are very intelligent and capable of reflecting back to us the true state of our whole well-being.

In her book "Heal Your Life" Louise Hay shares insights about the different parts of the body and typical physical symptoms that reflect the state of our emotional and mental health. Someone who is regularly suffering sore Achilles tendons may very well be struggling to step up in their life in terms of their personal growth. Regular lower back problems may also be a reflection of not standing up for yourself. Of course, the body is susceptible to real structural and physical ailments that may require medical attention. However, it is important to recognise that our overall health and well-being is not just the physical. All aspects of our being are interconnected, the mental, emotional, physical and the spiritual.

Our *emotional* well-being is equally important and very much connected to our mental and physical health. Too many of us have been raised to discount our emotions. We may have been taught or conditioned to believe that to be emotional is a sign of weakness or that emotions are irrelevant and prevent us from taking clear and concise action in our life. We were designed to have emotions for good reason. They are invaluable in giving us feedback to help us become aware of our thinking, what we are doing, and how we are responding to our world. The key is to notice and become aware of how you are feeling so that you can reflect and gain sufficient clarity to understand yourself before you take action to create change.

**Reflection: *Your emotional well-being***

If your feelings are letting you know that you are out of harmony with what you value or what's important to you, listen, notice and review what you have been recently thinking and doing.

- What needs to change?
- How are you perceiving the situation?
- Is it how you are using your energy or where you are focusing?
- Do you need more information, or do you need to surrender and let go what is not in your control or no longer serving you?
- Rather than do more in any particular area, do you need to do less?
- Is it time to rest and reflect instead of pushing the boulder up the mountain?

If you notice you are regularly becoming ill, suffering from headaches, putting on weight, not sleeping well, or you are increasingly more prone to injury, it's usually a clear sign you are out of alignment in other areas of your life.

- What could be troubling you?
- What is not working well or not resonating for you? Is it in your job? Is it to do with a relationship with a friend, family or work colleague?
- Are you putting your energy in an area of your life that is not serving you?

Whatever the issue, your health and your body will be a mirror or reflection of what is out of sync elsewhere. Naturally you must respond to the physical health issue first by seeking professional medical guidance. However, often the reason why the health complaint has shown up is due to your mental and emotional state that has attracted the lower energy and vibration that can lead to illness in the body. As we become more self-aware and present to our body and our emotions, and we take good care of our physical, mental and emotional well-being, we provide a clearer pathway to listen to our intuition and our inner knowing.

The key to having emotions is to use them as an indicator of your focus and where your attention is being drawn. It's not helpful to dwell in lower vibrational emotions, however we can use them as information to help us reflect on our life and our choices. When we choose to ignore the signs and take no action, we risk allowing an opportunity to pass to make a difference or to make an alternative choice. It may be wise to share with a close friend, seek a professional's opinion, or evaluate what you can do differently.

Our emotions can be a full expression of our how we are thinking and feeling, such as love, joy, fulfillment, compassion, as well as sadness, anxiety, confusion and fear. Often people associate emotions with negativity, weakness and feelings that are not controlled or understood. This is a limited perspective on how our emotions serve to assist us. It's possible that 'emotions' may have received a bad wrap in the past because of the emotion of 'fear' that is so prevalent in our world.

Fear-based thoughts are the cause for feeling confused and out of alignment with our true self. It is surprising how often we can entertain fear-based thoughts for a large portion of the day, even when we are unaware of doing this. Every moment of our day we are making choices to think, feel and do. Take time to observe your own thoughts and how your body responds when you are making a choice to do A or B. Do you feel at ease in your thoughts, in your emotions and in your body? Or do you feel unease, concern or a tightness in your stomach?

Debra Landwehr Engle's book *"The Only Little Prayer You Need"* shares her insights on how to recognise fear in our life and the simple way we can learn to replace fear with love. In this world of duality there is love, or there is fear. Only Love is real. Fear is an illusion. It's a difficult concept to grasp, however Debra helps to explain how any fear-based thought can be traced back to the same core fear: *I don't matter.* Fears may also surface around not feeling good enough, not feeling lovable, successful, valued and so on. Either way, fear is usually expressed in our body and in our emotions and will have a significant impact on the quality of our life. Most of the time our fear-based thoughts are all about anticipation of things that never happen.

To live in fear is to rob ourself of True Love. It lowers our energy and moves us away from the joy of Divine love, which is all that truly exists. Debra's prayer *"Please heal my fear-based thoughts"* is a way towards true healing and creating space within for expansion that is filled with love. The premise is that fear is not real and emanates from our thoughts, and that there is a higher power that can assist us with our healing, as long as we ask, and we are open to receiving the Divine healing.

As we come to recognise that the path to True Love involves the healing of our whole self, and a synergy between our emotional, mental, physical and spiritual aspects of our being, we are able to create more flow in our life. Our energy becomes lighter, and we begin to feel more at peace, and even joyful. When we are filled with joy, our spirits are lifted because we tap into our passion, our life purpose and our soul journey. Engaging in activities that bring us joy means we are living in the moment and no longer focused on the past, the future, or what is not working.

I was contemplating the other day what 'joy' really means. Most mornings I visit the beach to walk the promenade and wait for that glorious moment of seeing the sun rise above the ocean. There is a freshness to the air, as the sky begins to lighten and become the most incredible palate of changing colours, from deep blue to pale blues, pinks and oranges. The seagulls soar above in anticipation and the trees seem to lift up and open towards the sun as they wait for the golden rays to touch their branches at first light. It's pure magic. I feel and sense the energy of nature coming alive as the sun touches us all. The freshness of the morning and the way my senses come alive and tingle all at once creates a deep and expanded feeling of love and joy. In these moments I realise this is what joy feels like for me. Feelings of lightness and love fill my heart and my soul-being, as well as creating a new and uplifted energy in all of my body.

Joy is the culmination and synergy of Divine Love expressed physically, emotionally and spiritually. When we experience joy, we can only feel love, not fear. When we experience joy, in that moment there is only happiness, not sadness or judgment. Joy raises our vibrational energy so that we become open, expanded and aligned with Divine Love. We are always connected to the Divine, however when we experience joy it is as if we have turned off the mute button and opened the communication channels to love.

**Reflection:** *Your spiritual well-being*

Joy may be initiated in different ways for each one of us. It can be noticing the radiant beauty of nature, the connection we feel with animals, the deep soothing feelings evoked by beautiful music, or from the simple physical pleasures we can experience in small moments in our day. In whatever way you experience joy, you will notice it's not possible to feel fear or sadness at the same time. The light and love of joy radiates and dissipates all darkness.

- How have you experienced joy in your life?
- In what ways have you felt lifted and purely present in the moment, connected to your Soul and to the Divine?
- To experience more joy in your life, ask yourself what can you do differently that is more in tune with your values as an individual?
- What can you do that is more loving towards yourself, more enjoyable, and allows your heart to sing?

Becoming consciously aware of our thinking, what we are doing, and how we are feeling is the first step to making better and more informed choices that will lead to improved health and well-being. After all, isn't that what we ultimately want to have in life? Better health and relationships that are nurturing. Maintaining a deep sense of love and compassion for oneself is the key to experiencing a life that is joyful and fuelled by our soul-purpose.

## Our Vibrating Body

Our body is a miracle, a powerhouse of living energy that vibrates at different frequencies depending upon our mental, emotional and physical well-being. Understanding more about our energy-body can help us to learn how to adjust and manage our energy so we are living more optimally.

Our physical body is made up of energy that vibrates quite slowly and easy to recognise through the experience of touch. We also have a subtle body or energy system that is made of different layers of vibrating energy, each with its own specific vibration. The seven layers of the subtle body are known as the etheric, emotional, lower mental, high mental, causal body, soul body and the integrated spiritual body. Together the energy bodies work as a complete system. Each subtle body of energy connects into the physical body via an energy point or chakra, which directs energy into the physical body via the meridian system.

Anoeda Judith Ph.D, author of "Wheels of Life", explains in detail about the subtle energy systems of the body and how we can come to understand the interconnectedness of the energy centres for our health and well-being. Each of our energy centres (or chakras) is a vortex of energy that is a gateway for vital life-force energy from the subtle bodies to enter the physical body via the nadis and meridians. These vortexes of energy also provide an exit point for lower frequency energy to be released back into the subtle bodies for transmutation.

The physical body is dependent upon the vital energy flow to maintain optimum well-being. At different times our energy centres may become sluggish and they may lose their ability to flow well. When we are in a negative state for too long, holding onto rigid thought patterns and negative emotions, our energy centres will slow down and cease to function optimally. As a result, we will notice a drop in our physical energy when we are feeling mentally and emotionally low. This has a direct effect on our overall health and functioning physically, mentally and emotionally. It also effects our level of intuition and our ability to connect with our Higher Self.

When we learn to recognise the health of our chakras we can take simple measures to unblock and increase the energy flow so that we are in tune and re-connected with our soul, mind and body.

Crown Chakra — Spirituality

Third Eye Chakra — Awareness

Throat Chakra — Communication

Heart Chakra — Love, Healing

Solar Plexus Chakra — Wisdom, Power

Sacral Chakra — Sexuality, Creativity

Root Chakra — Basic Trust

There are seven main chakras in the body, that are positioned from the base of our spine to the crown of our head. (The base, sacral, solar plexus, heart, throat, brow and crown chakra). There are also many other smaller chakra points located around the body and in our hands and feet. Each chakra point vibrates at its own frequency and serves a particular function. When we understand the function of each energy centre and how it relates to our physical and emotional body, we can learn to manage our energy for optimal health and well-being.

The **Root or Base chakra** is located at the base of our spine and is represented by the colour red. A healthy base chakra enables us to feel grounded and stable physically, mentally and emotionally, promoting a sense of well-being and abundance. Energy in this centre tends to vibrate slowly and increases in frequency as we move towards the crown chakra. A blocked Base chakra however is likely to indicate a scarcity mentality and fears around meeting one's basic needs for living such as food, shelter, and our emotional, physical and financial security.

Taking care of your health by ensuring you have good nutrition, regular exercise and plenty of sleep, is a good step towards improving the flow of energy in your Base or Root chakra. If you are feeling particularly unstable or ungrounded you may choose to walk in nature, plant your feet in the earth, grass or sand, and connect with Mother

Earth. Spending time to ground through stillness and meditation, or connecting with animals, is also helpful for returning balance to your Base chakra. For a period of time you may choose to consume foods and beverages that are the colour red or surround yourself with more of this warm and nurturing colour in your day.

The **Sacral chakra** is located in the region of the pelvis and is represented by the colour orange. The Sacral chakra is connected to our creativity and sensuality. When the Sacral chakra is functioning well, we are feeling connected and in tune with our body and our physical surrounds. When it becomes sluggish we tend to feel disconnected from ourself and separate from our community. We may become more introverted and feel anxious and emotional.

To help improve the flow of energy and our sense of creativity, you can incorporate more movement into your day, such as through dance or listening to music, playing an instrument, or more creative and artistic pursuits. What do you love to do to create movement and creativity in your life? Do you enjoy sport, dancing, yoga, swimming, art, music, a warm bath or a relaxing massage? What helps you to connect to your sense of inner freedom to let loose and be in more flow? What do you enjoy doing that helps you to feel more nurtured and in tune with your Divine feminine energy? This chakra is not gender specific; it represents our ability to receive and to create.

The **Solar Plexus** chakra is represented by the colour yellow and is known as our power centre. It has a direct correlation to our sense of personal power and our ability to take action towards our goals and our dreams. This centre, when it is flowing well, will enable you to focus on your goals and what you value most. When it is not functioning well you may be feeling fearful, lacking in confidence and disempowered.

Creating more physical energy can help to clear any sluggishness in this chakra and assist you to have more clarity and purpose. When you feel emotionally and mentally low, you can shift and raise your energy by having a regular exercise program, and at the very least, create more movement in your day. This will help to improve your focus and mental clarity. It will also be helpful for you to be mindful of your thinking. Are you too focused on what is not working well for you? Shift your focus to the present moment and notice what you are blessed with right now. Remember, it is just as important to recognise and acknowledge your achievements and milestones to-date. Value what you have achieved, what you are experiencing in this moment, and what is present in your life right now.

The **Heart chakra** is represented by the colour green or pink and is located in the middle of the chest and thoracic region of the body. When the Heart chakra is flowing well, we are able to experience love in all areas of our life, to give and receive love and to recognise that love is created from within. When energy is flowing well through the Heart chakra we feel expanded mentally, emotionally and spiritually, and we feel a connection with the Universe and all that is. When the energy is blocked around the Heart chakra we experience issues around trust, difficulties breathing (tightness or shallow breathing), and feelings of depression or sadness.

Yoga is a very effective way of opening our chest and heart area to increase the flow of energy in the Heart chakra. If you have a moment to be still, try the following exercise in a space that is comfortable and quiet.

**Exercise: *Opening the Heart Chakra***

Lie on your back with a pillow behind your thoracic region of your upper back, and gently lay your arms open wide either side. This will help to expand the chest cavity.

As you do this, feel yourself relax and let go of the tight muscles in your chest and stomach area. You will notice that your breathing becomes easier and there is a sensation of wanting to let go.

With intention, feel yourself relax each muscle in the body, starting from your toes, ankles, calves, knees, thighs, hips, stomach, chest and back, fingers, arms, shoulders, neck, throat, jaw, tongue, eyes, forehead and ears.

As you physically connect with the sensations of your body and feel the benefit of relaxing you will notice a tendency to release mentally from the mind chatter.

As the mind calms it is common to experience an emotional release.

Give yourself time during this exercise. Don't be surprised if tears begin to flow as you come into your inner space and being.

Enjoy the bliss of stillness and openness. Allow the energy to flow freely within you.

Another way to open your Heart chakra is to regularly journal or write down your thoughts and feelings, without judgment or any attempt to modify what you write. This is not about perfection but allowing yourself to feel and experience what your inner self wants to express. It is a wonderful way to release what feels so pent-up in your heart which we are often not ready to release.

Recently my yoga teacher reminded the class that, love and peace do not come from our thinking; it comes from our heart. When you are feeling the need to experience more love in your life, ask yourself what you can do to nurture and love you. What things do you enjoy and help you to feel nourished, happy and well? When we give love to ourself and ensure we have filled our own cup, we are then able to give even more love to others.

I love to walk in nature, to receive a relaxation massage, indulge in a warm bubble bath, enjoy a beautiful meal, listen to calming music, buy myself something beautiful, take time out to read a book, and spend time with a friend over coffee. Whatever it is that you love to do when you feel the need to be pampered, give this gift to yourself. The experience of love comes from how we first give love to ourself.

The **Throat chakra** is represented by the colour blue and is connected to our ability to voice how we feel. It is the chakra for communication and so when it is functioning well, we will experience an ease and confidence in speaking our truth. When our throat chakra is compromised, we may be suffering from physical ailments such as sore throats, issues around the voice box, and challenges with speaking about how we really think and feel. When communication is blocked, we may experience difficulty in being our true authentic self.

There are times we all feel challenged in speaking our truth when in the company of others. However, living and speaking our truth can also be expressed in the way we give ourself permission to be our true self. It may be in the way you dress, the choices you make in your life, the principles that you live by, and how you articulate what is important to you. Are you living in a way that is aligned with your values, or do you make compromises to suit other people? Are your relationships reflective of your own value system? Does what you do in your job match your values and is in alignment with your own sense of truth?

Sometimes, giving a voice to our true self may not always be easy or appropriate, however the practice of journaling is a very liberating way to express how you truly feel. You don't need to be a great writer or fluid with your thoughts as you put pen to paper or fingers to keyboard. All you need to do is just start with something, as if you are speaking your mind freely and without inhibitions. Allow the thoughts and feelings to flow and very soon you will notice an ease and a release.

Sometimes singing (whether it's in the shower, on your own in the car, or with friends), is an amazing way of releasing the energy in the throat chakra. Recently I had the beautiful experience of learning some Hawaiian chants. The chants are designed to be sung with others and in harmony. As we sang the chants together and tuned into each other's energy, there was a wonderful feeling of unity and connection. This experience of feeling connected somehow opens the heart and there is a deeper release of all that needs to be expressed from our inner being. I'm sure it is our united connection with the Divine, which is within us all. The Throat chakra is our communication centre. When the energy is flowing freely here, we are able to express our true self with ease.

The **Brow chakra** is located between the eyes and is represented by the colour violet. This chakra is connected to our pituitary gland and is also known as the 'Third Eye'. A clearly functioning Brow chakra means our intuition is well developed, so that we can communicate and receive messages beyond the limits of our physical senses. A highly developed Brow chakra (or Third eye) will often lead to being able to see visual images in the mind that assist with the ability of clairvoyance (clear-seeing).

As mentioned previously, the vibration and frequency of the energy centres of each chakra increases as we move upwards and closer to the crown. To experience clear and free flowing energy in the Brow chakra we need to develop a practice of creating inner stillness of the mind and body, and to let go of distractions and physical attachments in life. Meditation is a very good way of developing the ability to go within and create stillness and peace. When we can be in a state of quiet, we are able to be a clear channel to receive spiritual guidance, which we often recognise as our intuition (*inner knowing without the need for conscious reasoning*).

Living a healthy life so that our body can best serve us, means we can improve our intuitive abilities. Good nutrition that includes a primarily plant-based diet, with little to no alcohol or caffeine or preservatives will also ensure our bodies are clean and receptive. A clean body means a clear channel for receiving messages and enhancing our ability to inwardly see, hear, feel, sense and know. This is known as clear-sight (clairvoyance), clear-feeling (clairsentience), clear-knowing (claircognizance), or clear-hearing (clairaudience).

If you are interested in crystals, you may wish to incorporate the amethyst crystal into your meditation practice or have it by your bedside, on your desk, or in your purse. It is believed that the energetic properties of the purple amethyst can enhance your ability to be in-tune with your Higher Self and your intuition.

The **Crown Chakra** is located at the top of our head (or slightly above) and is represented by the colours white or gold. This chakra point is a vortex that allows Divine energy, light and love, to enter our body. As we improve the flow of the other chakras in our body, from the base to the brow, we are preparing ourself to be a clear and open channel to receive Divine love and guidance from the spiritual realm. Through regular meditation, we can ascend and connect with the spiritual realm and experience our Higher Self, or soul-being. As the flow of energy increases in this chakra, and we become more open (less inhibited by our thoughts and our physicality), we are able to connect more easily with the wisdom and guidance that comes from the Divine, or a greater or higher power. As we connect with our Crown chakra, the limitations and the duality of our physical life falls away, and we can recognise our inner spiritual essence and our true self.

## Support for our Soul's journey

Having the courage to be myself was not only about recognising my own value and the importance of living my own truth. It was about taking personal responsibility and action to make changes that would help me to re-align with my authentic self. I knew that I needed to pause and take stock of how I was fairing, a measure of my spiritual, mental and physical well-being. Where was I out of balance? What aspects of my physical life needed improvement in terms of my fitness, my energy levels, my physical strength and flexibility, my nutrition, and my sense of connectedness with my body?

Whilst I was making some progress in my life emotionally and spiritually, I knew my physical health was waning. The body weight that I had carried for many years was like a ball and chain for me, weighing me down physically, mentally and emotionally. The heaviness I felt in my thoughts and in my spirit was directly impacting my physical health. Intuitively I knew I needed to move my body to release the heavy energy and to begin to inject new life into my physical being. I felt the urge to walk every day to create motion and momentum, to increase my oxygen levels and improve my circulation. My body was weak, disconnected and out of tune like a sluggish engine. To assist my spiritual and emotional transformation, I needed a stronger and well-functioning body to support me and to assist with increasing my vibrational energy.

As I was experiencing these new changes within, I became more aware of the necessity to be aligned and conscious of my physical senses; the way we give and receive communication through our physical body. The sense of touch and the need for physical release became more important to me. As my overall spiritual, psychic and emotional sensitivity was increasing, I also experienced more sensitivity in my body to energetic changes. I discovered that my hands and body were becoming more activated and that I could sense and feel the energy of others. Later this helped me with the practice of Reiki and massage to assist the body's natural physical and emotional healing. I quickly learned however that it was necessary for me to manage my energy and develop ways to protect my own boundaries in a healthy way.

The process of awakening and moving through a physical, mental, emotional and spiritual transformation has helped me to become a better witness of my own growth. With all of my senses more activated I have become sensitized to my physical and emotional needs, helping me to more easily recognise the state of my own energy levels. Over time and with practice I have become more adept at knowing how to manage my energy so that I can create and build positive and healing energy for myself.

If you are an empath, or someone who is a highly sensitive person (not hyper-sensitive), you will easily notice when you walk into a room if the energy is positive and uplifting, or heavy and draining. Some people that we know, either friends, family or work colleagues, may be what we call "energy drainers" or "energy vampires". If you feel particularly drained and low in energy after spending time with a person, you will know that this person's energy is a lower vibration to your own, and the experience will leave you feeling unwell, irritated, or very lethargic. If you know that your energy is normally lighter and more positive, then you may want to choose how much time you spend around energy of a lower vibration.

Rather than seek to gain energy from other people in order to feel good (which is what energy vampires do), it is best to learn how to manage your own energy levels. Become more observant about what makes you feel uplifted and more vital. Notice how you feel about your environment when at work, at home, socially or when you are in nature. You may have a strong response to the noise level, the lighting, the temperature, and the ambiance and activities around you. Be more conscious and aware of what feels good and what is in alignment with how you want to feel. We can manage our own energy by discerning the energy around us, as well as the energy within.

More often than not, raising your energetic vibration is as simple as doing more of what you love to do. When we engage in activities that create a feeling of fulfillment, peace, and enjoyment, we raise our own energetic vibration, and this brings more of the same energy into our life and our experiences. Maintaining a more positive and loving attitude and living with more gratitude for what is present in our life also raises our energy to levels that will help us feel lighter, more expansive and creative.

When we live and love unconditionally without judgment or self-criticism, we free ourself from the mental and emotional weight of unnecessary burden and anxiety. From this place we create mental clarity, we are emotionally grounded, physically in tune with our body, and we are connected spiritually with our Higher Self. Finding the *courage* to do anything is no longer the focus. We are aligned with our inner being, ready and open to *be our authentic self.*

As our ability to sense, feel and intuit increases, looking after our energy and our physical body is a necessity. Being in tune with my physical fitness has not been a natural orientation for me in the past. It was challenging because it was unfamiliar to me. I am working on maintaining a healthy fitness regime that specifically includes developing my strength and flexibility. Becoming more aware of the changes in my body has helped me to be more attuned to my body's needs and how this affects my mental and emotional well-being. The more I listen and take action, the easier it is to make the adjustments in my life so that I feel younger, healthier and vibrant. This is how I prefer to feel and live my life. Knowing the difference between adopting a mediocre approach to my health and consciously choosing to feel better is a 'no brainer'. I love variety in my activities, and one that I particularly enjoy is the wonderful integration of the physical, emotional, and spiritual aspects of yoga. For me, this is a great way for improving my health and well-being.

Becoming the observer of ourself is a wonderful way to increase our level of self-awareness for our healing and well-being. In the early stages of my transformation I began with an intention to be more observant of how I was feeling in my body and checking in to see where I felt pain, sluggishness, or low in energy. I then took note of where my thoughts were focused and whether I was engaging in positive self-affirming and creative thoughts, or whether I was more focused on worrying about the past or feeling anxious about the future. I also checked in with how I was feeling emotionally, noting my overall mood. Our emotions are a wonderful gauge for where our mind is focused and what we are regularly telling ourself. I also observed whether I was feeling connected with my Higher Self or whether I felt a general disconnection with my inner truth and intuitive self, separate from the world around me.

Checking in with ourself and reflecting on the status of our own well-being in any moment is a real gift. It's a simple way of honouring and valuing ourself, acknowledging how we feel, and what our soul, mind and body is needing in order to create optimal health and well-being. The path to True Love starts with this simple step. Know yourself and be true to you.

*"To thine own self, be true" (William Shakespeare)*
*"To know thyself is the beginning of wisdom" (Socrates)*

When we value ourself, and we consciously choose to really know who we are and what we need to do to feel good, we are on the precipice of creating amazing transformation toward True Love in our life. When we become a witness and an observer of ourself, we can make positive change to improve our emotional and physical well-being. For example, when I feel sluggish, I move.

*Motion creates motivation and momentum.*

Yes, it's that simple. When I have been sitting for too long at work or in the car, I notice my body feels like a heavy weight and this really affects my mood and my clarity. So, I get up and start moving. It gets the circulation going, the muscles and bones are working, and I'm breathing fresh air into my lungs. My brain becomes stimulated by new sights, sounds and smells, and I begin to feel more alert and uplifted. The choice to ignore my body means that eventually it leads to back pain or a body that struggles to move. I then feel mentally clouded, uninspired and inept at seeing opportunities in my day.

Every morning I get up early to go for a walk, because I love the sensation of moving my body and enjoying the feeling of the blood pumping around my body. It also helps me to connect my mind with my body, so I am feeling in sync with all aspects of my physical self. When I miss my morning walk it takes so much longer to raise my energy levels and to perform with any level of mental clarity and physical alertness. Improving my physical strength and flexibility is a work in progress, because I know the benefits I reap are for now and for a healthy future. I love the feeling in my body when I have completed a yoga class or when I have gone for a long vigorous walk. When I feel strong physically, I feel younger and more connected with my whole self.

It's essential to truly look after our soul, mind and body if we wish to live a life that is healthy, enjoyable and fulfilling. Now is always a good time to start by taking the first step towards changing our past habits and replace them with new ones that support the direction of our dreams. Without making specific changes in my weekly routine I will unlikely improve my physical health, and this will have an impact on my mental, emotional and spiritual well-being. My goal is to enjoy a good life with great health as I move into the last trimester of my life. This is not achievable overnight, however with every step I take that is loving towards myself, it brings me closer to living a life of True Love. Loving who I am is my inspiration. When we get too caught up with having to muster up 'motivation' to achieve our goals, then we are depending upon external cues and circumstances to create transformation in our life.

*"The journey of a thousand miles begins with one step"* (Lao Tzu)

Great physical health is empowering mentally and emotionally. It helps to raise our physical energy levels, which in turn triggers our body to create hormones that have an uplifting effect for our mood. This helps to raise our overall energetic vibration so that we can increase our intuition and spiritual consciousness.

Another method of improving and maintaining our physical health is to receive regular massages or therapeutic energy clearing sessions. I appreciate how important it is to relax the physical body to relieve muscular and skeletal tension, improve circulation, remove toxins from the body and promote oxygenation in the blood stream. It's not only physically beneficial it is also an effective way of allowing the emotional body to relax and release pent up energy.

Reiki therapy is another way of promoting and maintaining excellent physical health. It is designed to assist the body's natural healing process by releasing blocked energy and promoting a positive flow of energy that is vital for our health and well-being. I really enjoy the benefits of receiving a relaxation massage (such as Swedish Massage or Lomi Lomi massage, also known as Hawaiian massage) and the occasional Reiki session, as much as I love to give them.

Another aspect of maintaining physical health is to ensure you eat well. Good nutrition and eating plenty of plant-based foods that give natural living energy is really important if you are to live a life you love. If you indulge in eating processed food, it will leave you feeling depleted and drained of energy.

Doreen Virtue and Robert Reeves have co-authored a book called "Nutrition for Intuition" that provides helpful guidance on foods and beverages that will enhance your health and well-being for the spirit, mind and your body. I'm not an expert in nutrition, however I have made a conscious effort to become more aware of how different foods affect my body and my overall clarity and intuition. Notice what foods help you to feel more energetic and vital, and which ones leave you feeling sluggish and unwell.

Some people have very specific dietary requirements, and if this is you, working with a nutritionist will be the best step to ensure you are meeting your body's requirements to function optimally. We can improve our general health by becoming more aware of our body's needs and responses to food and beverages, and when we need to re-fuel. Eating natural foods that are grown in the ground and not processed is a good start. Staying hydrated with natural fluids is also wise, ensuring you stay clear of too much caffeine, alcohol and sugary drinks.

**Reflection exercise for your health and nutrition:**

Some helpful questions to ask yourself may include:

- Do you feel light and vital after your meal, or do you feel sluggish and bloated?
- Are the foods you are eating causing irritation in your stomach or digestive track?
- Do you feel mentally foggy or emotionally irritable after certain foods?
- Do you have adverse skin reactions to certain foods?
- Do you get headaches after specific meals or beverages?

Take note of what your body is telling you, how it is physically responding, and whether you are experiencing any changes in your mood after you eat and drink. As you become more in tune with your body, you will be able to naturally make better choices.

It's important to check how often you eat, and why you eat when you do.
- Are you really hungry or are you bored or wanting to satisfy another need in your life?
- Are you eating at a certain time of day because that is your habit or routine?

- Are you eating too much so that you feel full in the stomach when you have finished your meal? If yes, then you have eaten more than what your body is comfortable to consume and digest. Perhaps you are not eating enough, and you are lacking in energy and getting regular headaches. This may also be a sign of dehydration.

Being mindful of how and why we eat and drink helps to raise our self-awareness around our physical and emotional energy. This means we can choose foods and a healthy lifestyle that raises our energetic vibration, and also assists our intuition, and our ability to think, sense and discern more clearly.

# 8
## The Shift towards Self-Love

All of us may experience significant changes in our life at some point, not just at mid-life. There may be triggers as a result of a change in a relationship, loss of a job, the death of someone close to us, an illness or significant injury, or an impactful event that's occurred in our personal life. The change may have been anticipated, or the change may have occurred more suddenly and unexpectedly. Either way, it is human nature for significant change to feel incredibly uncomfortable and disconcerting, usually because what was previously recognizable as our personal reality has now changed permanently.

A few years ago, I remember reading a quote by Rumi:

*"Let the beauty of what you love, be what you do".*

Rumi's words resonate at the core of my being and remind me that life is too precious to live stressed out every day because I am not doing what I love or being the 'real' me.

So what does Rumi mean by these profound words? When we are doing what we love in life, we are in alignment with our true self, which means we are doing what's of most value to ourself and what makes us feel at ease in our core being. When we do what we love we can expect to experience good health, enjoyable relationships, and a sense of purpose and fulfilment in our life.

Sadly many people fill their life with doing things they don't love. The pressures and demands of life drive people to make choices based on economics, social expectations and cultural norms, rather than on what fills them with passion and joy.

How many people do you know who talk about how unhappy they are in their job or in their life in general? In Japan 'karoshi' refers to a very real condition where people die from overwork. When our life is out of balance to the point where we are no longer doing what we enjoy, the negative consequences can be huge. Over 10,000 people per year die from this condition, brought on by stress and overwork. Statistics are even higher in the U.S.

Lissa Rankin MD (Author of Mind *Over Medicine: Scientific Proof You Can Heal Yourself, Hay House, 2013*) found scientific and medical proof that doing work you don't enjoy will actually shorten your lifespan. However, spending time with close friends, enjoying laughter, investing in your relationships and generally doing what you really love are key factors that make a difference to a person's health and level of joy and fulfilment in life.

When we are stressed, our "fight or flight" physiological stress response is triggered in the body by the sympathetic nervous system, which then produces large amounts of adrenaline, cortisol and epinephrine in the body. These stress hormones elevate the heart rate, blood pressure and de-activate the body's natural healing and self-repair system. As a result, it leads to poor health and dis-ease in the mind and body. However, when we are doing what we love, the 'relaxation response' is activated and the parasympathetic nervous system kicks in, releasing 'feel good' hormones, enabling the body to relax and do what it does best, heal it-self.

So the question is – if we are not living our life doing what we love, then why not? Doing what we love can be as simple as laughing, dancing, listening to uplifting music, meditation, singing, playing with animals, taking a vacation, sleeping, doing your favourite hobby, exercising or pursuing a creative activity. Or it can be choosing a career or vocation that gives you great satisfaction because it matches your values and is moving you towards fulfilling your goals and dreams. When we consciously choose to do what we most love in life, we are living in a way that fosters a spirit of gratitude and love for the person we are. We are better able to attract abundance into our life, such as good health in our mind and body, loving relationships, and a life that is enriched and fulfilling.

What matters most is that we make *'doing what we love'* a priority and not something we do if we have time. It also means to live life consciously and on purpose. If you are feeling drained, unmotivated, or stressed, it could mean that you are not doing what you truly love in life. Now is the time to check in with yourself, not tomorrow. If you are not loving your life, then it's time to find out why and make some necessary changes.

When we do what we love, we reap the benefits of great health and a fulfilling life. It means we are living in a way that matches our values and brings joy and abundance to our life. At mid-life many people experience change, and this prompts them to re-assess how they are spending their time and energy. A great question to ask yourself is – Am I really doing what I love and is it giving me meaning and fulfilment? Are you having fun in your life? If not, why not? It's easy for anyone to slip into an unconscious way of living, where we become accustomed to the same routine, without really questioning the direction we are going.

Rumi's words are poignant, and for me they had the effect of giving me a kick up my rear-end, causing me to question if I was really living as my authentic self. For a long time, I was doing what I felt I *'should'* do, but underneath I felt empty and unfulfilled. Over a longer period, I became filled with doubt about my own abilities and this affected the relationship I had with myself and others, leaving me feeling down, low in energy and motivation, and unhappy. I was looking at my life through a lens of scarcity and deprivation, focusing on what was missing. Needless to say it didn't lead me to a path of joy and happiness.

One of the first things a Life Coach will tell you is that *'if you want things to be different in your life, you need to think, believe and do things differently'*.

My own personal transformation has been a slow transition from seeing myself as limited and not good enough in many areas of my life, to living life in my own way and accepting myself exactly where I am on my soul-path today. I am now much better at feeling gratitude for the blessings and abundance I experience every day, for I know that deep down, only I am responsible for my happiness, not other people or the 'things' that I can easily convince myself I need to have to feel happy and loved.

## When the Heart Sings

At mid-life we often realise life is too precious to waste time putting energy where it doesn't serve or nourish us. Making the change in my life meant not just talking about it, but actually doing something about it. So why don't we put energy into doing what makes our heart sing? Why do we have a belief that it's not okay to be happy and that we should take care of our duties first? If you believed in your own happiness, would you do more of what makes your heart sing?

*There is a difference between knowing your soul-*
*path and walking your soul-path in life.*

We can invest a lot of energy into thinking and knowing things about ourself, but nothing changes until we actively and consciously do something about it. When we are doing what we most love, we are able to make better choices in life because we are less stressed, and we can think and see more clearly the options available, and what is good for us.

*We create health and abundance in life when we do what we love*

Doing what we love activates the feel-good hormones in our body – dopamine, serotonin, oxytocin, estrogen, progesterone. This means we can experience feeling good both physically, mentally and emotionally when we are doing what we love and being our authentic self.

Did you know that when we engage in doing something creative and using our imagination, we naturally relax? When I get lost in my 'happy place' of doing what I love, I see more beauty and abundance in life. I notice details in my surroundings and in people that were previously invisible to me. I am more appreciative for what I have, rather than worried about what I believe I don't have. Friendships are more cherished, and every day experiences are enjoyed rather than taken for granted. As my mind settles into peace and calm, stress leaves my mind and my body. Motivation and inspiration return fuelling my sense of purpose and mission. I feel a zest for life and gratitude for who I am. Rather than making life happen, I allow my inner light to shine, and I am able to focus on being 'me'.

*When we 'still' the noisy mind we hear the answers from within.*

If you have trouble finding the 'real' you inside so that you can do what you love, it may be because your chatterbox mind is ruling the show. If that's the case, it's time to let go. Let go of the rules and restrictions you put on yourself and you will find that your Higher Self will step forward. You will hear your inner voice speak the truth of your Soul to you.

Many of us are not accustomed to letting go of the need to figure everything out. It's a bit like an addiction to the need to constantly think or reason our way through life, and to get those answers we believe will give us certainty. The truth is, there is no certainty in life, so we may as well enjoy what we are doing. We become so focused on problem solving that we lose touch with what most inspires us.

We all have the answers inside. No one else knows you better than yourself. All you need to do is trust yourself. Don't be afraid of being the real you. It's your life, so make it count and do what you love. Be purposeful and enjoy your life.

When we listen to our heart and soul, and do more of what we truly love, we focus less on the past or what *could* be in the future, and we can live in the now, which is really all we have. It's in this space we can be our true self. When we are doing what we love, there is no effort or resistance, there is joy.

Are you being your true self and doing what you love in life? If not, what can you do, think or believe differently so that your life is lived with a bit more *spice*?

## The Possibilities

One of the most important lessons I have learned is looking at life through a different lens to what I have always been accustomed to doing. It's difficult to change what is well embedded and familiar. Often, we are conditioned from an early age to think, feel and see our world in a particular way. Our upbringing and our environment can have a significant influence in shaping our perspective and the way we see and interpret people, places and events.

I was reminded recently that our perception on life is a gift to ourself. Our reality, our experience of our life, is how we think about it. Two people can be in the same scene, experiencing the same event, but have a completely different perspective, with different interpretations of what is taking place. With different perspectives, and alternative meanings, it can either open or close doors to new possibilities and opportunities. It all depends on how we choose to see and experience our world. Do we see a greater vision with fresh opportunities for growth, expansion and learning? Or do we see only obstacles that limit our options?

*Your perception on life is a gift to yourself ~ Linda Thompson*

My mid-life transformation has certainly tested my resolve and provided countless opportunities for me to reshape my thinking. There were days when I felt very low in energy, and my perspective on life was very dismal. I found it difficult to see my way out of the drudgery and the problems I was experiencing. My mind played havoc with me and presented only problems and 'what-if scenarios' that just seemed to loom bigger and bigger as the day passed by. The more I tossed around the dilemmas in my mind, the more I seemed to be chasing my tail and getting no-where. Admittedly, we can all experience this kind of 'mouse wheel' thinking at any time in life.

Have you noticed when you are feeling low, your day seems to attract more of the same low vibrational energy? Obstacles and resistance to flow seem to follow one event after the other. At the same time, this low vibration tends to attract other people with the same mindset and attitude, compounding your negative experience. When we notice we are caught in a loop of negativity and limited thinking, it's important to find a way to shift the energy and raise the vibration in order to return to flow and harmony. How we think, believe and respond to our circumstances is all about our attitude and our perspective of our current reality, as well as how we choose to interpret our past and present situations.

During my own personal challenges, I have many times been overly focused on what wasn't working for me or what I perceived to be a negative situation. The more I stayed stuck in this energy, worrying about my circumstances that had either passed or not yet happened, the more difficult it was to see the blessings or the possibilities from a positive viewpoint. This energy can become addictive and repel opportunities to manifest abundance in our life.

Developing a possibility mindset may require some practice if we have conditioned ourself to respond to our circumstances in a way that is either limiting or self-sabotaging. We may need to develop the muscle of patience (temperance) as well as trust, and practise new ways of thinking and believing. A persistently negative mindset is illustrative of well-conditioned neural pathways in our brain, highways of thought that we have used so regularly that our mind continues to travel down that road each time we are presented with a new thought or idea. Research has shown that our brains are highly flexible and adaptable, and we can change our neural pathways to develop new ways of thinking. Bruce Lipton's book "The Biology of Belief" (2015) and Dr Joe Dispenza's book "Breaking the Habit of Being Yourself: How to Lose Your Mind and Create a New One" (2013) are excellent resources on this topic.

There are many suggestions for how we can change the way we think and believe, however it ultimately depends on our decision and choice to change, to desire more. Yes, it means we require patience, perseverance, and trust in ourself that we can do this, and a great life is possible. However, we also need the desire to change our old ways of thinking. When inspiration and motivation come from a place of conviction, from our heart and soul, and not just the mind, then change in the way we see ourself and life then becomes sustainable.

After so many years of pain and feeling lack within my heart and soul, transformation was more than just shifting my perspectives. Unless I love myself enough to want to experience greater love and a better quality of life, no amount of strategies and tactics will last the distance. I had a choice to either sink or swim. I could continue to see myself as a victim of my circumstances or believe that I am the creator and author of my own life. How big can I dream? Well, it will always be up to me. No-one else can write the script to my life accept me. My good friend would often remind me – *Be the author of your life, the star of your movie.*

He was right. It took practice for me to shift my perspective and to look at the possibilities. The ego, that part of your mind that consistently reminds you of how you are no good and that life will continue to find ways to trip you up, will work hard against you, and is driven by fear and the need to survive. It is our Higher Self that lifts us up to 'possibility thinking' and allows us to see beyond our belief systems and limitations.

Each time I give myself permission to *believe* what is possible, I find myself tapping into the realm of creativity. No matter our passion in life, we are all born with the ability to be creative. It's part of our human nature, since we are in essence, *creating* and *creation* all the time. Being creative is 'day-dreaming' of the possibilities. Young children are fabulous at doing this with ease. They have no filters or belief systems that tell them that they 'can't do something' or that 'it serves no purpose'. Day-dreaming or imagining is a wonderful way of stretching the muscle of possibility-thinking. When you have lived your life focussed on what you believe won't work, it comes from a lack of belief and self-love, and not from an understanding that all is possible when we see through eyes of love. Our dreams and a life of peace within is possible when we recognise our unlimited Divine potential, when we know that our soul-being is capable of living, loving and seeing beyond our limited thinking, to what is Divinely possible.

There are no tricks that we need to employ to convince our mind to think differently. However, if we open our heart to receive, and tap into what our Soul knows, we can open ourselves to creativity and possibilities. We can open doors that seemed tightly closed or not even in existence. When I am playing with possibilities, my day flows with ease, and I recognise how the Universe is working with me to resolve issues, complete projects or bring good energy and people into my life. As the saying goes – *like attracts like*.

The Law of Attraction is based on the principle that our focus, energy and the perspectives we adopt, will attract more of the same into our experiences. It seems to be a conditioned habit of people to focus on what is not working, or what they don't want more of in life. What we don't realise is that the more attention we give something (a thought, situation or people), we will experience more of this. Our attention and focus *is* what creates our reality. So, doesn't it make sense to focus on what we really want to feel and experience in our life?

Believing in what is possible is trusting that we can manifest (draw closer) from the Universe what is available to us. When I feel gratitude in my life, I always experience more joy, peace and inspiration. This opens my heart to greater self-love and seeing Divine Love and possibilities in others. Life is *creation* and we are always *creating*. All is possible when we believe. What's important is to not allow our mind (or ego self) to tell us otherwise or restrict how things are brought into manifestation. It's our energy (our level of vibration) that makes our experience of life possible, whether that is an awesome experience of unlimited possibilities and great love, or whether it is a life of restriction and restraint.

It's human nature to doubt what we hope is possible, until we experience the evidence for ourself. Some of us like to have the evidence or the proof that something works before we are willing to invest our time, energy or reputation. We are also very prone to forgetting, and to falling back into the same patterns of believing, thinking, speaking and behaving as we have always done.

So much of our spiritual growth and maturity is centred around our willingness to trust and listen to our inner voice. It is our logical mind that likes to resist, provide limitations and is more comfortable with evidence-based thinking (which has its place in other areas of our life). However, this type of thinking means that our reality is limited to what we currently know, rather than open to expansive thinking and increased awareness of other possibilities.

Choosing how we want to think and believe is how we create the life we want to live. So often we limit the possibilities by tuning into what we think we know or focusing on what we believe can't happen. This comes from a place of fear and doubt. Elon Musk succinctly puts it when he says "If you get up in the morning and think the future is going to be better, it is a bright day. Otherwise, it's not.".

## Your Creative Genius

One of the keys to raising our energy is to do things that make our heart sing. When we are doing what we truly love, there is no effort or resistance, only awareness of the present moment. When we do what we love we access our creative genius, which means our Divine potential. It's as if we open a portal to our soul that enables us to activate and utilize our very core essence of who we are. All of our gifts, talents, strengths and wisdom seem to interplay to create something magical, which only you can do. All you need to do is what feels natural to you.

Being creative may feel foreign or unfamiliar for some people. Did you know that from the moment you wake up you are constantly creating something in your world. It may be the thoughts and ideas you are creating, the meal you are preparing, the work project you are innovating, or the hobby you are indulging in.

*The act of creating is life-giving and therefore it raises our energy and our vibration, helping us to connect to our spirit essence and Divine nature.*

Creation and creating is an act of the Divine. When we dare to let go of wanting to control our thoughts, our world and other people, we are effectively telling our mind to stop the chatter and listen, to create a space of receptivity. Creating stillness within helps to create an openness and vulnerability that will allow awareness and exploration of ourself and our world.

The unconscious mind is a place that is timeless and yet filled with infinite possibilities. This is the space that we enter when we receive ideas and from where innovation is born. It is also the space where the lessons and wisdom of our past come to the fore, to help guide and inspire us.

Why is this important? Because this is where we come to understand our soul-purpose in relation to recognising our inherent gifts and talents. Our creativity or our ability to 'create' is connected to our emotional and spiritual intelligence, which simply means the depth at which we intuit and understand concepts beyond our reasoning and our need for physical evidence.

Our emotions inform us and as move us in ways that enable our spirit and soul to be expressed without restraint or inhibitions. Think of a time when you have become absorbed by your favourite song or expressed yourself through dance, art, music, writing, gardening, when excelling in sport or through passionate lovemaking. Our ability to sense, feel and intuit is the language through which Spirit works, and the way in which we connect to our spiritual core, bringing forth creation in our tangible world.

When we speak about creativity it involves our emotions and our ability to feel and respond to our world and our experiences. Many people fear their emotions because they are afraid to feel things more deeply. They reason that if they do feel or sense, then they may be compelled to step out of their comfort zone to believe, think or do something different. Our creativity actually opens the door for greater possibilities beyond our fears. It's not possible to live in this world without experiencing fear. Fear is an emotion as well as a belief about what we think may or may not happen. Used wisely our emotions are a guide to a deeper understanding of ourself, which leads us to possibility thinking and enlightenment.

I have experienced fear of not being good enough, fear of being alone, fear of not achieving anything worthwhile in my life, and fear of not being loved. However, I know deep down that denying my fear will only keep me in a dark place for longer. Embracing your fear takes courage, but if you are willing to go there it is liberating.

Through tapping into our creativity, we can reverse the effects of fear. The act of creating is life-giving and gives birth to insights and wisdom either as enlightenment or in tangible form. Fear and Divine creativity cannot exist at the same time. When you go into a dark room and switch on the light, the dark disappears. The brighter the light bulb (your inner light and love), the more quickly the dark corners disappear.

When we are in a state of fear, we doubt ourself and our ability to create and see the possibilities in life. In fear we see only darkness and limitations. In these moments we need to remember that what we believe and what we think will determine how we feel and the perceptions and experiences we create. When we live in fear, what we regularly speak about and the actions we take is a reflection of our doubts and our anxieties. Our thoughts, speech and our behaviour reinforce those fears and create more of this experience in our life. We always have the ability and the choice to think, believe and do differently.

*To create change and possibility in our life, tap*
*into what makes your heart sing.*

What gets your juices going? What lights your fire? Have you stopped to think about it lately? Do you remember what *you* love to do? Going back to basics and keeping it simple is a great place to start. We can easily become distracted in life by the 'shiny ball syndrome'. That's when we become fascinated by too many choices and we take on many projects and interests at the same time. Yes, they may all appear fun or interesting, but juggling many activities at once is not the answer. The aim is to get back in touch with what is truly 'your thing'. Not what other people put up for a suggestion. Look back at the activities you have enjoyed in the past and notice the recurring theme. Do you love connecting with people? Do you love to potter in the garden? Do you love to be with animals? Do you love numbers, sport, helping people or, do you love to make things with your hands?

When we better understand what we love to do, it helps us to see where our strengths lie. More importantly, it's information that helps us to reflect on how we can use this to fulfil our life purpose. As a foundation, our life purpose is to become a better version of ourself and to enjoy our life. To enjoy life, we must learn to love our true self. Beyond that, our life purpose becomes our contribution to others.

Tapping into your creativity is like a pipeline to your soul. It's a direct line to your heart that opens up your ability to receive, especially love and wisdom. If you are feeling disconnected and separate from others and the world, accessing your creativity is a great way to reconnect with the inner you. When you shine the torch of your attention to what brings light into your life, the darkness and fear disappear. Creativity gives birth to new ideas, innovation and possibilities.

Whenever you feel stuck or you feel like you are at a crossroads and you don't know which path to choose, take time to imagine the possibilities. You will need to ignore the monkey-mind-chatter that reminds you of your fears and the stories that you create when you don't have the answers. Daydreaming is a gift that knows no bounds or restrictions to imagined possibilities. When you set yourself free to imagine and do what you love doing, you release yourself to express your heart's desire and your soul's intention. This is true liberation.

**Soul Reflections -** *tapping into your creativity*

List some activities that you love to do, gets your juices going or lights your fire.

Some ideas could be:

• Do you love connecting with people?
• Do you love to potter in the garden or go for long walks in nature?
• Do you love to be with animals?
• Do you love sport?
• Do you love the healing arts, giving or receiving massages?
• Do you love helping people?
• Do you love to build things with your hands?
• Do you love reading, writing, art, jewellery making or music?
• Do you love numbers and problem solving?

There is no need to limit yourself. Create a list and enjoy thinking and feeling into the idea of these activities, then choose one and create some time to explore what you enjoy. When we allow ourself to switch off our busy mind and move into our creativity we can tap into our spirituality and discover the freedom of feeling connected with in-spir-ation (spirit in action).

# 9
## I Choose to Believe

Usually when we reach the moment of saying - 'Hold everything, I *am* good enough', it's that moment of realization we no longer want to continue to feel the same way or experience the same circumstances over and over. Why is it that we allow ourself to put up with negative thinking and toxic situations for so long?

Over a longer period of time, living with stinking thinking, toxic relationships, poor health, recurring injuries, or disruptive circumstances can lead to believing we are a victim of life's cruel intentions to make us suffer. Getting caught in the trap of believing that our circumstances will never change or improve leads to making assumptions about what is or is not possible in life. This perspective comes from a core belief that we are controlled by other people and external circumstances, which places us in the position of being the victim of what appears to be a cruel world. It limits our ability to seek alternatives, to dream big and to see the potential in ourself and others. It's the opposite of possibility-thinking. It's a belief that we are not creators of our reality or how we experience our life.

When we have been conditioned to believe and think about ourself and others in a certain way for so long, it can be difficult to see, think, do and feel differently. Our brain and neural pathways become hard-wired to habitually respond the same way to every thought and situation in our life. It's a bit like driving your car down the same super highway every day. Very rarely do we deviate through the side roads, because we are used to going the same path and it's a known route and outcome every time. Over time our habits create a specific level of energetic vibration which attracts similar vibrations and experiences, reinforcing and delivering evidence of what we believe and perceive in our world.

When we adopt a flexible attitude and approach to life it enables us to think and do things differently, providing us with new options. As human beings, we do not yet fully understand the power of our imagination and that our ability to create our reality is unlimited. When we allow ourself to deviate from the usual route of our thinking and responding to life, we exercise our ability to think of other possibilities. Making different choices brings different results in life. So why do we keep doing the same thing over and over, getting the same results and wondering why we are still so miserable?

We do it because of a host of reasons. Fear of change is a biggie. It's human nature to want to stay with what we know, because it feels like a safe option. Why change what you already know and provides a certain outcome each time? When we are driven by the need to avoid fear and change, it means we are driven by the need to have certainty in our life. We tend to choose the option that feels safe, has a low level of risk, and there is a smaller chance of being hurt, or having to deviate from our familiar path. However, if what you are choosing to think and do every time is not giving you peace of mind or happiness, then why do it?

I am reminded regularly that *life really is very simple*. It's not that complicated, and yet we create and attract drama into our life because we are afraid of facing our own truth which may cause us to change what we have been doing all this time.

*'Simplicity is the greatest form of sophistication' ~ Ralph Smart*

It's often the case that until we have reached a point of feeling completely fed up with our circumstances, that we are prepared to change the way we see and do things differently. It requires honesty and courage to do what is true for ourself, and a deep desire to alter our course towards the path that better serves our well-being and our soul-purpose. It also requires the commitment to be more loving and compassionate with ourself, and a belief we are worth the effort. It is not merely to make a change from a cerebral or psychological level. It's making a decision that feels true in our mind, our body and in our soul. When we experience peace in our thinking, calm energy in our body, and alignment with our soul-truth, then we know that the path we are travelling is where we are meant to be.

It's not wise to make a change in life just for the sake of change, or because you don't know what else to do. Deeper reflection about what resonates with your true self assists with the choices you make for a more enriching experience in life, helping you to attain wisdom, and greater love for yourself. Releasing and relaxing into your life instead of going at full speed will alter your perspective and energetic vibration and create space for you to see and experience the way with more clarity.

I have learned the hard way, often repeating the same lessons, because I have been too stubborn, too fearful of change, and of what I may miss out on. As human beings, despite our story, context or personal landscape, we all limit ourselves because of fear. Fear so often drives our choices even though underneath we desire more love in life. When we convince ourself to stay the same and we continue to hold onto the firm belief that life is unfair and we have no control over our experiences, then we will truly create a life of misery. Life will feel like ground-hog day. This path does *not* lead to more love.

I have often reminded myself to hit the pause button and stop being so insistent that progress means to do more, and to do it faster. Sometimes transformation requires us to cease doing what we have been doing, or at the very least, slow down. I developed a pattern in my life of pleasing others by insisting I could support them, fix them,

manage them and make them feel better. I didn't realise this is a form
of control and that I was making a judgment that they were not capable
of helping themselves. I now understand I was also driven by a desire
to feel loved. My unconscious belief was that if I help, fix, support or
please the person of my attention, then they would love and support me.

My heightened sensitivity usually means that I can often feel and
sense what other people are feeling and where they are in terms of
their soul growth. In my earlier years I would attempt to take away the
pain that person was experiencing by solving their problem or offering
ways to improve their situation. It came from a heart of love, but I was
ignorant and did not understand that my motivations were coming
from a place of fear of not being needed, not being good enough, and
fear of being left behind. I felt an overwhelming desire to help others
because I have a big heart, and underneath I wanted to be rewarded with
more love. Wanting to help and support others is not wrong or bad in
itself. It's wonderful, however we must be aware of our intentions, and
come from a place of healing and self-love, not from our own personal
need to fill a void of our own.

It took me a long time to realise that my actions were self-serving
and unhelpful to both myself and the other person. Unless we are asked
for assistance, we need to allow others the time and space to travel their
own soul journey, and to experience the soul lessons in their own timing
and in a way that empowers them to make their own choices. If we are
asked for assistance and guidance, then we know that the other person
has freely made the choice to do so when it feels right for them.

I needed many experiences to understand that the best way to give
love is to let go and learn to 'be' with people in their sorrows and their
joys. For years I tried to numb my sensitivity, so I would not feel the
emotion or pain of others, and yet my un-resourceful behaviour of
seeking love and trying to fix others kept re-surfacing over and over.
Knowing how to be loving and compassionate without being driven to
change others is a key milestone for all of us on our soul journey. The
path to True Love is travelled by the way of our own choices.

This growing self-awareness helped me to realise that I *am* good
enough just as I am, flaws and all. I have experienced many set-backs

emotionally, and the pain of being hurt did run deep before I was able to heal my own wounds. However, from my own experiences I have learned that we always have a choice to either sink or swim in the depth of our pain. We can learn to use our emotions to increase our awareness and become conscious of what we tell ourself, or we can allow our emotions to create inner confusion. Life is not about avoiding pain. We will always experience pain and fear in our life, but we always have a choice as to how we respond.

During the most challenging times I was tempted to give up on the idea that it was possible for me to heal and to feel love for myself. However, despite the pain and the loneliness, I was determined to get back up, dust myself off, tend to my wounds, and allow myself the time I needed to cry, rest and reflect. I'm sure some of my friends thought I was taking the hard road when they would have chosen the easier option to return to life as it was before. However, I knew this was my soul path, and that I was learning to be strong and resilient, not in spite of love, but because of Love.

We all have soul lessons to learn and our own soul journey to walk. Deep down I knew the pain of my inner growth was teaching me so much about myself. Rising up to meet Love and to see myself as worthy of Love, helps me to appreciate the contrasts in my life. Every day I am remembering to listen to the wisdom of my Soul, and to be more compassionate with myself.

Choosing the path of resistance, or refusing to embrace the lessons, can turn our heart cold and delay us from reaching a deeper level of love, understanding and wisdom. When experiencing pain and confusion, it can feel like it's an easier option to shut down our emotions rather than risk feeling more pain. However, the emotions we experience allow us to bring to the surface what we need to address for our soul growth. Our emotions serve to shine light on what is motivating our thoughts and driving our behaviour. With a deeper level of understanding of ourself, we can then make an informed choice about whether we need to make a change.

Like anything in life, we can choose to use information and our senses to assist us in our journey, or we can choose to believe we are a victim of our emotions and allow them to take control. Even though I wanted to feel relief from heart-felt pain, I did not want to allow it to control me. I wanted to become stronger, wiser, and a more liberated soul.

Feeling the full range of my emotions since the end of my marriage, was exhausting at times. When I sank to the depths, I needed my friends to be there with me, not necessarily to solve anything or take away my experiences, but to remind me of my worth and that I was not alone. Their love, compassion and their presence, was food for my soul. Each of them gave me their love and support in their unique way. It has been comforting to experience such supportive friendship, but this is also how I perceive my world, sensitive to the presence and energy of others. Deep and meaningful connections have enriched my life and are also the measure of how I show my love and appreciation of others.

In the first couple of years of my transformation friends provided the mirror and context I needed through their own example, to help me raise my self-awareness and remind me we are all connected at the soul level. We are in each other's life to love and support each other, through the power of our presence and from living from our soul-being.

The realization that the contrasts in my life were there to move me towards True Love was a significant part of my soul growth. The life lessons have not been like switching on the light in the darkness, but more like turning up the dimmer switch, slowly raising the voltage to increase the clarity of my vision and my understanding of what I was feeling, sensing and experiencing.

Over time I have come to appreciate myself at a deeper and more compassionate level. Every learning experience is helping to reveal the real me whilst uncovering the parts that I kept buried for many years due to my fear of not being good enough. It can be confronting, however developing courage to face my shadow self is helping me to grow in wisdom and experience a new-found sense of liberation. When life gives me tasteless fruit, I reassess what I can do better, or what not to do next time around.

I have had some tough lessons, and I know that life will continue to provide contrasts so that I can learn and grow. When I choose to see and feel only the pain of disappointment, I tend to receive more of the same in return. It's a dismal way to live, as misery begets misery. Our choices in life, what we believe, our interpretations and our perspective will always be reflected back to us in our relationships and our life experiences. When we can learn to not take things personally, we will experience the freedom that comes with personal accountability.

Don Miguel Ruiz Jr. offers some sage wisdom in his book "The Five Levels of Attachment" that advises to stay clear of having expectations of other people in life. Basing your happiness and sense of fulfilment on what someone else may or may not give, is setting yourself up for guaranteed disappointment. We have all experienced feeling let down as a result of our own expectations about how others should treat us, and how we believe life should deliver fair and reasonable outcomes. However, letting go of such expectations and taking responsibility for my own growth and happiness means I choose my life path and soul growth, and I accept the consequences of my choices. Some things in life are not in my control, but I can surely choose how I respond to these circumstances.

In the past I recognise that I have run a pattern of giving too much of my time, energy and support to others. I know that I do this because I am a caring and loving person. However, at a deeper level I was seeking to gain attention, acceptance, love and a sense of self-worth from others. When we seek to give in order to gain, especially to a degree that surpasses the personal boundaries of what is considered healthy, it can lead to dependent relationships. The pattern of behaviour I was running was out of a fear of not being loved, and not feeling good enough. I feared feeling disconnected and alone. I was seeking love and acceptance from others, rather than finding this within myself.

When we are driven by fear, we can easily lose sight of our own self-power and magnificence, which can lead to the belief that we cannot manifest a life that is fulfilling. Fear can drive us to make compromises and impulsive decisions that are not in our best interest. When I felt particularly vulnerable, I would often allow my mind to slip into negative self-talk, which would frequently tempt me to give up on myself.

We all suffer from negative self-talk on occasions. In these moments we can easily choose to avoid what feels uncomfortable or requires a little self-confidence to step up. It's helpful to pause and reflect on our options, and to listen to our soul's wisdom before we take action. There have been many times when I have felt fear and I have been tempted to criticise someone's behaviour because of my own discomfort. If I had chosen to act impulsively at the time, I could have damaged the relationship or missed an opportunity to understand something I had not previously considered. I'm sure there were times when I missed the mark and made a hasty decision. Fortunately, I have learned to slow down before responding, by either stepping away from the phone or keyboard, or holding my tongue when I really wanted to vent my opinion.

Fear will cause us to judge ourself and others, and to react spontaneously with aggression and from a wounded place. When we pause to listen to the wisdom of our Higher Self, we have the opportunity to see things from a different perspective. The art of stepping back from the situation will often give us time to process our thoughts and adopt a calmer energy to see things from a different angle, and with greater clarity.

With a renewed level of self-awareness, I am able to adopt a more loving perspective of myself when challenges now present themselves. When I feel the need to impulsively react due to my own fears and insecurities, I wait for my inner storm to calm down before I respond, if indeed I choose to respond at all. I have learned that sometimes it is wiser to let things go and not feel the need to respond to everything. Sometimes life just happens and all we need to do is observe and accept what is, rather than judge and react. In this way we develop self-control and resilience, and we give ourself the opportunity to learn from the experiences. This is how we grow in wisdom and spiritual maturity.

## Love, Forgiveness and Self Compassion

The inner transformation of our soul journey is not all roses. It's a challenging path full of obstacles and the path is not always clear. Our past wounds, our ego mind, our self-doubts and our lack of love can become obstacles that block our path. The more we focus on the obstacles, feeling frustrated and distracted, the more we will lose sight of what is important and our true direction for our soul journey. When all feels lost and hopeless it is usually because we have allowed our fearful mind to take over and cloud our heart's desire to show us the way.

On our soul journey there are times we will need to re-assess where we are going and to remove the baggage of the past that is slowing us down or holding us back. That baggage may be old beliefs, conditioned patterns of behaviour, ingrained negative self-talk or a desire to stay focused on memories of the past. We often choose to hang onto these old ways because they are so familiar to us, and perhaps there is some ignorance as to how to do things differently.

As we go through transformation, we may notice that what was once relevant, of value and of interest, is now changing. Over time, our preferences slowly evolve and change. With new information and lessons learned we gain more wisdom and we adopt new perspectives that enable us to make choices that are more in alignment with our true self, and our new level of self-awareness and understanding. As we master specific soul lessons, our interests lead us toward other experiences that better serve our soul growth and help us to spiritually mature.

Transformation or soul growth comes from a desire to feel happy and to reconnect with our essential Divine nature. The Divine inspires us to experience more love and to move towards greater Love. We may recognise this when we feel our connection with others or with nature. Through our experiences and heightened awareness, we can develop a renewed appreciation of our life, it's purpose and meaning.

Making the decision to improve your circumstances is an acknowledgment that you want to feel better in your life, and that change needs to come from within. At first, when we feel the pain of our challenging circumstances, it is easy to look outside of ourself and focus on how other people have caused us to feel pain. However, the external manifestation of the problems are a symptom and reflection of how you think and feel about yourself, and where you have been focusing your attention and energy in your life. When we let go of attributing blame on others and manipulating others to solve the problem in order to feel safe, loved or validated that we matter, we can be open to adjusting our own perspectives to create change. Change in our external world happens when we recognise our own soul-power to manifest more love and abundance in our life.

The path towards True Love is through love, forgiveness and self-compassion. The only way to combat our fears and to create change in our life is to discover this love within ourself. Self-love is non-judgmental, kind and caring. When we can fully accept our true self, without criticism and with a heart of compassion, we can experience forgiveness for our soul-being. Forgiveness is an act of love and acceptance of all aspects of our true self.

It's possible our life circumstances may not have provided us opportunities to experience love from others, and so we may not have learned what it is to love ourself. So, it may be a very unfamiliar experience and something that you may have difficulty imagining or feeling. A step in the direction of self-love is to practice acts of kindness to yourself. Be gentle with yourself. The moment you notice your self-talk is sounding more like criticism and self-judgment, find something to acknowledge that is good about yourself in that moment, no matter how small. Focusing on gratitude for what exists in and around you is a beautiful way to slowly dispel negativity and to shift your focus towards possibilities rather than limited thinking.

## Healing Meditation

To bring peace and connection with your heart and soul, find a quiet place to sit comfortably for a few minutes and do the following meditation. You can also access guided healing meditations on my website, www.livingwithspice.com.au

*Close your eyes and place your hand on your heart.*
*Breathe deeply for a few moments, until you feel yourself settle into a slower rhythm.*
*Feel your heart beating as your chest rises and falls.*

*Feel the blood pump through your veins, through your head, ears, hands, body and legs.*
*Breathe and listen.*

*You are alive. You are here in this moment, as living energy.*
*Be in this moment, and recognise you are loved.*
*Your life is an expression of love, of pure creation by the Divine.*
*Listen to your body speak to you.*
*Feel your heart pumping and the rhythm of your breathing.*

*Through your living body feel the connection with your heart and your Soul.*
*Feel the presence of the Divine that exists within you. You are loved.*
*Breathe.*

*Focus on the rise and fall of your chest and your stomach as you breathe deeply.*
*Listen from your heart and hear your Soul speak to you.*
*What does your Soul want to say to you?*

*Pay no attention to the obstacles of your mind.*
*Breathe and feel your chest rise and fall.*
*Ask your Soul to guide you.*
*Notice what feels good, what feels certain.*
*Feel your heart, it is the physical manifestation of your Soul.*

*Here in your heart, in your Soul, is Divine Love's guidance.*
*Here is the soul-light that will guide you through what has felt like a maze in your life.*
*Trust what you feel and what you hear from your Soul.*

*Your past is not your present or your future.*
*You create your path from your heart and Soul, not from your fearful mind.*
*Breathe.*

*With your hand on your heart, feel the love inside melt away the fears, the past judgments and self-criticism.*

*Allow yourself to feel what you feel. Take your time.*
*Feel the touch of Divine Love within you and the peace that comes from this love.*

*Know that you can access this Love and peace at any time.*
*Let love be your guide in your life.*
*Breathe and say, .... I love you (your name), .....I love you (your name), .....I love you (your name).*
*Open your eyes, and say ...... thank you, ....thank you, ....thank you.*

## The Mental Grip

When we are feeling the most pain and it feels that we are at our lowest point, it is an easy temptation to give up on ourself. It's often in these moments that we believe the worst of ourself, of others and of our circumstances. This is fear shouting at us, and its grip on our inner being can be crippling if we let it take hold. If you are a parent and you have witnessed your child sobbing uncontrollably and they are taken over by their own emotions through a fit of anger, you know they are feeling the full force of their own fears. With patience you wait until they calm down because you know that in that moment, they are overcome by their emotions, their sadness, anger or fear. You know they have created this reality for themselves and yet you know it need not be this way. You know they are still loved, lovable, and that all will be clearer and calmer when the force of their inner storm passes. In the same way, we need to remind ourself of this when we are feeling the fullness of our own fear and lack of self-love. This is not the time to

127

be making life-changing decisions. It's in this moment we need to stop and pause. There is wisdom in going within and reflecting on what is going on for us.

Our inner storms come, and they go. However, we can learn to develop some resilience and remember that they will pass. The storms don't change who we are, our value, our uniqueness, our potency or our lovability. In many ways, weathering the storms of our life strengthen us. They show us that no matter the chaos, noise, and force that we may feel in those storms, we are more than this. Our soul-being is capable of rising above the storm to see that there is an expanse that goes way beyond the weather we are experiencing.

With every dark night that we go through, the sun rises the next day to show us the truth. We can use the blanket of the night to provide us calm and a period of time to go within and feel what needs to be felt and hear what needs to be heard from our inner soul. When the sun rises, we are reminded that light exists beyond the shadows we create. In every present moment, in each new day, we have the opportunity to start fresh. Use the energy of Love's light to guide you.

There is nothing wrong with you. When we see the child crying and in despair, we still know that this child is perfect, and we see their greatness and potential beyond what they are feeling in that moment (their light and their shadows). Know that you too are perfect exactly as you are in this moment. You are not missing anything inside of you. Everything that is in you, is in me. Our differences are coloured by our personalities, experiences and what we choose to notice in our life.

Our life is also a result of our very active mind that will easily create scenarios that become our perceptions and our interpretations of our experiences. The mind is powerful and if it is not quietened it can lead us down a path that is away from our soul's purpose. The ego part of ourself desires to seek safety, and in doing so it is often focused on avoiding what we fear, and therefore inevitably creating more experiences of fear in our life. What we think about most becomes our reality, and then we begin to experience those matching emotions, which is reflected in our body and our physical and external world. What we see and what we think about becomes our internal world. If we are not mindful of this, we can quickly find ourself shrinking and contracting, no longer open to the love and expansion that our life offers us.

The quickest remedy to this malady is to quieten the mind. I find walks along the beach and in nature, a wonderful way for me to still my mind and connect with my Soul. The sun, trees and the ocean are healing and help to cleanse me from stressful thoughts. Meditation and yin yoga is another beautiful way to calm my mind and connect with my body. It is an effective way to relax and release the build-up of mental and physical toxins. When we quieten the mind, there is peace and room for us to be our authentic self. We live in a world that is over-stimulated, fast paced, and competitive. Our mind is usually racing to keep up or stay in front. When we believe we are lagging behind, we can quickly resort to fear-based thinking, and before long we are experiencing lower levels of energy and even depression.

Freeing ourself from the mental grip of our fear-based thoughts is not so hard. We often convince ourself that change is difficult and that we are not good enough or able to experience anything different. This is fear manipulating our thoughts and influencing our behaviour. When we go to the gym, we know it will take some time to develop strength and flexibility. It doesn't happen overnight. The way to success is consistency and taking one step at a time towards our goal. Keep your eye on the bigger picture and how you want to feel and what you want to experience. Transformation is a process, and it requires us to develop patience, perseverance and a strong desire to experience a more fulfilling life. There is no room for self-doubt, as it is a powerful form of self-sabotage and will not help you to create more love and expansion in your life.

We all experience the strong holds of our mind at various times. Recognising when we are in that low energy space (what I call a 'funk') is a good start. Sometimes, if I allow myself to slip, I can often feel paralysed by my thinking, and I struggle to shift the fear-based stories that I play over and over in my mind. When this happens, I know I need to switch to spending more time self-nurturing and quietening my mind. Involving myself in activities that I enjoy or being with friends that are uplifting and supportive is an excellent way to get out of my head and out of my own way. Showing kindness and love to others is also incredibly powerful and will instantly lift your energetic vibration. Physical activity is also very effective for shifting your energy and raising your level of thinking. Whatever your preference, get moving and you will experience a change for the better.

Embracing change was initially a scary concept for me. When I had that moment of realization that my life needed to change direction in a significant way, I knew I was at the point of no-return, leaving what was no longer serving me in my life. I was frightened of the unknown, fearful that I may not cope or that I would not find love for myself or happiness in my life. Deep down I knew that taking a different path would require courage and inner fortitude, because the changes I wanted to make were so different to my previous ways of living. Yet, I was at the same time feeling a sense of peace within because it felt right to be finally listening to my inner truth and the voice of my Soul that was calling me to be my true self. I knew there were experiences I needed to have to spiritually mature. Feeling scared is being human, however I know that sometimes I scare myself way more than I need to. It's all in the way we think about our circumstances and ourself. My transformative soul journey has been a pilgrimage of learning to trust and grow in self-love.

What we know is constant in life, is *change*. So, it's interesting that so many of us are averse to change. Perhaps it comes from a belief that change must be painful and to be avoided. In my own experience I have come to appreciate these moments. I now realise I am not a 'victim' of change but rather an instigator of change. Change is still at times painful for me and I don't always feel brave. However, I have learned the value of love for myself and living for the way of love.

We are the creators of our life. Our orientation, our focus and our energy either attracts or repels people and circumstances in our life. It may feel as though some circumstances are completely out of our control, however there is also a likelihood that whilst we have not caused some situations to happen, they may have arrived in our sphere of consciousness to assist us in some way. It may be to draw our attention to something we need to learn or provide an opportunity for soul-growth and wisdom.

Change and transformation is inevitable and necessary for soul growth. The energy that enables us to expand spiritually is Divine Love. Many of us make the mistake of seeking love outside of ourself. We've heard many times, that the secret to true joy is *not* found externally, in things or other people, but within. So, what does this really mean?

We are all students of life, seeking answers and desiring to experience more love, but often we are looking in all the wrong places. True Love resides in our heart and in our soul and is affected by the way we think about ourself. When we are no longer busy pre-supposing the future, or re-hashing the past, we can find peace in the moment and be open to the guidance of the Divine. In the stillness within it is easier to release our mental strongholds so Love's energy can flow through us again.

If you have been used to allowing your mind to rule in a way that distracts and lowers your energy through negative and limited thinking, then it is likely that the current of Love within may feel murky, stifled or blocked. What we are aiming for is an energetic flow of love that feels abundant and free flowing. Learning to be still and receptive will assist you in becoming a clear channel and a vessel for love that will open you to the experience of abundant joy and a life that is fulfilling and expansive. When we remember to spend more time doing what we love in a way that is true to our way of being, we can very quickly open our heart and soul to let love flow.

The secret to true joy is allowing this energy to flow through us and not become blocked, stifled or stagnant. We are living energy in flow, just as the animals, birds, plants and every other living thing is energy in flow. When we consciously connect to the Divine Love within (the experience and feeling of love), we can use it for our soul's healing and growth. Preparing ourself for being the best possible vessel for Divine Love is the key to allowing this healing energy to flow through us so that it nourishes our mind, our body and our soul-being.

Being in flow is recognising when it's important to let go of the thoughts that keep us bound and the habits that don't serve us well. Our thoughts can become self-torture, and I know from my own experience that I can quickly descend into feelings of hopelessness and despair if I don't manage my thinking. It can lead to fogginess and confusion, and as a result my actions come from a place of fear rather than love and self-empowerment. When in fear, we are more likely to resort to forcing an outcome or solution in order to re-gain control or a sense of security. The more we 'push' the more we repel love's peace and joy in our life.

How often have we heard ourself say, '*no matter how hard I try I just can't seem to make it work*', or words to that effect? When we are feeling out of sync with ourself and the circumstances in our life seem to offer up too many obstacles, this is a sign that it's time to *pause* and stop trying so hard by coming at life with push-energy. It's time to take our hands off the wheel, our foot off the accelerator, and step back to reflect on what is happening. When there is no flow it's the Universe's way of saying this path is not the best way forward.

We may have many moments when the road feels particularly bumpy. We may question if we are going in the right direction or that we can even find the right direction. There is always a clear path forward, even when it's not apparent. This is a perfect time to reassess, gather more information and even gain a different perspective. We may even benefit by waiting for better timing. I still recall 20 years ago when Sr Eily said to me "Let go and let God". In other words, pause and listen. What is your Soul saying to you? Listen to your inner voice. There will be a message from Spirit to clarify things for you. Then, allow God to assist by accepting the opportunities that are given to support and guide you on your way forward.

We are very conditioned to be busy, to think too much and to believe we must always be doing something. We feel compelled to have an opinion, state our case, or claim our place for fear of someone jumping in front of us. This kind of mindset comes from a belief there is not enough for everyone in this world, and that *we* are not enough. So, we go into over-drive and adopt an energy and intention of forcing an outcome. It takes wisdom and practice to balance our energy, knowing when to receive (yin) and when to actively give (yang).

The best way is to tune into our heart (our intuition), pause, and then examine (with our intellect) the options before us. Give yourself time to re-assess the situation and notice your perceptions and intentions. Are you coming from a place of fear or love? If there is no flow, and only confusion and agitation, it's likely you are coming from a place of fear and your energy is out of balance. When we are coming from our heart, we experience ease and flow, and an inner peace that increases our awareness of ourself and others. (A more detailed explanation of how we use our yin and yang energy is explained in Chapter 11.)

## Simple meditation techniques to quieten the mind:

1. **Focus on the breath**

   Sit comfortably in a chair with your back straight (not rigid). Close your eyes and your mouth and relax your shoulders. Now breathe. Notice your breath going in and going out through your nostrils. Take a moment to sit with this. Now, slow down your breathing to a comfortable pace. It may take you a minute or more to relax your body and your breathing.

   Wriggle your toes, clench and release your fists in your lap, clench and release your shoulders.Come back to focusing on your breathing, feeling the warm air coming in and out of your nostrils, with your mouth closed. As you breathe in, count for 4. As you breathe out count for 6. Keep doing this for a few minutes, feeling the breath coming in and out and the soft air on your upper lip.

   *When you are focused on your breathing, the mind relaxes and is not focused on anything other than the breath. Within 3-5 minutes you have created physical, mental and emotional calm in your body.*

2. **Focus on an object, such as a candle**

   Using the same technique above, you can bring your attention to an object such as a candle. As you gaze at the flame of the candle, breathe slowly and gaze into the light. Notice its luminescence, the flicker and the changing patterns of light intensity in the flame. Relax your body as you gaze gently at the light. Do this for 3-5 minutes until you feel calm and relaxed. You may find your eyes wanting to close. This is fine.

3. **Walking meditation**

Using the same technique as above, focus on the movement of your steps as you very slowly and mindfully walk. Notice the placement of your foot on the ground in front of you, feeling the pressure against the heel and the ball of your foot, and the release as you move forward. Notice the movement of the muscles and the bones in your feet, your knees, and your body, as every part moves in synchronicity. Walk for 5-15 minutes slowly and mindfully and feel the benefits of your mind and body reaching a place of calm and inner peace.

*Meditation is an act of self-love. Whenever you are feeling hurried, stressed or in overwhelm, take a few minutes to calm the mind and body using any one of the above techniques. Perhaps you have already found a technique of your own that you know works for you.*

*Namaste.*

# 10
## Release and Surrender

The way toward greater love in our life is to release what binds us and to fully accept all of ourself, with love and compassion. To do this may feel somewhat difficult, particularly if we are so focused on what we perceive to be our shortcomings. However, to experience unconditional love means to accept our true essence without the limitations of self-judgment.

The path to self-love is simple, though at times it may not feel so easy, especially when we have experienced years of conditioning, either as a result of our family background, negative self-talk, or the persistent messages we receive from others that we have chosen to believe and internalise. Developing self-love requires a willingness to release and surrender our story and all that keeps our heart and soul captive. Our *story* is made up of the philosophies, beliefs, justifications and conditions that we hold onto because we are determined they are right, and they give meaning to who we are and our way of being in the world.

When we are so focused on the personal judgments, the analysing and comparisons with others, we are unable to see our own magnificence, only what we see and desire in others. It is only through acceptance of ourself that we can experience self-love, forgiveness and appreciation of our uniqueness. It's a difficult path to walk when we live to feel the approval of others, and the desire to be liked and understood.

The path to greater love is a healing and transformative journey that requires releasing the strongholds of our mind, understanding and managing our emotions and surrendering to the gift of Spirit. This has the power to liberate us and bring us forever closer to Divine Love. It begins with learning to recognise the limiting ways in which we think about ourself and others. Our thoughts have the power to bind us or set us free. What we 'think' about a situation or another person is how we create our physical and emotional reality, through our beliefs, perceptions, interpretations and internal experiences. If we have thoughts of resentment, judgment, sadness or hurt, then that is the experience we create. The secret to happiness and the path to True Love is dependent upon what we choose to think, and therefore create in our version of reality.

The path to greater love can feel confusing, especially if we feel as if we are in a perpetual state of longing for something that will finally bring us happiness. We may believe that happiness and fulfilment can only come from the successful career, a certain amount of money that will make our life easier, the relationship that will give us the love we want to experience, the perfect and harmonious family, the new car, a holiday experience, or the new dream home. These external manifestations may certainly help create a feeling of happiness for a while, however they are momentary and not long lasting. Experiencing greater love in our life is more about experiencing 'joy'. Joy is that radiant Divine spark that lights us up from the inside and gives us meaning and purpose for the long term. It's a way of being that comes from an eternal soul-connection, rather than experiences we feel in our physical reality in the short term.

The belief that certain conditions in our life will bring us happiness is only an illusion. If we become so focused on this illusion it will put us in a place of eternal separation from what we believe we don't have. It will leave our heart constantly aching, with a feeling of deprivation that resides under the surface of our thinking, driving our attention and energy away from what we have been blessed with every day. Over time this creates stress and anxiety. The compound effect of a stressed body and an unsettled mind can lead to sickness, injury or an ongoing physical or emotional distress.

The truth is, we already have what we need for our soul journey. In each life time we are in the process of remembering our true self. Most of us have forgotten our spiritual essence, our Divinity and the love that resides within. Our physical life is an opportunity to remember and grow in love through soul lessons. Unfortunately, we have a tendency to subject ourself to a lot of 'un-love'. The process of loving ourself comes through releasing, surrendering and accepting all aspects of ourself. Unless we cease the never-ending longing for happiness to be given to us from our external world, then we will not find peace in our heart, mind or body.

The way towards recognising that Divine spark of love within is to become the observer of our life so that we can witness the gifts, talents and our own lovability. It's also about adopting a perspective of love that enables us to feel grateful for who we are and what we can manifest as a result of our perspective.

If you choose to always desire to have something else in life or to be someone else, then you will rob yourself of the joy you can experience in being your unique self. We are always blessed with gifts that many of us choose not to recognise. It is not helpful to ignore what we have been blessed with, for the sake of being modest or humble. This is ignorance, and a lack of appreciation of what we have to contribute and share with others. Our joy comes from being our authentic self and sharing our gifts with others. This is living life with True Love.

The experiences we have in life, good or bad, are usually the result of our energy, focus and perspective. Our energy and focus emit a particular vibration, and so we will have a tendency to attract more experiences of a similar vibration. If we are sad and depressed (heavy energy), we are more likely to attract more experiences that are similar to this energy. Have you noticed when you are having a bad day, that things just seem to compound with similar experiences?

The sadness, pain, and joy we experience in life is usually a result of what we have attracted into our reality. The way we choose to respond to situations, events, and interactions with people determines what we are likely to experience. Wayne Dyer suggests there are no problems in life, unless you perceive things as problems. When we see only problems, our mind creates the illusion of separateness and some kind of deficit. Our experience then becomes a reflection of this perspective of lack, which can become a perpetual dis-ease in our mind, in our body, and in our reality.

As spiritual beings we are all connected, which means in truth there is no experience of separateness or any deficit. When we choose to see opportunities or solutions rather than obstacles, this uplifts our energetic vibration. The Universe responds to this energy by offering up more experiences of the same vibration. As we raise our sights and we focus on the positives, we create an energy of attraction that opens doors and reveals new opportunities.

*When we release ourself from the entrapment of
our mind, we can experience connection,
Divine Love and freedom from what binds us.*

It requires trust in ourself and trust in the Divine, to release and surrender our mental strongholds and our desire to control our experience of love. It's about knowing that God has our back and is ready to support us. When we try to hold onto things or people, we can block the energy flow in our mind, body and soul, and this prevents us from being able to experience what is already available to us. Parts of our life become stuck and that's when we notice we are looping with the same problem, or we are experiencing recurring health ailments, or having difficulty with the same issues that come up in relationships, our finances or in our work environment.

Whatever you are holding onto will be showing up somewhere in your life as a recurring theme. It will be a repetitive way of thinking and behaving that you slip into without a moment's thought. It will be those patterns that, in the first instance, may feel good, but ultimately lead you down a path of self-doubt, dependency and melancholy. Until we release from our fear of losing something or the dependence upon something or someone in order to feel safe or loved, we will continue to feel like we are on a downward spiral of never feeling strong enough or good enough in ourself.

Loving our challenges and seeing our situation as a blessing and a teaching moment, is a great starting point for letting go of what is holding us back and preventing us from experiencing more love in our life. As we learn to release and surrender the need to control people or situations in our life, we experience greater levels of freedom and inner joy. What we release will in time flow back into our experience, as long as we maintain an energy of love and not attachment.

## Creating Stillness Within

The process of releasing and surrendering our mental strongholds can be greatly assisted when we can learn to be in the gap of silence. Wayne Dyer refers to 'being in the gap of silence' as the place that is between the 'noise' of every moment. As we identify the difference between the noise of our mind and the silence between the noise of our thoughts, we can learn to create stillness that enables us to tune into our Divine nature. It is in the silence of 'being', rather than thinking or doing, that we can reflect and understand what is most important to us in terms of our soul path, and to also experience powerful healing and Divine love.

Our minds are often very active, and it can be difficult sometimes to quieten the inner chatter. Most of us have a constant running dialogue of thoughts and words that carry meaning and emotional energy. Our thoughts can have a significant impact on our sense of well-being, our self-esteem and our experience of self-love. Every word we utter externally or in our self-talk, conjures up an image in our mind that elicits certain feelings and emotions. These emotions create a frequency or vibration that affects what we manifest into our experience. Words that are self-deprecating and negative, carry a heavy energy, closing down our ability to be open and receptive to love. However, when we choose to think and speak lovingly about ourself and we come from a place of self-acceptance, we raise our energetic vibration to attract more love into our life.

Being comfortable in the gap of silence may take some practice, but it's the only way to connect with our Higher Self and God. Busy minds and rampant tongues are a reflection of someone who has not learned to sit in the comfort and peace of stillness. Fear is what drives our minds to loop and ponder all of the past choices (good and bad) and worry about the possibilities that could arise in the future. This is not self-love because we are not trusting that our Higher Self has the answers to teach us and guide us towards Divine Love. It is only in the stillness that we can hear, feel and experience the voice of God and our Higher Self.

*Be still and know I am with you. (Psalm 46:10)*

## Living Now

Learning to be still and in the present moment enables us to create an energetic vibration that allows us to feel the presence of the Divine in every moment. As we sit with the 'gift of silence' we become present to ourself, no longer focused on the past or the future. There is only 'now'. The past no longer exists. All that you think you said and did is no longer there. It cannot be repeated or relived, unless you choose to dwell in the past and re-create those experiences in your mind.

When we constantly dwell on what was, past relationships or past experiences, we tend to embellish them either for better or for worse. As we relive those memories in our mind, our subconscious believes they are real present moments being experienced again, and so our physical and emotional body responds as if our thoughts were real. If we identify those past memories with negative feelings and limited thinking, we keep creating the same energy in our present life. Our transformation and soul growth then become stuck or put on hold.

When we let go of our self-limiting thoughts, we can remain in the present rather than drift off to thoughts about the future and the possibilities of who, what and where. Being overly focused on the past or the future will drain our energy and pull us away from the experience of Divine love in this moment. We only ever have the present moment. Everything is only ever 'now'. Our joy, our sense of who we are and how we choose to think and feel comes from what we are thinking, feeling and doing now.

## Choosing Trust over Control

In a television series that's set on a horse farm in Canada, I was reminded that the path to self-healing comes from letting go of control and learning to trust in the power of Love. Part of the training of a wild horse is to work with them so that they become familiar with you, and ultimately develop a relationship of trust. If we use force, control and punishment to manipulate the horse, it can limit or even damage that relationship. However, when we use our energy to communicate with the horse, and show patience, confidence and love, we can create a synchronistic connection and a lasting bond of trust.

It is the same with people. When we project our own ideas, thoughts and feelings onto other people, expecting that they should think and feel the same way, we are exercising a form of forceful control. This is not trust. It comes from the desire to manipulate others so that we feel justified in our way of thinking and doing. When we are motivated to make others more like ourself, we are exercising a form of control to suit our own needs. In an effort to feel more powerful and in control, we actually give our power away. This is because our desire to feel good becomes dependent upon that person complying with our conditions or fulfilling our desire for approval. We also give our power away when we attempt to rescue, fix or heal someone when they have not requested our help. This is a form of control and a lack of trust in the ability of others to help themselves.

We are all free-spirited beings and any amount of control of another (or our circumstances) will only shut down our ability to trust, and to give and receive love. Control is when we have expectations of how other people should think and behave, and how they ought to respond to our needs and situation. How many times have you noticed yourself get upset when someone has not given you the response you were hoping for? It may have been attention, affection, approval, or even significance. Expectations of others will only ever lead to disappointment and negative emotions such as resentment, anger, or the internalised pain of rejection.

As justified as we may feel about our own viewpoint or personal rules about how other people should behave, it's important to remember that they are the product of our own construct and reality. What we believe we see in others, is what is already within ourself. Our perception and judgment of others is what is occurring in our own vibration. Our energetic vibration attracts the same energy into our experience. Our beliefs, rules, expectations, personality quirks and our feelings belong only to ourself and are therefore not part of someone else's reality.

When you learn to release and let go of the need to control others, only then can you truly learn to love and value yourself and experience spiritual, emotional and physical freedom. However, transformation doesn't happen overnight. Like most things in life, it takes time to develop this level of self-awareness. Be patient with yourself, stay vigilant and persevere with love and self-compassion.

Holding onto pain and expectations of others, including the memories of your past and your concerns for the future, is just another form of control and self-torture, it is not self-love. As we release and let go of people and situations in our life, we send out the message that we trust and love ourself enough to direct our own path. Our happiness, the joy we experience, and the peace that comes from loving our true self, does not come from someone else or our circumstances. It comes from knowing that we are a reflection of Divine Love, just as we are. In time, as we learn to love who and what we are, and trust that we are enough, we can heal within and open our heart so that we are drawing more love and trust into our life.

When we are able to see love in ourself, and at the same time accept our shadow parts, we come closer to seeing the same in others. Are you in the habit of only seeing the flaws in other people? What we see in others is a reflection of how we feel about an aspect of ourself. Seeing a lack of empathy, care or love in someone else is because you are struggling to trust and love yourself at the same time.

*Loving all aspects of ourself becomes a gift of self-love and healing.*

As we realise we are worthy of love, we allow the process of healing to take place. Healing takes time, and we all need to heal and reconnect with our true self in our own unique way. You may feel uncomfortable or even impatient with the inner silence and stillness needed for self-healing and self-love. We are very used to allowing the Spirit of distraction to create busyness in our mind and in our life as a way of avoiding our deeper emotions and seeing our inner truth. However, the Divine resides within each of us, and so there is always an intention of True Love emanating from our soul, guiding us toward spiritual upliftment and peace for our highest good.

## Choosing Love

Love is not an idea, a fantasy or just a feeling. The origin of Divine Love comes from Source (God), and it is this love that feeds our Soul and our Higher Self. Love is never separate from us or sourced from someone or something else. It lives within us, is a part of us, and is our spiritual essence. We feel the experience of love in many ways, more known to us as physical and emotional expressions of love in the physical realm.

Love is a choice, and the opposite is fear. God reminds us to release our fears and know we are loved, created from Love and, so we *are* Love. Love is not something that we have to find or conjure up. So many of us spend a lifetime searching for love, believing it will appear if we try hard enough. However, love already exists within. It is simply a matter for us to tap into our soul and ignite that spark of Divine Love and choose to *live as Love*.

We have a choice to love, and to experience greater love in our life. In her book "The Choice to Love" (Hay House, Inc, 2017) Dr Barbara De Angelis says *"We're all fluent in the language of the heart. We just don't speak it much"*.

God's angels of the spiritual realm are always there to offer their support. All we need to do is ask for their guidance, and then let go of the need to have all the answers. Our angels are with us throughout our life and it is their mission to hear and respond to our prayers when we ask for their support and guidance. It's our choice to trust they have heard our prayers, and to listen for the promptings in our soul. When we ask, they respond.

We are never left alone to walk the path of our soul-journey, unless we refuse to ask and receive the guidance given to us. God and the angels love you. Whether you choose to believe or not, you have the choice to love *You*. You can either reach your Divne potential or you can hide under a rock and refuse to shine. You may tell yourself you are not worthy of love or that you are not as intelligent or as good as the next person, but this is not the truth. You are no more or less worthy than anyone else. Love and full acceptance of all of you will allow you to grow and heal. Fear will only reverse the healing and send you back down the path of mistrust and low energy, and this will attract more fear and anxiety into your life.

I recently spoke with a friend who has a very big heart but a troubled mind. In his attempt to find answers and clarity in his world, his mind raced, searching for answers, love and forgiveness. His energy was erratic, and it made his body and mind tired after years of living without peace within his soul. He was full of self-judgment and to compensate he had spent much of his energy trying to please others. He had the most amazing amount of love and compassion for others, and an incredible amount of wisdom learned from years of challenges and inner reflection, and yet he still struggled to love and accept himself.

*We can break free from our self-imprisonment through self-love.*

The way to release from our self-imprisonment is to see that love and peace come from within. The path to peace and to greater love is through quietening our monkey-mind, self-acceptance, and through conscious awareness of being in the present moment. We are made from Source (God) and so we have all we need within us already. We may not feel lovable or good enough, and maybe we have spent years feeling resentment, regret, blame, or self-judgment. These beliefs and feelings only disempower us and give us the illusion that our soul is imprisoned, separated from Divine Love.

This is an unnecessary and painful choice, however it's possible we have become so conditioned to feel this way that we don't realise we are choosing this option. The magic is in realising we can release ourself from the prison of self-judgment and the conditions we succumb to. There *is* an alternative. Today we can choose to lean towards love and compassion. Our worth, value and lovability are not founded on our successes and failures in life. We don't need to prove ourself to anyone. All we need to do is love all parts of ourself, and as we do, our perceived troubles will melt away.

Love is a choice. When we make the conscious decision to choose love, we automatically begin the process of releasing what is 'un-love'. So, what happens when we experience resistance to letting go? What if letting go feels difficult, or even scary? What I can assure you of, is that love is the only way to peace and liberation.

I have experienced deep peace in moments of surrender, where I have allowed my Soul to step forward and my ego mind to fall into the background. Yoga and meditation have helped me to experience this inner peace. With daily practice I can experience these moments on a regular basis. As I let go, I feel great calm and peace within and my energy vibrates at a higher frequency, closer to that of Divine Love. This is when I feel connected to my Higher Self. I feel lighter and more open in my heart, and through trust and self-love I feel a sense of expansiveness and loving vulnerability emanate from within me.

There are always opportunities to make changes in the way we see ourselves and others, so that we can move towards greater love. In doing so we are able to make room in our spiritual and physical life for uplifting energy, loving intentions and healthy opportunities to come forward. With such an opportunity put before us, why do we find it difficult to let go of negative ways of thinking and being?

Choosing love and letting go, is about making a decision to no longer pay mind to those beliefs that tell us we are not good enough, or that our life will not improve. When we struggle to let go, our ego-centric mind wants to focus on what we believe we are losing. It is easy to slip into thinking more about what we don't have, and to come from a mindset of lack, scarcity and comparison. When we fall for this level of thinking we can disconnect from our own sense of truth and veer off our soul-path. Our mind will trap us into old mental patterns that influence our emotions, which then shape our decisions around how we choose to respond and behave.

Our resistance to change or to letting go of control comes from fear and affects the health of our mind and eventually our body. Maintaining the belief we are not good enough keeps us locked into a particular pattern of thinking and behaving that limits our growth and the opportunity to experience more of our true potential.

When we realise there is no place for fear in our life, letting go of control becomes a decision and an act to release, surrender and just 'be'. As we come to truly love who we are, we realise we are not separate from God or the Universe. There is nothing to let go other than our illusions. We are Divinely connected to everything already, so there is nothing to gain or lose. As we tune into our Divine nature and recognise the Divine light and the love within, we are able to know our true value and worth. Why would you want to do or think in a way that prevents you from experiencing this pure Love?

*"Let all that you do be done with love" (1 Cor 16:14-22)*

What are you doing in your life that is drawing you away from the experience of peace, love and abundance? What are you thinking about that causes angst in your heart and mind? What rules do you hold onto about your world and others, that creates feelings of frustration, conflict and irritation within you?

When we more closely examine our intentions (our reasons and justifications) for what we choose, we may be surprised to learn that many of our thoughts and decisions come from fear of losing something or feeling we are not good enough or deserving to receive.

When we reflect upon our life with the intention of releasing what is no longer in alignment with our true self and our soul-path, we can progress to the next level of spiritual awareness and soul growth. During the process of our transformation we may choose to release ourself from unhealthy relationships, unfulfilling jobs or self-sabotaging habits. It's important at this time, not to confuse our own self-awareness with a desire to discredit or blame others on their own soul-journey. Our soul growth and transformation is not about what others choose to do or believe.

Releasing the material things in our life will help our transformation. However, what's more vital is the need for self-examination, and to surrender the limiting beliefs, illusions and mental strongholds that alter our reality and affect our path going forward. We have the power to choose what we focus on and what we keep within our energy field. As we release false perceptions and attachments, we will experience peace, alignment with our values and clear access to our soul-path. God and the angels will guide us to release only what is not serving our highest good.

# 11
## Becoming Friends with Fear

It may feel scary to release and let go of what is familiar, especially when it has been key to the way we habitually think and respond. Our thoughts, beliefs and feelings are how we unconsciously form our personal identity. When we are asked to give up something we have always done, it feels like we are being asked to give away a part of ourself. Wow, instant discomfort!

So why does it feel so hard? There have been many times when I have attempted to let go of negative thoughts and habits, and yet, I have repeated the same way of thinking, believing and responding over and over again. When we notice we are looping in our habits, it is usually due to some level of resistance which causes an undercurrent of tension and conflict. Do you recall feeling this way at times? Have you noticed that when you attempt to let go of an unhealthy way of thinking, such as being focused on blame, resentment, and negativity, you end up doing the same thing again, receiving the same unfruitful results?

Some people become experts at looping and after a while they become so unconscious of their own actions that it feels as though this is normal. When you frequently find you are getting poor results in your life it can be easy to believe that life has it in for you, so why bother putting in the effort? When we take on board the victim-mentality we can forget that we have the power to make changes and think and do things differently. There is no benefit in attributing pain, discomfort and ill-fortune to other people and circumstances. Believing we are not responsible for our own outcomes can lock us into the illusion that 'life doesn't get any better than this'.

When our mind seeks to find peace, relief, or fulfillment external to ourself, eventually we disconnect from hearing the wisdom and voice of our Soul. Our mind takes over and our heart can become closed, receding into the background so that we lose touch with our Higher Self and our soul-purpose. This habit of externalizing our reality will eventually repel opportunities to grow in wisdom and understanding and create a state of dis-ease that can manifest as poor health issues.

Fear is what keeps us trapped, so why are we afraid to release and let go of what is hurting us? Why don't we see the blessings and benefits of creating space for peace and abundance in our life? When we hold on to fear we are holding onto what we know so well, and what feels familiar and comfortable. It's like holding onto the partner that is abusing you or staying in the same job and allowing your boss to bully you each day. Or it may be that you have been refusing to move away from people who are negative and draining, because this is all you know and to change your own pattern of behaviour feels difficult and uncomfortable. Or it may be that you have lived a life telling yourself that you are not good enough, because that's what you believed as a child, and to believe anything else is strange and unfamiliar. Holding onto something consistently when you know it is doing you harm is similar to the addiction condition.

Could it be that when given the opportunity to release what is not good in your life, you are afraid that you will have nothing left or you will feel like a failure? Are you fearful of what will happen next when you let go of the toxic relationship, the unhealthy habits, the negative workplace, the expectations or dependency on others? Have you heard yourself repeating the same story (excuses) that you have relived for years and allowed this story to stop you from progressing? This kind of fear will keep you trapped, as you repeat the same behaviours and patterns that have given you the same outcomes over and over.

If you want your life to improve, and to get back on the path of self-love, then trust is the way to inner peace and growth in love. Trust in your Higher Self and your Soul, and trust in the Divine that you are being taken care of. You do not need to believe that change is hard or challenging. With the changing seasons comes new life, beauty, and growth in new ways. Lift your gaze and your perception to see that life is supporting you through love, not fear.

Trust is not an activity of the mind, for the mind is what creates fear and doubt. Trust is deeper and comes from the heart. It is the release of fear and an intention of allowing Spirit to flow within us, so that our energy emanates from a place of love, even in the presence of not knowing or understanding.

We can develop trust by choosing to see with new eyes and opening our heart to Divine Love. As we create that inner shift, we can develop our muscle of courage to face our truth, what needs to be released, and where to devote our energy and focus. With trust, our level of confidence grows, and we can begin to witness the Universe always supporting us. It takes practice, and a desire to live with love for ourself. It's not about 'getting it right' or counting how many times we miss the mark. It's accepting that we are fallible, and that over time and with practice, we will learn, grow from our experiences, and recognise our amazing value and self-worth.

To begin with, become the observer of your life. Let go of needing to have the answers. Let go of over-analysing yourself and others and 'be' the observer. Bring your attention to all that you enjoy in your life now, and what you love in you. See your own goodness. You are a magnificent being. Observe what is beautiful in you, what makes your heart sing and lifts your soul.

We are all unique in the way we present ourself to the world, each with our own flavour, expressed through our personality, perceptions and experiences. Sit back in your life and breathe. See what is also magnificent in your surrounds and in other people. See the light in others, not their mistakes or limitations.

Our self-imposed limitations cloud our vision and taint our experiences so that we become unaware of our powerful potential. The Divine Love is within us, waiting for us to see it and use it to live an abundant and meaningful life. The way of love is healing; it is the remedy for our soul to wash away the darkness we have been experiencing.

Fear is insidious. If we allow it, our mind will have us believe we do not live in fear. Observe your life as it is now. How are you feeling? What are you perpetually focused on? A lack of money, poor relationships, health problems, routine stress and anxiety that manifests as health issues, self-doubt and a belief that success cannot be yours in this lifetime? Fear is prevalent in our lives, but we have become so accustomed to its existence that we no longer recognise it as our limiting thoughts, unhealthy coping mechanisms and patterns of behaviour.

Your Higher Self can be accessed within you when you tap into the essence of your being, where Divine Love dwells. When you trust that your Higher Self knows the path to love and peace, you have no need to fear that you will have nothing in replace of what you are letting go. Trust that your Higher Self knows what is best for you, and that as you release what is not needed, you are making room for all that will improve your well-being and lead you toward abundance in your life. Do not waste time and energy by staying in a place of fear. Fear comes from negative thoughts of what we imagine is real or will happen in our life. If you have the power to imagine the worst, then you have the power to imagine and create what is the best for yourself. You have the power to be a better version of yourself every day. All it takes is the smallest of steps toward the Light on a consistent basis. The Light is the Divine spark that emanates from True Love; all that inspires.

# What do you see?

Our physical eyes and what we perceive can lead us towards True Love or create distance in a way that causes us to see ourselves as limited and separate from the Divine. We are more than what our physical senses respond to every day. What we see with our eyes is interpreted by what we believe we are seeing, and what we choose to think and feel at the same time. What we perceive is not just the physical objects of colour and shape; we see our world through a lens that is coloured by our experiences and our expectations. Our beliefs and interpretations create a particular energetic vibration that is reflected in our subtle energy bodies. When we see our world through our heart and through the eyes of our Soul, we vibrate at a higher level than the lower vibrations of our physicality.

We can alter our energy anytime when we are aware of how we are thinking, believing and feeling. When we tune into our Higher Self we can tap into the world of Spirit. With a still mind and an open heart we can align our physical senses with our inner-sight and intuition. In doing so we lift our awareness, open our psychic senses, and raise our energetic vibration to a higher frequency, which opens us to the guidance that comes from the Divine.

Take note of how you are feeling right now in this moment. Tune into your body. Does it feel relaxed and centred, or tense and unsettled? Where in your body do you feel this? In your chest, back, knees, neck, stomach? Our body gives us clues as to how we are feeling emotionally, which is a response to where we have been focusing our mind and what we are perceiving. *(Refer to Chapter 7 – The Energy Shift)*

We are able to manage our vibrational frequency by choosing what to focus on, what to believe and what to think. When our vibrational frequency is high, what we perceive will be a reflection of things vibrating at a higher frequency. We are likely to physically feel more energetic, more positive and open to growth and opportunities, and we have an attractive appeal in terms of our appearance and demeanour. However, if we are dwelling in self-doubt and anxiety, our energetic frequency drops and our lower vibration manifests as sluggishness, low motivation and a lack of clarity. We may also feel greater fluctuations and intensity in our emotions.

Beyond our physical sight we are constantly interpreting our world and responding to what we think and believe. Are you regularly noticing the irritations of others around you, the loud voices in the office, the mess on the floor, the inconsiderate employee? Or are you feeling frustrated by the many slow drivers on the road today, the rude woman behind the counter, or the child screaming next door? What are you noticing? When we are perceiving the negatives or the lack in our life, we are operating with low energy and a low vibration, and this will tend to attract other people and situations that are also resonating at a low or similar vibrational frequency.

However, if your focus is on gratitude and appreciation, your vision and perception will likely to be clear, and your outlook will be focused on the possibilities rather than obstacles. You may observe how amazing the water is reflecting the sun today, and how the birds sound particularly sweet, as if they are singing specifically for your pleasure and enjoyment. Or you may marvel at how beautiful our environment smells after it has been raining. You may remember the wonderful blessings you have in the support of family and friends, and that you have a roof over your head and a bed to sleep in tonight. Whatever it is, your attention to feelings of gratitude will greatly influence your energetic vibration and what you are more likely to attract into your experiences in life.

When we are resonating at a higher vibration our energy will help to facilitate flow in our life, where we experience synchronicities and an ease with which events integrate and interact. Our relationships with other people will feel more at ease and more in alignment with our own frequency, and more closely matched with our own values and interests. As we vibrate at a higher frequency, we are able to develop and maintain peace within, so when there are disturbances, we are less affected, and we are not taking that energy into our own aura or energy field. It is a pleasurable state to be in. When our vibrational frequency is high, we feel calm, peaceful, open, receptive and more consciously aware of our connection with the Divine.

Love is not infatuation with another individual, as we would perhaps imagine in a relationship. True Love in the first instance is the 'truth' of love, which in its purest form is spiritual in nature, unconditional, and expressed through Divine creation. When we operate at a higher vibration, we are able to see, feel and experience love in ourself, in others and in our world. Love in its purest form enables us to connect with all that is living, as well as the spiritual realm. The essence of love is unity and communion, not separation, although love can be experienced uniquely as an expression of who we are in spirit and through our physical form.

## Self-acceptance

When we are in a state of True Love, we are able to accept ourself in entirety, without judgment or expectation, with all of our idiosyncrasies, foibles, past and present experiences, and our unique qualities. Self-acceptance is key to experiencing love in our life. So often we are conditioned to believe that love must come from outside of ourself, either through a relationship or our material world. So much of our energy is geared toward seeking the attainment of love and to feel loved. When we are focused on seeking love from others, we are telling ourself and the Universe that we are not enough, and that we do not have love within. With a belief that there is not enough love, either within our being or in the world, our energy reflects our belief there is lack in our life, and so we end up attracting more of the same experience. What we believe, is what we will experience in our reality.

It is human nature to want to be loved, to feel lovable and to give love. The first step to create this in our reality is to see love in ourself. What do I mean by that? Well of course you love yourself. But do you? Do you think about yourself in a loving way? Do you treat yourself in a way that is caring and compassionate? Are you forgiving of yourself when you mess up or do you expect to get it right every time?

What about when you tell yourself that you are not as good as the next person, or that for all your efforts you will never amount to anything in life? Or when you say to yourself that you are only worth 'x' amount and you will never have enough money to achieve the dreams you have for your life. This is not demonstrating love or acceptance of yourself. Many of us have an ongoing conversation in our mind that berates our ability and self-worth. As a result, we often make choices that reflect our low value and low self-esteem. This is not 'self-love'.

Self-love does not come from the Ego, where we may have an over-inflated evaluation of our worth, our appearance or what we possess. It's also not about the ego that is steeped in fear and self-doubt, always working to limit us due to our insecurities. Our measure of self-love is our willingness to accept all of who we are, and to live in a way that is aligned with our inner truth and what we truly love and value in life, rather than from a position of compromise or mediocrity.

The measure of our own worthiness is also not dependent upon the opinions of others, our successes or failures, or even the circumstances in our life. It's our ability to love and accept our warts and all. It's an unconditional love that comes from the heart, from a recognition that we are more than how we appear, who we hang out with, or what we possess in life. It's the desire to be our best, and to be consistent in how we think, what we say and what we do in a way that supports our growth and well-being.

Whenever we go through a significant transformation, we are often faced with thoughts about our self-worth and our measure of self-love. Challenges are marvellous opportunities to bring us face to face with our inner truth. However, it's still our choice to hear, see, feel or experience this truth and to act from a place of integrity for oneself.

One thing is certain in life, and that is change. Change is happening all the time, in our environment, our jobs, and in our relationships. This is life, and for the most part we can be flexible enough to adapt to the changes. However, embracing inner transformation can bring us to a deeper level of self-awareness that may create a feeling of greater vulnerability. Inner transformation opens the door for us to face our soul-truth, our true essence and our 'raison d'etre' (our reason for being). This kind of transformation is more of a spiritual experience as it involves our soul's growth, which is beyond our intellect, our personality or our physical body. Our soul's growth is where we learn soul lessons and grow in wisdom and spiritual maturity.

Our physical life is the landscape on which we experience our soul's journey, a journey that takes us closer to Divine Love. As we experience changes in our life, whether it's around issues of health, relationships, career, finances, family, or our dreams yet to be fulfilled; the experience will often bring us to a point of self-reflection. One of the basic human needs in our life is to experience love, along with food, shelter and safety. If we have not already developed a strong sense of self-love when challenges come our way, we are going to struggle to manage the stormy weather.

Self-love is being compassionate and accepting of ourself. It's agreeing to not accept the values and judgments of other people. It's having love and respect for ourself, by living in a way that honours what we believe is right and good for our soul-being. It's making choices that do not compromise our integrity or our ability to be our true and authentic self. Self-love is self-acceptance, which means we are not driven to seek love from others to fill a void or a perceived need or personal lack in ourself. As we see and acknowledge the Divine goodness and love in ourself, we are then able to see the same Divine love in others, accepting them as they are without the desire to change them.

We are all unique and the way we perceive life is how we create our own reality. When we cultivate a natural appreciation and gratitude for the unique person that we are, we develop a mindset and attitude of flexibility and self-acceptance, as well as the heart and desire to nurture our soul-being through kindness and compassion.

When I chose to take a different path in my life, my measure of self-love was at an all-time low. I knew I was equipped with a good dose of common sense, and that I was an intelligent person, emotionally and spiritually aware, loving and supportive of people in my life. However, I had not developed a measure of self-love or self-worth. My estimation of my own value was very low. At this time, living with poor self-esteem was crippling me and holding me back in most aspects of my life. I could not see this in me at the time. I needed to come face to face with my soul-truth. I experienced the growing pains of many challenges and experiences that stretched me in every possible way to help me learn. I made a lot of mistakes, which in time helped me to better reflect and understand what wasn't working, and how I could do things differently. I regularly hear Wayne Dyer in my head saying:

*'Change the way you look at things and the things you look at will change'. (Wayne Dyer)*

The road I was travelling was not an easy one for me. I mentally understood the lessons however it took much longer for my emotions to catch up, and for my doubting mind to settle down. I needed many repetitive experiences to gain a deeper level of awareness and to learn my soul lessons. I have since realised that the obstacles and the heartache we experience in life is greatly affected by the way we perceive ourself, our level of resistance to moving forward, and our willingness to embrace love for our soul-being. We are human, and therefore we do experience pain. That is inevitable. However, learning to have self-compassion and forgiveness is part of our soul's growth.

When you feel low, and it feels like life can't get any worse, you may have uttered to yourself – *'Why does this keep happening to me? What have I done to attract all this bad luck? When am I going to get that break? Why does everyone keep telling me to be patient, haven't I been patient enough?'*

In time I began to develop an understanding as to why my thinking, my beliefs and my perceptions were creating my reality. I was building a reservoir of personal experiences and resources that provided me with a lot of 'aha' moments, insights, new skills and supportive people in my life, all of which were helping me to think and feel more uplifted. More importantly, I began to see that my choices and my measure of self-love was determining the quality of my life and my level of abundance.

On an intellectual level I knew what I needed to do, which was to manage my energy, adjust my focus, and believe in myself. However, it was still taking me much longer to heed the lessons and change my outcomes. At the time I didn't understand why this was happening and it was so terribly frustrating for me. I now know it was because I had a measure of resistance to change which was coming from a deep-seated belief that I was not good enough to experience improvement in my life. I believed I would never be successful and that my circumstances would never be any different to what it had been all my life. I also knew that this was a reflection of how I was not loving myself. When we let go of all that rubbish self-talk and we pause to notice the beauty within us and in our environment, we can realise we are so much more, and that life truly is abundant.

## Love and Abundance

When we are passing through any kind of transformation in our life, it's important to realise there are no shortcuts. When we choose the path of soul growth there is only one way, and that is to go through the experience. When we are confronted by change, it's a human phenomenon to want to avoid it or circumnavigate around it. For most people the idea of change is equated to pain and suffering, which is something most of us do not want to experience. However, this belief is a product of our fearful mind. We fear change and so we attract all the negativity and suffering we can imagine.

Choosing to embrace our soul's growth does not need to be a sufferable experience. Yes, it requires us to be stretched and challenged as we learn new ways of being. This can cause discomfort if we are very resistant to change, however the way in which we approach our own soul growth has a significant effect on how we experience our own transformation. If we have chosen to make a change, then the best way forward is to trust the process and know that we always have Divine Love as our guide and our spiritual support. With an open heart and a measure of courage, knowing we are loved and supported, the way forward will open new doors for more love, happiness and growth.

Learning to release and surrender is an act of faith and trust. It's not about being submissive to a greater force against our will because we have lost the strength to resist. It's precisely the opposite. It's surrendering to our own resistance because we realise we are being held in the palms of the Universe with love, supported in a way that empowers us. This awareness expands and nourishes our soul's growth as we move towards greater Love.

Letting go of our fears and our desire to control is like clearing the fog away from our mind and the blindness in our eyes. Spiritually the effect is releasing into the arms of love and trusting that our needs will always be met. When we are able to embrace love and compassion, we enter new realms of possibility for abundance and spiritual wisdom.

Abundance is the experience and the expression of love in our life, physically, emotionally, mentally and spiritually. It encompasses everything that we perceive and energetically feel with love. It is the inner experience of the Divine and the connection we have with the Holy Spirit. It's knowing we are completely whole as we are, created in Love and eternally connected to Divine Truth.

For me, living the outward experience of abundance is as simple as witnessing the glorious sunrise each morning and feeling gratitude for its beauty. When we experience abundance in our life it is uplifting and inspiring. When we let go of the confines of our mind and recognise that abundance is more than just money in the bank, we enter the Universe of abundant thinking and living. Abundance is the manifestation of energy that is already in existence and in motion. It moves according to our perception and how we chose to either draw it closer to our living reality or repel it from our experiences.

True abundance becomes apparent when we are able to make the connection between the mind, our heart (soul) and our physical experience. It requires trust and a willingness to be open to the possibilities, with a desire to perceive our world differently to the way we have done so in the past. We must see ourself and our world through eyes of love and infinite possibilities to know true abundance.

We are energetic beings and our experiences in life are about how we draw energy towards us or repel energy. Our energetic vibration and focus will determine the experiences and people we attract into our field of awareness. Energy cannot be destroyed or cease to exist, it only changes form. What appears to be in our experience one day, and then gone the next, is not because energy, such as love, has disappeared. All forms of energy can change at any time and is not something we can hold onto or possess.

To attract loving energy into our experience we must first *be* that energy of love. When we give love, we vibrate at the frequency of love. Have you noticed that when you give your time or talent to someone else in need, you have the experience of feeling fulfilled? You receive an energy exchange or the return of the same energy of giving or contribution, either from that person or in some other form. Such as energy returned through the kindness of a friend, a gift of a colleague's time or expertise, a compliment or a favourable opportunity that comes our way. When energy is in flow, we experience this as equal exchange through giving and receiving.

The key to happiness, health and abundance is to be in flow with the energy of life. Energy is constantly flowing from person to person, from one living creature to another, from spirit to spirit, regardless of time or space. When we use energy wisely, we can live a sustainable and abundant life. This means, gratefully receiving gifts and blessings that come our way, using them to assist our soul growth, and then passing on these gifts (of knowledge, wisdom, skills, experience, healing) to others when they have served their purpose in our life.

The gifts we receive in life are exchanges of energy. An example may be the arrival of a person in our life to assist with specific soul-lessons or to provide support and guidance at the right time. They may appear on our soul-path for a brief time, or they be there to travel with us the for long term, depending upon our soul contracts. Other gifts may be more material, to help us with our material needs. Everything can serve a purpose for a period of time, however it's important to let them go, share them or move them on when we no longer need them. When we hold onto energy (the gifts of life), we can experience blocks or disruption to the flow of energy in our life. It's important to release attachments to energy (people, gifts and opportunities) so we can pass on the blessings to others when they have served their purpose in our own life, and restore the balance and flow of energy in our life. When we are in flow, we will experience less conflict and turmoil, because we are living in a way that is giving and receiving.

*"There is a time for everything, and a season
for every activity under the heavens."*
*Ecclesiastes 3:1*

When we give and receive Love as energy in flow, we not only benefit from the fruit that Love bears, we can also share this gift with others. The gift of love and abundance is shared by our own gratitude and intentions, with a willingness to share what we have received, learned or gained as a result. In this way we stay in flow with the energy of Divine Love, transferring and transmuting this love from receiving, to giving love and abundance.

## From Darkness to Light

We are living in flow when we can embrace the transformational and birthing process that we go through as we move from one phase of our life to the next. The transformation is usually challenging and often painful, but like a mother in labour, she knows that there is an end in sight and a new life is to be born. The transformational process is as important as the new version of who you become. Most people associate pain and struggles as something that is bad and to be avoided. However, when you know that the Divine is there to only love and support you, then the energy and expectation around the birthing process can be lovingly welcomed and embraced. All struggles are an opportunity for transformation to bring greater love into our life, as well as spiritual and emotional growth and a deeper understanding of ourself, and our purpose in this life.

The caterpillar is earth bound and has limited movement and sight, and its primary focus is to ensure it has enough to eat each day. When it has fed on as many nutrients as possible, the time comes for it to go into a resting state in readiness for its transformation to the next level of beauty and awesomeness. Cocooned in an elaborately woven silk covering, the caterpillar goes within, withdrawing from the world it has known, and prepares to transform to a new version of itself that will bring greater freedom, expansion and new opportunities. The chrysalis process is powerful, and non-reversible. It appears to be exhausting and perhaps even painful. It takes time, and there is a definable beginning and end to the process. If the process is interrupted the caterpillar will certainly die prematurely.

When we go through any period of change it can feel uncomfortable, unfamiliar and even frightening. There is uncertainty when we step into the unknown, but when we go let go of the need to know how things will turn out, and we surrender to the ebb and flow of life, knowing that the Universe is always working in our favour and for our growth, then we can embrace change with an expectation that all is well and for our greater good. The caterpillar does not resist change. It instinctively knows that this process is necessary and is a part of living its life to the fullest extent.

Fear is an illusion that keeps us bound, small and unchanged. It's the place we stay and never come to realise our true beauty within, or our unlimited potential. It's a tragedy for the caterpillar to miss the opportunity to transform into the amazing beautiful butterfly it was intended to be. Butterflies are radiant, light, unaffected by the gravity of life. They are creatures free to fly, and their purpose is to multiply so that there is more beauty to be shared ongoing.

So why do we stay in that place of fear and limit our own potential? I have spent many years of my earlier life living small and not seeing my own potential. When I did finally open my eyes and my senses, my initial awareness of my own beauty and potential felt a little confronting. I realised that when we avoid transformation for the purpose of our soul growth, we inevitably experience constant dis-ease and internal conflict, and this can feel like a heavy emotional and spiritual weight that drains our energy and dims our soul-light. In time, our spirit suffers what feels like a slow and painful death in our heart, mind and body.

*When the veil of darkness and ignorance lifts and*
*the light of self-awareness burns within us,*
*the voice of our Soul grows louder and stronger,*
*calling us to step away from fear and move into greater love in our life.*

We can be reminded of our fears on a daily basis, however when the call of our Higher Self speaks to us it can come in a variety of ways. The calling may be from synchronistic events or repeated signs we receive to remind us to take action in a certain area of our life. They may be conversations with friends, something we hear on the TV, the words of a song on the radio, or what we notice in our environment. Signs can also come to us in our dreams. Dreams are a visual representation of how our soul may be speaking with us, mixed with our feelings, emotions and desires that surface from our unconscious mind, asking to be expressed, noticed and heard. Dreams are not necessarily meant to be taken literally; they are often clear signs of what is calling for our immediate attention. For a long time in my life I did not dream. Perhaps it was a reflection that I had shut down my sub-conscious self, suppressing it in all its forms. It felt painful to live like this, though I was not aware why it was happening. I just felt a constant pressure on my chest and in my soul, with a knowing there was more and that I was not living as my full authentic self.

In time the call of my Soul became too strong to ignore. The moment I began to open the door to explore more, the sunlight filtered through the cracks and shone on the darkness inside me. Like a moth to a flame, our Divine self cannot help but be drawn to the Light. When our soul feels, sees, touches and experiences Divine Light, it craves for more.

As I let more Divine Light into my life and into my soul, I felt myself going through a transformation and an awakening. It was both painful and liberating at the same time. Although I experienced periods of resistance, I also had joyous moments of embracing the changes happening within me, experiencing the deep healing that came as I released and accepted the parts of me that I had hidden for so long. The light exposed recesses in my mind and in my old Soul, and my body began to transform, slowly releasing toxins and the weight of years of self-doubt, bottled up pain, and karmic lessons of the past.

Each of us may have past experiences that are shaping our decision-making today and influencing our thoughts and emotions. Whatever our soul journey has been, what is common to us all is that we are all ultimately striving to move closer to Divine Love. This is built into our spiritual-being. As we move closer toward the Light, we come to better know our true self, and experience joy that uplifts and nourishes our soul.

Living with a limited view and appreciation of our soul is sad and a waste. We are designed for so much joy and pleasure, with the ability to expand and grow in wisdom, love and peaceful communion with Spirit. In truth we are limitless beings living in a limited way. When we have courage to listen to our Higher Self we are Divinely guided on our Soul's path toward True Love. Become the butterfly and be willing to go through the transformational process with self-love, compassion and patience with yourself. Know that you are worth it and the challenges you experience are there to assist you, not punish you.

Find your voice, sing the song of your heart and Soul. Don't stop. Don't hesitate. Speak your truth and be all that you can be. Refuse to see yourself as anything less than all that you are. See through the filters you place over your eyes that cause you to compare yourself to others. There can be no-one like you. You are unique. You do not need to conform to anything or anyone because only *you* can create your version of life and your reality. Live it. Be it. Take a step forward, one at a time, but whatever you do, don't look back. Why? As Wayne Dyer says, the wake of your boat cannot drive you forward, only your engine can do that. Put some fuel in your tank (love who you are) and let it ignite the fire within you to get going. Life is precious and what matters is this moment, right now.

We can be masters of hesitation, procrastination and self-doubt, but this energy becomes toxin in our fuel tank and will cause our engine to splutter and in time, conk out. We must be the master of our own life, set a course and go. There comes a time when all the planning and preparation is done, and it is time to let go of the rope that holds us back and set ourself free. There are worlds within our soul to discover and experience. We can hold on and lament over what we think is missing in our life, or we can take the leap and recognise that life is an adventure to explore and there are endless opportunities for us to experience love and abundance. Our measure of self-love determines the quality of our experiences, our soul-growth and our ability to give and receive love.

We can get so caught up in playing the *'yes, but...'* game that we miss the calling of our Soul. While we're hesitating, life is passing by. We can become so distracted about what's 'out there' and what other people are doing, that we forget to focus on what we want to create for our own reality. To create the life we want, we must purposefully choose to see, feel and think about the experiences we want in our life now. This has the greatest impact on the way our life will unfold going forward.

The question is, are we amplifying all that is amazing in our life, using our gifts and talents to bring greater joy to ourself and others, or are we living a life with filters of scepticism, resentment, and victimhood? Do we want to grow and expand our life so that we are living to the fullest, or do we want to stay as we are, or even shrink over time? Whilst we may fear change, it is the transformation that change brings, that allows us to grow spiritually, emotionally and mentally. Why not live life as the greatest version of ourself? The alternative is to live in order to die.

# 12
## Embracing the Divine Feminine

As I entered my mid-life transition and a somewhat meaningful period of soul growth, I realised I was reconnecting with my personal identity as a woman. Through my own gender experience, I felt a strong desire to connect with my Divine Feminine as a way of reaffirming my identity, my sense of self, and my soul-essence. It was an important part of my soul growth as I had felt disconnected from my personal sense of self for so many years. I had become lost in the routine of my life, and I had, like many other women, lost touch with who I was or what was of value to me. In my re-awakening, I felt that very human need to reconnect with my core spiritual essence and the Divine Feminine within.

Like a lotus flower unfolding I came to see, sense and feel my soul awakening. I felt it in my body, in the releasing of mental strongholds and powerful self-beliefs, and within my spiritual core. I heard my inner voice and my Soul calling me to come forth, to live and breathe into my humanity. As I revealed the inner most parts of my being, I began to feel a connection with the Divine Feminine, that creative and nurturing aspect of our Divine self, seeded in our soul and expressed through Divine Love in our physical experience.

Along my journey of self-discovery and reconnecting with my true self I slowly became more proficient at acknowledging all aspects of myself, my thoughts, emotions, my sensuality and my spirituality. For a long time, I was so used to living from my head that I had not realised I had become disconnected from my physical well-being. I had not seen how my body is so vitally connected to all aspects of myself.

Our body is a key communicator of our inner world, all that we think, believe, intuit, interpret and feel emotionally. When we disconnect from our body, we become numb or unaware of the signals our body reflects back to us when we are out of balance. When we live in a way that is contrary to our health, well-being, and the values of our soul, it will always show up in our body. This is why our body is so often referred to as the *temple of our soul* or spirit. In our physical world it is our body that is the home from which we live and experience our world as spiritual beings.

General signs of being out of balance and disconnected from our body and our soul may show up as regular aches and pains, recurring illnesses, and a general dis-ease that creates a feeling of being unsettled and unwell. Perhaps you can relate to this experience but have not yet understood the powerful effects of your mind, your thoughts and beliefs and how this can affect the state of your physical well-being. Sometimes illness or injury is unexpected and out of our control, however at a deeper level there is also a possibility that we are creating and recreating a general dis-ease in our body that causes our chakras (energy centres) to not function optimally. As a result, we can feel low in energy, and blocked emotionally and spiritually.

With personal reflection and perhaps the aid of professional guidance you will be able to ascertain whether your self-beliefs and state of mind (your habitual thoughts and mental strategies) are contributing to your ill health. Our body is a reflection of our mental and emotional well-being. When we are living contrary to our values (what resonates and feels in alignment with our true self, our soul being), it is usually expressed in our physical body.

As I became more consciously aware of my own soul growth, I recognised I was out of tune with my physical body. I had accumulated weight and I felt sluggish and out of touch with my femininity. I was physically disconnected from my body (my sensuality, my physical strength, my flexibility and general well-being); and I felt disconnected from my spiritual self, feeling somewhat weighed down and restricted from expressing my true sense of who I am as a Divine spiritual being. I yearned to be free from the confines of my rigid exterior, to express the fullness of the Divine Feminine within. I wanted to feel alive and to fully experience my emotional, spiritual and physical connection.

I realised there is more to me than just my active mind and the depth of my emotions. My body and physicality could not be denied in this process of transformation that involves the integration of my mind, my body and my spirit.

I came to realise there is a flow to our human experience, through the flow of yin and yang energies. Our Yin energy represents the feminine aspects of our being, the receptivity, the nurturing, and the creative aspects of who we are. Our yang energy is represented by the masculine aspects of our being that is expressed through our focused energy to produce, achieve and outwardly express through our actions and purpose-driven behaviours.

What makes a woman unique is her ability to harness both her yin (feminine) and yang (masculine) energy. In one moment, she is able to embrace her Divine femininity, softness and compassion, yielding to truth and love; and in the next, she can access her powerful, strong and courageous energy to achieve her intended purpose. The same can be said of every man, who has both elements of yin and yang energy.

Love and beauty are intertwined naturally, since all that is True Love is pure and beautiful. No wonder a woman's beauty is so alluring and seductive. As human beings living a physical life our sense of sight, touch, taste and smell is so powerful and an intimate part of our earthly experiences. The ability to live in the tangible moments are a gift, and when we are able to express our very inner being through a physical life, it is the soul expressed in physical form and reality.

Life is beautiful because we are given the gift of being able to physically connect with all that is living. Our spiritual essence synergizes with the physical essence of life - in people, nature, animals and in our surroundings. When we are able to experience this intimate connection, we feel the presence of God, the Divine and the Universe. In this space we sense there is so much more. Our Soul yearns to be expressed, as it brings us closer to our experience of Heaven or Divine bliss; all that is joyful, beautiful and pure love.

A woman's goddess energy is her connection to the Divine Feminine that enables her to create, give birth and embrace life with her full essence and wisdom. When we are in tune with our Divine Feminine we are able to connect our physicality with the knowledge and wisdom of past experiences and past lives. This becomes the power that is the fuel from which we can create and give birth to new form, ideas, and movement in our life. It is a vital way to share, influence and give to others. A woman who is connected to her yin and yang energy and is able to tap into and utilize this energy appropriately and with discernment, is a woman who is as much grounded as she is connected with her spiritual essence and Divinity.

Our intimate relationships also provide men and women a way to connect with the Divine energy of Love. For a woman, she is designed to 'intend' as well as 'allow'. When she is in her feminine energy of receiving, her essence is that of nurturing, embracing and receiving. She is highly intuitive and perceptive, able to recognise her own frequency and vibration, as well as that of others. When she is connected to her *yang* energy, she is equally powerful as she applies her intuition and wields her influence and connection with the Universe for the good of all.

A woman is her most authentic self when she is connected to the ebb and flow of her yin and yang energy. This is often affected by the bio-rhythms of her monthly cycle with the varying levels of hormones that influence her temperament as well as her natural reserves of energy. She will also experience the beauty and freedom of surrendering to the giving and receiving flow of energy in the exchange of love and shared intimacy with another. When we are able to fully accept our true nature and all that is from our heart and soul, a woman is able to powerfully create, influence and support others.

Understanding our Divine nature and energetic self is to embrace and accept our own design and creation. When we accept ourself we are able to love and appreciate who we are, with compassion, emotional intelligence and wisdom. As we consciously choose to let go of control of the need to be perfect or good enough, and embrace the spirit of acceptance, we are on our way to loving ourselves deeply and unconditionally. Only then can we experience connection with our true spiritual nature and know through our experiences that we are all connected as one. This is the path to True Love.

There are perhaps many ways to describe our spiritual nature. It is the Divine and eternal essence of who I am, that enables me to connect to my Higher Self and to Divine Love that is shared by all. Divine Love is not from our 'person' but is the pure love from God (Source, the Universe) that we tap into, the loving energy that connects all souls. It is not something easily translated when we are conditioned to think and experience in terms of our physical reality. Our spiritual essence has no need for the physical elements of time, space or matter in order to exist. It's the universal energy and essence that is inclusive and embraces all. Our spiritual nature is the outward expression of this Divine Love that informs and infuses our being with knowledge and wisdom, helping us to understand, connect and share with others.

*The path to True Love is acknowledging, accepting*
*and living as our authentic whole self; our spirituality*
*lived through the physical expression of our soul.*

As spiritual beings living a physical reality, we have the power and ability to attune our energy and focus our intentions so that we can design and create the life we wish to experience. Creation comes into being when we utilize our feminine and masculine energies, our yin and our yang. Whatever we want to experience in life, whether it is ultimately more love, more joy, or a greater sense of fulfillment, we can embrace and utilize our yin and yang energies to achieve this. It's all about connecting into the rhythm of our life and flowing with the dance of our Soul to create what we truly desire.

## Creating Your Desired Life

The first step is to become clear about what it is you want to feel within yourself, and what you want to experience in your life. Remember, you are the Creator of your life. Through your self-awareness you have recognised that there is more to who you are. You feel it deep within you and your Soul is calling you to move towards your authentic self and your souls' purpose. You are ready for transformation, which means you are no longer content to just ride the train and go wherever the tracks may take you. It's time to get off everyone else's train and design your own path for where you want to go.

When we know that we want and need more clarity on our journey, it can be difficult to step off the runway of life and disconnect from all that distracts us or drains our energy and attention. However, the only way to connect with our true self and understand our soul-purpose is to move away from the noise of life that clutters our mind and wears our body down with exhaustion.

I have always found the most effective way to ground myself and step into the energy of my Soul is to take a walk outside, barefoot on the grass or sand. I go to nature, where the energy is pure and unobstructed by the toxic energies of our working life and other people who can become energy drainers. It's not that we need to take an approach of being separate to others. When we create stillness within it enables us to be more receptive and open to tapping into the Divine loving energy. This Divine essence is within everyone and in nature, but we are not always vibrating at the same energy frequency for a healthy or meaningful connection.

Another effective way of shifting away from your busy mind is to engage in some form of physical activity such as walking, swimming, yoga, gardening, or whatever is your favourite pastime. It's a simple way to distract the minds' focus and create calm and re-connection with yourself. Essentially what you are aiming to do is to free yourself of your monkey-mind so that you can make space for daydreaming, imagining and ideation. In this space you can hear the voice of your Soul and tap into what resonates with you.

Ask yourself – what do I want to feel? What do I want to experience right now and in my future? Where am I headed and is it in the direction I want to be going? This is how we create clarity. It doesn't need to be more complicated than that. Avoid leaping into writing out your goals and plans, as this takes you straight back into your head again. For now, it's better for you to let go of your busy mind and tap into your heart and soul. Feel what you want to feel. Notice what is happening in your body. How do you prefer to feel? Slowly you will discover that you are becoming clearer about what you want, and you will be able to articulate this for yourself in your thoughts and in your words. Just keep it simple.

When your energy increases and your experience of feeling good lifts, you will become more receptive for allowing love and abundance to flow towards you. When you are ready to 'allow' it means you are ready to receive the goodness that life has to offer. This is not the time for 'forcing' things to happen. Your personal energetic vibration (influenced by your thoughts, feelings and intentions) is what you are going to attract more of, so if you are feeling stressed or anxious, then do what you can to calm the body and the mind.

The key is to *slow down*. You literally need to physically change your energy so that your mental and emotional energy can mirror a calmer state within. There is no need to rush to achieve a calm and mindful state of awareness. Take your time and allow the energy of your mind and body to shift at their own pace.

When we are *calm* we are in a state of receptivity and it is easier to be clear about what will best serve us. As we become clearer about our purpose, we can create an energy of *allowing*, clearing the energetic obstacles on our path so there is room for the new energy and what we intend for our life. This is how we can utilize and synergize the balance of yin and yang energies within ourself, for the purpose of creating and manifesting what we desire in life.

**Pause. Ponder. Reflect.**

To consciously create the life you desire, we need to increase our self-awareness. It may be helpful to journal your answers to the following questions:

- How do I want to feel? *For example, "Today I'm feeling low in energy and I want to feel comfortable within myself. I want to experience feeling nurtured, so I can increase my energy and create feelings of joy and happiness."*
- What can you do to help you feel this way? Pick one or two things you can do now.

Next, consider the following questions:

- What do I want to experience *now* and in my future?
- Where am I headed now?
- Is this the direction that will best serve my soul growth and purpose in life?

These reflections will help you to gain more clarity and assist you to more effectively utilise your feminine (yin) and masculine (yang) energy to manifest what you want to purposely create and bring into your life.

## Harnessing the Yin and the Yang

Attuning to our yin and yang energy is like making music in our life, and dancing to the rhythm of our own soul. As we become more in tune with the natural energies and vibrations of nature and the Universe, we are able to more authentically know who we are and what we want in life. Ultimately this is the state we need to be in to connect to our soul-purpose.

When we focus on our intentions and we are ready to take action toward how we want to feel in life, we simultaneously tap into our masculine (yang) energy. In the first instance I am referring to how we want to feel rather than what we want to obtain or achieve in life, since the first step towards creating a life you love is to know how to create fulfilment from within.

Utilizing our yang energy helps us to focus and manifest our desires. When we are clear about our intentions and what we want to manifest, we can experience more love, more joy, more satisfaction and fulfillment. Where our attention goes, our energy flows. As we focus our attention, and then release from the outcome, we attract more of what we want to experience in our life.

Like anything in life however, we can become out of balance in the way we use our energy. If we are too much in the receptive mode (yin energy), waiting for life to give us what we want or depending upon others for the way we want to feel, then we are likely to create a negative energy of scarcity and dependence. If we are too much in our yang energy our focus will be on our external world, which will eventually leave us feeling drained and unfulfilled, creating more resistance which will lead to disappointment.

The over use of yang energy may appear as someone who is continuously active and projecting a strong assertive energy to push for their own agenda or to have their physical, mental or emotional needs met. They may come across as manipulative and controlling, insisting that their own agenda is a priority. Someone who is overly dominating in conversations and demands to be heard is also demonstrating an over-use of yang energy.

However, a person with effective leadership skills, someone who is confident and discerning, will be able to utilize their yang energy to take appropriate action to lead a team or to achieve particular goals and outcomes in their work or family life. An example of someone who has a good balance of yin and yang energy will be a person who is well grounded and able to give and receive when appropriate.

When we misuse our energy we become unbalanced, and this can affect our mental, emotional and physical health, as well as our relationships with others. When we seek to use our energy to manipulate or control other people or situations, it comes from a place of fear. The same can be said for when we choose to sit back and wait for others to tend to our needs, failing to take responsibility for oneself. This kind of behaviour usually illustrates there is a deeper belief that we are incomplete or that we do not have enough within ourself to feel happy, fulfilled and loved. When we believe that love, joy and fulfillment can only be obtained or experienced from the outside world, we become dependent on other people, places and things to provide our needs. The key is to integrate the two energies, recognising that we can enjoy the abundance in our external life, as well as create great joy within by tapping into our authentic self.

It's important to be in tune with what we value about ourself, and to understand our own point of focus for our life. When we feel out of balance it is usually because we have drifted from our authentic nature and our soul-purpose in life. We have forgotten to be our most beautiful self, exactly as we are. In these moments I have often reminded myself to come back to my centre, to return to what is important to me, and not what is necessarily urgent or important for everyone else.

I learned a wonderful lesson about valuing myself in a beautiful meditation exercise where I visualized a huge mountain before me. It was majestic, tall, strong and very stable looking. This mountain symbolized all that I desired in terms of certainty, wisdom and strength in my life. I recalled how in the past I have associated other people in my life to be this 'rock' upon which I could rely and trust. They became my focal point of admiration, certainty and dependability. Then, the moment came, when that solid rock, crumbled before my eyes. All that appeared to be certain, trustworthy and solid, was no longer.

It's a fact of life that we will be disappointed when we place our expectations on other people or circumstances in our life. Life changes and people are fallible. I realised my soul's lesson - I did not need to see the rock of solidity and certainty in someone else. The rock (or the mountain) was me. I had reached a point in my life where I knew I had all the resources, self-love and wisdom that I needed to be that mountain. No matter the weather or seasons that come and go, I would be able to stand firm and steady, and draw upon what I have inside of me, and yet flexible enough to go with the flow of waters in and around me to withstand any changes that come and go in life.

## Riding the Ebb and Flow

One way of learning to get in tune with our own energy and ensuring we are in flow with our values and purpose, is to become consciously aware of the ebb and flow of our masculine (yang) and feminine (yin) energy.

Even though women may be expected to be all 'feminine energy', the truth is that we all live with a measure of yin and yang energy according what is needed. There are times we need to create and take action, fully utilizing the energy of intention. This is what we call 'yang' energy. Then there are times we need to tap into the feminine 'yin' energy that is more nurturing, patient and receptive, as we co-create with Spirit, allowing the Universe to work in unison and harmony with all that is.

We can learn to balance our focus and energy by utilizing our feminine energy of 'receiving' and 'allowing'. Sometimes we can become so conditioned to 'do' and 'produce' all the time that we are unable to switch off that strong masculine energy that drives us to achieve and progress in life.

Today, women are more empowered in our culture, and they are being encouraged to achieve more in their careers, in their home life, socially and financially. The expectation of women in the working world of western society is that she needs to be a professional, multi-talented, multi-skilled 'wonder woman', full of energy and on the go, at the ready to produce, meet the needs of others and still remain compassionate and understanding. Yet she feels drained and unappreciated most of the time, with little or no energy left in her cup for herself or anyone else. The Alpha woman will typically demonstrate these traits.

Women are incredible. They are powerful when they balance their masculine and feminine energy and become the true Divine Feminine goddess they were designed to be. When she is able to connect into her authentic self and come from a 'healed' place and not a 'wounded' place, she can tune into her own rhythms and move with her natural energies to achieve what she wants to feel and experience in life. A woman creates. She was designed to create life and so this is a natural state for her. Just as the man was designed to build and protect, his energy helps him to focus on his purpose. Whether we are male or female, we all have the capacity to tap into our yin and yang energy as we need. Learning to be in tune with our energy and knowing how to use it to our advantage is the key.

Understanding and effectively utilising our energy is powerful. Our personal energy is made up of our mental, emotional and spiritual intentions that flow or emanate from our heart and Soul. It is the force that is driven or ignited by our spirit that urges our being toward the light and the experience of True Love. Of course, that same energy can drive us to our demise as well, when it comes from a place of fear and doubt.

All living creatures (people, animals, plants, minerals and all substances on earth) are filled with life-force energy (also known as chi or prana). It is the fuel in our tank that enables us to experience life, learn, grow and contribute. There is no doubt that it is powerful, but it is not to be feared. Many people become concerned about the word 'power', and perhaps conjure up images that are negative and illustrated by mis-use of energy and intentions. However, when we appreciate that 'power' is merely the fuel for our vehicle (our mind and body) then we can get on with being the driver and setting the course for our life.

A woman's energy flows very differently to a man's energy. She is governed by the natural rhythms of her female body, which is influenced by the ebb and flow of her hormones and emotions. Resisting the natural ebb and flow of being a woman only causes more of a disruption to her ability to harness and utilize this beautiful energy. Like the waves in the sea, a woman's energy peaks and troughs so that she flows from an empowered creative state to a more receptive and restorative state of being.

Understanding and recognising the ebb and flow of her rhythms enables the woman to love and appreciate her design. Depending upon our background, culture or conditioning in our life, we may have come to believe that the female energy is inconsistent and not to be relied upon. If we compare a woman's energy flow to that of a man, then we are going to notice a distinct difference. A man's energy flow is more consistent, and this is a part of his unique design that enables him to be in a state of powerful readiness more often so that he can build, achieve and protect his domain (work, family etc). It's not to say that he is always on the go and utilizing his yang energy. Men and women need to balance the ebb and flow of action and rest – yang and yin energy. A woman's design and purpose is more multi-functional, where flexibility and flow are necessary for her to be her natural authentic self.

For a woman, the path to love and acceptance of our true self is to honour our unique female design and work with our natural energy flow. It's less about achieving a 50/50 balance of yin and yang, and more about being sensitive and receptive to the dance and flow of our life-force energy. There are moments when we need to tap into our 'goddess' energy that is powerful and strong. It is forthright, warrior-like and protective, and comes from a place of clarity and grounded certainty. Then there are other times when we need to drop back into our feminine yin energy of receptivity, compassion, and nurturing; the state that allows us to listen, notice and be open to learning, receiving, reflecting, and restoration.

When embracing her 'goddess' energy, a woman can become powerful in her own right, unleashing her ability to give and receive, and truly come to appreciate her own value, worth and uniqueness. Being in tune with your 'goddess' energy happens when we let go of the urge to want to take control of everything in our life, all the detail, the outcomes, the people and so on. Goddess energy is having the wisdom to know how to use our energy and intention in a way that brings life and love to ourself and to other people. It's that balance of knowing when to let go and surrender to the supportive love of the Universe, and when to step up to take directed action to fulfill our purpose.

In many ways the principle is the same for the Divine Masculine. Having self-awareness of our energy flow is key to creating balance and being able to effectively draw upon our resources as required. The grounded energy of the Divine Masculine produces clarity and the ability to store up wisdom and energy for when action is required. Periods of restoration and dropping back into yin energy is essential for recuperating physical and mental stores. As the Divine Masculine refills his cup, he is now in a state of readiness, powerful in mind, body and spirit, and able to create and fulfil his purpose in life.

There are times when we all want life to go our own way and to be on our terms. There is nothing wrong with wanting to live life on our own terms, but we need to remember that we are not isolated human beings living for just ourself. Everything we do, say and think produces an energy and intention that is felt (consciously or unconsciously) by other people, near or far. Our personal energy not only matters to ourself, as it affects the quality of our living, but it also affects other people, animals and our environment. We are connected energetically and at a soul level. What we say and do and think has a ripple effect on all living beings. If you want more peace and love in your life, *be* that peace and love, and you will attract more of this.

Do you recognise when you are in tune with your goddess energy? When we feel aligned with our authentic self, we feel empowered, grounded and unshakeable. It's that sense of knowing that you don't need to put energy into defending your position because you have already created healthy boundaries that allow you to live by choice.

Learning to accept and love ourself is how we live in our Divine Femininity. There is nothing that needs altering or fixing, adding or subtracting from the beautiful soul that you are. You are already created by Divine light and love. Unveiling the real you and living by choice is all that is needed. We tend to make our lives complicated, believing there is a huge mountain to climb that will change our life, so we are the perfect version of what we are meant to be. That's a myth, so breathe and relax. All that you need is within you now. As we move through life we learn how to live with more love, and this helps to shape our thinking, our minds and our body. The transformation we choose is a natural process and not beyond the scope of anyone's imagination or ability. At no time do we need to put pressure on ourself to be something or someone that we are not.

Living with goddess energy is knowing and loving who you are. When we exude that love for ourself and for life, we share our intention to live harmoniously. Our very vibration is what draws more of the same into our life, as well as sending ripples of love out into the Universe. There is no need to be apologetic for who you are. Love and embrace your Divine Goddess within and embrace your femininity that creates, loves, nurtures and aims to work cooperatively and in harmony with the Universe.

## A Woman's Rebirth

There is a moment in every woman's life when she realises she is more, and that she is moving into her true essence. Her first birthing of her individuality is when she becomes the young woman, having emerged from the naivety of her adolescence. There is a period of time when she explores her femininity, sensuality and sexuality. She explores and learns about her strengths and weaknesses, testing the waters through relationships, life experiences and the challenges of life's lessons. If her circumstances allow, she slowly develops an understanding of who she is and becomes aware that she has the potential to be strong and powerful in her own way. Giving birth to children or perhaps her career, she further develops an understanding of the scope of her skills, and along the way she is able to learn from the feedback she receives, which helps her to grow in knowledge, wisdom and understanding. In an ideal world she learns courage, determination, inner strength, and what it means to love and care for her well-being.

The diversity of our background and life experiences colour and influence the kind of lessons that are offered up in our life, and our response to these determines the course of our path. There is a lot of activity and focus on producing results in the 'morning' of our life, which hopefully assists our spiritual development and raises our level of conscious awareness. Unfortunately, we often become so busy that we can easily miss the call to stay on our true path, the course that helps us to grow closer to our potential and serve our life and soul-purpose.

As time passes, we reach that moment when life begins to turn from morning to afternoon, and we notice that the sky looks different, and the shadows are cast in a different light, revealing what we had not seen before. What was once of value and important to us, slowly changes as we adopt new perspectives, redefine our preferences and alter our choices to better suit our soul-growth and wisdom.

There is beauty in every moment of our life, and there are blessings that await us for when we are ready to believe, see and receive. Change is inevitable, either as a result of our personal growth, or the circumstances of our life. With change comes an opportunity for transformation when we recognise that our needs are shifting, and our focus alters to accommodate our new way of being. When we approach a turning-point, we may feel uneasy or even inclined to resist changing from what we have always known. Depending upon our own beliefs, moving towards something that looks new and unfamiliar may be welcomed, or it may represent something that elicits fear within.

When we are in sync with our soul's purpose, we will recognise the upcoming change as an opportunity to grow in wisdom and expand in Love. When we choose to follow the call of our Soul, we are likely to experience more flow in our life. However, when we choose to respond with resistance, often our experiences become more turbulent and conflicted.

In many ways, when a woman moves along her soul-journey there comes a time when she experiences a rebirth. If we can accept and allow the change, there is the most beautiful gift of new life waiting for us. It requires a settling in the soul and an openness to loving oneself. As we are able to expand our consciousness, we are able to open our heart to an even greater degree so that love pours in and love flows out to others. A woman who embraces her femininity is free to live her truth and the wisdom of her years, and she is able to share this abundance with others. Doreen Virtue reminds us to ask ourself each day *'What would Love do?'* What a beautiful way to begin each day and how to approach life when we are uncertain about what steps to take. Our response to life can be to simply ask 'What would Love do'?

As a woman draws closer to her authentic self, she can discover the loving and powerful goddess within. Kuan Yin (Quan Yin, Guan Yin or Kwan Yin, known as the Buddhist feminine goddess who is the embodiment of compassionate loving kindness and mercy) and Mother Mary (or Miriam in Christianity) can help us to tap into our goddess energy, showing us the way to being open to love without compromising our values and remaining true to ourself and our soul's path. The calm and peace we find within is the door to living life with more wisdom, self-awareness and love. Our receptivity to love and our ability to discern expands, and so too does our power to see, feel and influence the world around us.

> *The calm and peace we find within is the door to living life with more wisdom, self-awareness and love.*

A woman's rebirth may be triggered by specific changes in her life or she may have simply arrived at a time of transformation quite organically. Either way, it does not necessarily mean she surrenders her power and gives way to submissively accepting whatever life presents and thus resolving she is no longer able to significantly make a difference in her life. She is now ready to relinquish or move on from what was her previous focus and redirect her course toward new opportunities to learn, grow and be.

With years of experience, knowledge and wisdom, she is clear about who she is and what is important to her. If she has not had the opportunity to gain this clarity, now is the time to do so. Armed with a stronger sense of purpose, she is willing to dive deeper to discover more and find inner serenity and soul-fulfilment. When she aligns her energy (mental, emotional, physical and spiritual energy) she becomes one with her true self. Her desire to live with focused intent and a stronger passion now drives her to live out her soul-purpose.

## Soul-Power

An aspect of our journey towards True Love and liberation of our soul is to give full expression to our voice and the creative life-giving energy within. Man or woman, our ability to give expression to our Soul is our birthright. There comes a time in our life when we are ready to articulate the life-force and light within. There is a strong desire to give a voice to our soul-purpose and to express this with passion and action. When we are living our soul-purpose we are no longer driven by the demands or illusions of our external world or even the fears conjured by our active mind. We are giving birth and full reign to the calling of our Soul, living true to the essence of our spirit.

Having gone through my own *dark night of the soul,* I have seen in my life journey how this experience was part of my soul-growth, albeit painful. Like the metamorphosis of the caterpillar to the butterfly, its destiny is to allow the natural process of life to unfold. There is a stretching and growing as it transforms to a new level of beauty and ultimately self-expression. My transformation was painful, but I always knew that I was moving towards something more powerful and more magnificent. As long as I was prepared to surrender and release the binds that were holding me back, I knew the process was helping me to grow in ways I had not imagined or experienced before.

I believe we go through multiple periods of transformation in our life, not all of them so big. Every month or year of our life we are constantly being stretched as we learn to face our inner truth. We choose to respond by either walking the path with love and compassion or we crawl along as if wading through the heavy weight and resistance of thick mud. These moments often feel very uncomfortable, as we wrestle between our mind, body and spirit. The opportunity for personal transformation is a gift as well as our soul birth-right. The Universe offers this gift, it is not forced upon us. It is our choice to receive the gift and to accept the opportunity to grow in Love and wisdom.

Events that occur in our life show up as a result of our focus and intention. They are merely a reflection of what is going on inside of us, and an indicator of where we are on our soul-path. When we are presented with the contrasts in life, we have an opportunity to use these moments to our advantage. They may show up as physical challenges in our health, relationship struggles, work dilemmas, financial issues, or simply the daily battle with our ego mind that seeks to survive at all costs. If we choose the path of ease and flow, we can learn how to release our resistance to the process and embrace the gems of what the contrasts reveal, to facilitate our soul growth with ease and compassion. These are valuable growth moments for wisdom, understanding and connecting with our inner truth.

Every experience is an opportunity to plant seeds of wisdom in our life. Those seeds, if watered and nurtured, can break through the soil to sprout with more inner growth, revealing our souls' truth and our Divine purpose in this life. If we apply what we learn from our experiences, we become stronger and wiser, and we are better positioned to contribute to others. However, when we procrastinate or avoid opportunities to grow, we miss the chance to move closer to our full potential, and the experience of receiving blessings of Divine Love in our life.

Sometimes the sequence of our life experiences can feel like a never-ending search for something outside of ourself. At the core of our search is the desire to come back home, to where our Soul knows only True Love. However, our life is a physical and tangible one and we live in a world of dualities and contrasts. Through these contrasts we find ways to measure and reflect upon our experiences of what moves us closer to Divine Love or what distracts us from our soul-path.

In our physical life it is easy to forget that we are firstly spiritual 'beings' having a physical life. Our physical reality can draw our focus outside of ourself and it can be easy to fall into the trap of searching for comfort and love, abundance and freedom, through other people and in material things, as well as through the subtle and intense experiences of life. As we focus more on obtaining happiness outside of ourself we can believe that this is the only way to achieve our dreams. If we do not believe that love, happiness, freedom and abundance are already available within us, then our desire to obtain and hold on to what we find, can increase with great intensity. If we truly believe we are in a state of lack, this focus can become more like an addiction that we need to satisfy.

As we become more focused on fulfilling our desire for love we can form attachments to the idea that what we want is something we must 'obtain' in order to be happy. The search for and the attachment to the idea we must 'have and hold' on to what we seek, can become our own self-imposed ball and chain. When we are in a mindset that we do not have what we seek, we create an energy field that repels what we truly desire, because we believe we do not have it already. Conversely, if we truly believe that love, freedom and abundance already exists within, then that is what we will receive and experience. Napoleon Hill succinctly states that: "Whatever the mind can conceive and believe, the mind can achieve". We truly are very powerful, and our mind can either serve our highest good or it can diminish us to less than our Divine potential.

Powerful as we are, we have the ability to create our own experiences and our version of reality. On the path towards True Love, what most serves us is to stop searching for the experience of love outside of ourself. That's difficult to hear when you are still in a state of wanting and desiring to share love with someone else (or others) in your life, or if you currently do not have enough money to pay your bills and you are in a state of anxiety and worry about how you will have enough to live within your means.

What most serves us is to let go of worry and know that the key to freedom lies within. When we feel lost or confused, or we believe we are lacking in the love, truth and the freedom we desire, we can return to our centre and remember our Spirit rather than focus on our physical experiences.

It is helpful to surrender by quietening our mind, nourishing our body and soothing our soul. When we loosen our grip on life and let go of all that we think we know, all that we think we own, and all that we think we need, then we can begin to see the True light and personal power within. We are not separate from Divine Light and Love. It's already in existence, however it depends upon whether we choose to see it, feel it and experience it. If we are not separate, then we have the resources of the Divine to support and guide us in all circumstances.

Freedom is not an illusory dream to have what we want, do what we want, when we want it, and at the expense of others. Freedom is a spiritual state of being. It's the opposite of feeling entrapped by your thoughts, feelings and things that you believe you must have in order to be fulfilled and complete. Freedom is knowing that you are complete already, and that the Universe (God, Source) is working to support you always. It's knowing that living as your authentic self is a dynamic process, not an ultimate destination.

My own stormy struggles were turbulent and at times painful. I came to intimately know that the way of transformation is experienced through challenges, emotional highs and lows, and periods of intense pain, fear and doubt. However, I was frequently reminded that eventually the storms pass, and the sun re-appears through the clouds. All is not lost, and despite the struggles, we are all Divinely supported.

It is through the difficult times we can discover our own internal resources to get us through. No-one likes to endure painful times, and as much as we may wish the storms to never appear, there is usually nothing we can do to speed them up or send them away. We must learn to go through them. Resistance is tiring and only causes us to harden our heart.

Often the storms in our life manifest as difficulties in our relationships, finances, health or when circumstances don't turn out the way we were expecting. Learning how to see the challenges from a different perspective, and to see perhaps the hidden truths, can be enlightening and give us a gift we may not have otherwise acknowledged or received. When we are open to what the storm can offer us in the moment, it's energy no longer feels like an enemy we must fight. Observing the strength and the power of the storms in our life can help us to see what the contrasts can reveal to us. When we let go of the struggle, we can recognise our own strengths, and draw on what we know and have learned about ourself. This is the moment when we discover our true soul-power and soul-wisdom.

Storms are not only the external circumstances we experience in our life. They are the storms that brew in our heart and soul. When we are prepared to face those storms within rather than resist them, we have the opportunity to look squarely at the truth of ourself. This can be confronting, because perhaps we will be too frightened by what we will see. However, when we do embrace that storm in our heart and in our mind, and we face the truth, the revelation is freeing. Giving up the fight and seeing the truth of who we are and accepting all of our being (past and present), is how we learn to walk through our storms and develop that inner strength, and soul-wisdom. It is an act of self-love.

Storms eventually dissipate and what follows is a new light and freshness that helps us to see and feel things differently. They also help us to develop fortitude, courage and a new sense of value for the beautiful (and not-so-perfect) being that we are. Throughout my own personal storms, I knew I needed to trust in Divine Love by loving and trusting in myself. This is the power of our Soul. Transformation is all about change. Our measure of self-love is what makes the difference to our experiences in life and what we make of them. What is certain is that nothing in life stays the same. We are forever evolving, no matter our level of resistance. Our Soul is always calling us to move towards greater Love.

Our soul lessons in life often teach us to return to the openness and vulnerability we had when we were a child. To be like a child, is not to be as a child without the skills and resources to make discerning choices. To be as a child is to embrace being open, with awe and wonder of the world and of ourself. It's about trusting ourself and learning to connect with nature and the Universe, which offer the wisdom of the Divine. Children have an open gateway to their intuition and Higher Self that allows them to feel and explore their inner and outer world. They are more easily in tune with their creativity and their imagination, and they can hear their soul speak to them without the barriers or limitations that we learn to adopt as we grow older and more dependent upon our external world. Their vibration is aligned and open to the vibrations of the Divine.

As adults we can return to this state of openness any time we choose. However, we need to be willing to trust that we are not separate from Divine Source; rather we are connected as one. We have access to the knowledge and wisdom of the Divine any time we want to tap into it. Until then, our vibration will be more aligned with living in a state of fear and doubt that will only limit our potential.

Walking the path towards greater Love is the way to freedom, however it doesn't always feel so easy or straight forward. We can often veer off the path because we have become distracted by our fears, or perhaps the illusion of dreams fulfilled by other things and other people. This is part of being human. It is not a failing, it's feedback that shows us the contrast we need in order to course correct and adjust our travels. Unless we slip up, we cannot be fully aware of our direction and take the necessary steps to come back on our soul-path, back to our centre of being where we are living as our authentic self.

There have been many times I have stumbled, but I have learned from experience to get back up and be thankful rather than feel defeated. When I view my challenges with gratitude, it strengthens me. I realise it is all for my benefit even if it takes me a while to reflect and notice the gems in my current experience.

## Soul Lessons

We are all affected by the cycles of life, and by our feelings and emotions that take us up and down, as we respond to life's situations and our beliefs about ourself and our circumstances. There are astronomical and environmental influences that can powerfully affect our feelings and perspectives. Women are also particularly influenced by the cyclic nature of their physical and emotional body. The changes in her hormones each month can affect her energy levels and significantly influence the emotions she experiences.

However, whether we are male or female, and in addition to the external influences in our life, we can learn to observe and embrace our natural way of being and respond in ways that are more accepting and in tune with our natural flow of energy. Expecting our energy and emotions to be constant and unchanging is not realistic. However, we can learn to better manage our energy so there is more flow and harmony, and more peace within. Developing a less reactive and resistant way of being and replacing this with an energy of allowing and acceptance, helps us to open our heart to experience self-love, compassion and the soul lessons we need for our spiritual growth.

When my energy wanes, it can feel tempting to take on the role of the victim and believe that life is happening to me instead of for me. This only causes me to feel more self-pity and then I feel sad and despondent. I know this is not my true nature or representative of my greater potential. When I step back, pause, and quieten my monkey-mind, I am able to find peace within. It is only when I cease trying to figure everything out, that the teaching moment becomes apparent. I recognise that it's time to nurture my mind, my body and my soul. Rather than deny my shadow side, I have learned to be more compassionate towards myself and acknowledge that I am not perfect, and that's okay.

So often we can torture ourself through the constant desire of wanting to have all the answers and to understand what and why events occur in our life. The key to peace is to let go of that addictive desire and realise that it is not necessary to understand everything. We can adopt a spirit of curiosity about life, rather than an intense need or desire to know and understand everything. We can choose to be grateful for what is and realise that what shows up is there for us to learn from and is revealed at the right time for our soul growth.

Some of the greatest pearls of wisdom have been revealed to me from the ashes of my own inner fire and torment. In these moments of reflection, the nuances of God's deep love and healing for my soul washes over me. It is often better for us to be emptied of all of our 'stuff' - our limiting beliefs, our victimhood, our fears and doubts, our stories, our anger and self-pity, before we can begin to re-fill our being with unconditional love and acceptance of all that is. This draws me closer to experiencing true joy and more freedom in my life and in my soul.

Every time we experience hardship, there is an opportunity to know there are lessons to help us, not hurt us. Without a doubt, each lesson aims to lead us in the direction of greater love. Our soul-lessons are never to punish us but to show us how to love more deeply, in a way that brings greater awareness, compassion and wisdom. If we are truly loving toward ourself, we will apply the knowledge and wisdom gained to facilitate our soul growth as well raise the loving vibration in the world for others.

Discovering and revealing our true self is an experience of connecting with our spirituality, the essence of who we are, beyond time and material reality. If we have been unconscious for a long time, it may feel strange or unfamiliar to go deeper and journey within. The process means to listen to your soul and tune into the essence of who you are. To begin, you can ask yourself - what do you truly enjoy doing and experiencing? Tune in to what you are feeling about a situation rather than what you are thinking. What moves you emotionally and spiritually?

The aim is to grow more adept at tuning in to your intuition rather than habitually turning to your thoughts. Why? When we respond to life only from our thoughts, we have a tendency to rationalize and reason our experiences, which shuts down our ability to intuit or hear the voice of our Higher Self. There is an opportunity to get to know yourself more deeply, and to develop new associations and connections with your Soul or Higher Self. You can start with spending time with yourself. You don't need to necessarily be by yourself to 'be' with yourself.

Remember, if you have been in a relationship with someone for a long time you may have learned to identify yourself with the concept of 'we' rather than 'I'. It may take you some time to unravel your previous emotional and physical connections and build new ones with your true self. On a daily basis you can begin by choosing to do something that you did not do before and develop new associations with activities that you love and enjoy. Learn to experience being 'you'. Get to know you, and along the way you may ask yourself how you feel as you try new things. Do what inspires you, makes you feel happy, expanded and loving towards you.

As we learn to spend more time in our own presence, that inner space where our spirit resides, we develop the sense, skills and ability to fulfil our own cup of love and happiness, rather than rely or depend upon others to fulfil our needs. From this place we can experience a deeper connection to our true self.

As I live more authentically as the 'real me', giving myself permission to enjoy what I truly love in life, I feel myself moving closer toward the experience of Divine love, that universal essence that is all loving, all knowing (omniscient), and all powerful (omnipotent). The Divine is always working for us and for our highest good. When we choose to focus on loving ourself and seeing Love in all of our experiences, we invite abundance and more love into our life. When we have the courage to surrender our fears and to see only Love, we are brought face to face with our inner truth. In so doing we open our heart to expose and remove the strongholds of our fearful mind, giving ourselves permission to express our Soul and make room for greater Love in our life. This deeper self-awareness is what precipitates change and soul growth in our life.

*Awareness precedes change.*

Perhaps we may question why we need to go on such an inner journey of self-discovery. As human beings we are highly motivated to avoid pain, so we side-step, deny, and cover up the truth of our authentic self so that we don't need to feel the pain of what we imagine could be uncovered and revealed to the world. When we are faced with our inner truth and we have not yet experienced the safety and expansion of True Love, all we know is how to avoid being hurt. We build walls around our heart, and we steer our conversations to topics that feel safe. We engage in activities that allow us to feel confident, and we associate with people who will not threaten our sense of safety. We even choose careers or jobs that will not challenge us too much for fear of failing or having to deal with people, places or situations that will leave us feeling personally vulnerable or inadequate.

However, the pain of living a life that feels like ground-hog day is not the experience of life that I want to have, nor do I want to face a deep sense of lack of fulfillment on my last day, realizing that there was so much more inside of me that I did not express or experience. I love Wayne Dyer's reference to the expression of our soul and spiritual vitality as *the music within* us. Let's live to our Divine potential and express the music of our Soul.

> *Don't die with the music still in you.*
> *(Wayne Dyer)*

Expressing our true self is how we can experience liberation of our soul and come into alignment with our soul-purpose. As we give voice to our true essence, we give life to our 'reason for being'. When what we do matches what we are saying to ourself, the Universe responds by providing opportunities and situations that are aligned with our energy and expectations. When we are in flow with our true purpose, we are no longer resisting or blocking our potential, and we become magnificent manifestors.

When we are faced with increased awareness of our soul's deeper purpose, we can feel either compelled to run and hide, for fear of what we may now need to do, or we may feel energized and inspired by our soul's calling to draw closer to our spiritual home.

When I found my inner voice, it was not like a light switch that I turned on, going from darkness to light and then suddenly finding all the answers I wanted to hear. My awakening was more like turning up the dimmer switch. Slowly I was seeing more, and feeling closer to my true essence of being, and at the same time sensing I was connected to every other soul and living creation. I recognised I had companions with me on my journey, both of the earthly, spiritual and angelic kind.

I have had many joyous moments in my life, and there is so much I am grateful for, including my family, my work colleagues, my friends, my health, and the wonderful learning opportunities I have experienced that have facilitated my spiritual development. My darkness was not any of this, it was the shadow in my heart of not living according to my own truth or giving expression to my Souls' purpose. My metamorphosis came when I heard and responded to the calling of my Higher Self, in readiness for the next stage of my life, to move towards greater Love.

When we let go of our fears and we willingly trust, even when enduring the storms of our life, we can become one with what binds us all together, the inescapable essence of Divine Love from God. When we step out of the shadows toward the light, there is a release that happens within, and the gateway to love is opened. As that light grows inside, so too does our world brighten before us. So much becomes revealed in a light we have not seen before. It is as if the landscape unfolds like a majestic field all around, and the sky is revealed as a huge expansive dome that liberates our soul. As strength and energy rises from the earth through our body, it bursts open from our heart in a way that fills our being with love and light. In this moment we feel connected to our earthly nature and the Divine Source, and our voice gives expression to our Soul, a re-birth of our true self.

## Soul Sandwich

Discovering our true self is learning to tune in to the true essence of who we are.

On a daily basis you can begin by choosing to do something that you have not done before and develop new associations with activities that you love and enjoy.

Learn to experience being 'you'.

## Exercise

• List some examples of activities that you love and enjoy.

As you explore new activities, ask yourself how you 'feel' when you have a go.

• List some of the feelings you had when you tried something new.

## Pause. Ponder. Reflect

• What inspires you?
• What makes you feel happy, expanded and loving towards you?
• What leaves you feeling bored or unfulfilled?

# 13
## Connecting the Mind, Heart and Body

Our mind is very powerful and capable of creating either great drama and sorrow, or incredible heights of joy and gratitude. The key is to understand how the mind works and to recognise that you can choose to let it control how you experience life or not. The way we perceive all of our experiences and how we choose to interpret these experiences is what creates our reality, our beliefs about ourself and our world, and how we feel.

The first realization is recognising we are not our 'mind', despite its powerful influence. A person with psychosis or dementia is suffering the negative effects of the mind, but the essence of that person is unchanged, since their soul never diminishes. We are able to choose to master our thoughts and perceptions, but as Don Miguel Ruiz says, we need to become an even better huntress than our mind, which seeks to master (and connect with) our soul-being.

The more we allow the mind to dominate our thoughts, the more we will continue to experience that which we think about most. Do you recall feeling stuck in a looping pattern of thought, as you try not to feel or think about something? The more you tell yourself you don't want to think about it, the more amplified your thoughts become around that issue.

So how do you make the shift? How do you stop the merry-go-round of spiralling thoughts that serve to drain you rather than uplift you? It starts by making a connection with your heart. Your heart is that place within you that represents your spiritual and energetic essence that is life and love itself. It's where you feel there is no barrier to the truth of who you are and to the experience of love and appreciation for yourself. Love is not a thing you possess or have, but a way of being and experiencing. Love is the radiating vibration that is you and all that is life. When we drop into our heart, we are able to connect with the Spirit of Love. As we open to Spirit (the Divine) we shift our energy so that we are receptive to Divine wisdom, truth and unconditional love.

The mind serves to work you tirelessly through busyness and problem solving. When we are so caught up over-thinking and over-analysing everything it's easy to find ourself, back on the merry-go-round and into overwhelm. The key is to learn how to manage our thoughts that often take us down pathways that don't serve us well. Our mind is designed to problem solve and ensure our safety and so it is geared towards seeking immediate comfort. However, the mind will tend to move towards fear-based thinking, looking at all the possible negative scenarios, and as a result create more self-doubt and confusion. Relying only upon a logical answer to a situation is not necessarily going to guide you towards the path of growth, love and wisdom.

To move towards greater Love, we need to understand how to connect our mind with our heart. Fear-based thinking will not lead to inner peace or True Love. Creating a state of calm and stillness in and around you, is the fastest way to create a state of receptivity for guidance from our Higher Self.

Whenever we feel our energy has dropped, and we notice our thoughts are looping and creating more restlessness and confusion, then we know that the *spirit of fear* has taken a hold of our mind. Clarity and peace of mind is not possible when we are in this state. However, there is a way to shift our thinking and move towards connecting our mind with our heart. We can do this by first connecting with our body, which prepares us well for connecting with our heart or our inner guidance.

Meditation and focus on the breath is a simple way to calm both the mind and body and useful in any moment when feeling confused or mentally stuck. No matter where we are, we can close our eyes and for a few minutes just focus on our breath, ensuring each breath is slow and deep. The following meditation exercises are repeated to assist your practice.

## Exercise 1 – Breathing Meditation for the Mind

Use the following exercise to help you manage your thoughts and create inner calm. It will help you to reconnect with yourself and your heart-centre.

*If possible, find a quiet place where you will not be interrupted, close your eyes and breathe.*

*Focus on your breath, gently noticing the breath going in, and then the breath going out. Allow your body to calm as you sit quietly, breathing.*

*Count to 3 or 4 when breathing in through the nose, and then count to 5 or 6 when breathing out through the mouth. Do this for a few minutes and you will notice your body relax and your mind slow down. When distracting thoughts enter your mind, visualize the thoughts floating towards you on a stream of water. As they approach, notice the thought, then without attempting to mentally solve any problems or issues, just watch them float by and let them keep going. As each thought approaches, notice it and then let it float past you.*

There is no perfect way to visualize or do the meditation, it is purely a practice to assist you to gain experience in managing your thoughts so that you can create a state of calm in your mind and body. If the visualization is not working for you, bring your attention back to your breath. With practice you will be able to still the mind and prevent it from distracting you.

## Exercise 2 – Mindful Walking Meditation

This form of meditation may be helpful if you prefer not to sit still.

*Give yourself 10-15 minutes to walk a short path (say 5-10 metres) back and forth. As you walk, gently focus your gaze downwards so you are not distracted by your surroundings. Begin with standing still and take a deep breath to go within.*

*Feel your body calm and your shoulders relax. When you take a step, do it very slowly and mindfully. Notice the placement of your toes, the ball of your foot and the heal, as it touches the ground.*

*Observe how the muscles and bones in your body move and adjust as it automatically compensates to keep you balanced.*

*As you walk your path slowly, focus on your breath and be aware of your energy. When your mind wanders off on a tangent to think about a particular topic, bring your attention back to your body and your breath.*

*At the turning point of your walking path, stand still for a moment to notice, breathe and reflect before turning around to continue on your path again. You will find that as the minutes go by, your mind will calm, and your ability to be aware of your body and sense your surrounds will have increased.*

Another very effective way of managing our mind is through physical activity. When the body is in motion, our vibrational frequency is raised with the assistance of the increase in naturally occurring chemicals in the body. Feel-good hormones are produced as our body moves and the blood circulates, oxygenating all of our organs. As a result, we feel an increase in our physical energy, and our mood is uplifted. We are now feeling lighter and clearer in the mind and the body. I find my early morning walks and evening yoga classes to be a great way to help me create a state of calm and clarity. In this way I also become more open and receptive to receiving guidance and wisdom from God, my spirit guides and my Higher Self. Mastering our mind is about creating synergy between the mind, the body and our spirit.

There are many methods of meditation and this may be a good time to learn a method that suits you. There is no perfect way to meditate. What's important is that it helps you to achieve a state of calm and openness. Learning to create calm within is a process of learning to manage the busy mind and bringing it to a state of peace that is in tune with your body, and thus prepares you for a receptive heart and increased intuition and awareness. In time you will come to better understand yourself at a deeper level and reach a state of calm quickly and at any time. Remember, the process is not about perfection, but rather what is working best for you.

When we aim to harmonize and synergize our mind, heart and our body, we create alignment and balance within, allowing us to return to a place of love rather than fear. Fear will always keep you trapped, and so as long as you are in this state of mental confusion and disconnection from your heart, you will be unable to experience love and commitment for your Soul's growth.

With an energized body and a calm mind, we can create mental clarity, making it easier to redirect our attention away from fear-based thinking, to thoughts that are coming from a place of love. Sometimes it's not easy to create the shift in our thinking, and so learning to tune into our body through exercise or yoga, or managing our energy through our chakras (as discussed in Chapter 7), or using techniques such as meditation and practising gratitude, are very effective techniques to help us connect with our heart-centre.

As we learn to connect our heart with our mind and our body, we can step into our soul-power. The experience helps to create more certainty and clarity within, so we are able to sense and intuit our world more clearly, helping us to make wise and discerning choices for our life.

Learning to master the mind takes practice, so don't expect perfection. When children first learn to ride a bike, it's typical to have a lot of mishaps, and after getting back on the bike and refocusing on having fun, they get on with it, eventually mastering the skill of staying upright. One day the child and the bike become one and they no longer need to think about how to ride, they are just doing it and enjoying it. The same goes for connecting with our heart and becoming in-tune with our mind and body. It takes practice. Most importantly it requires our love and compassion, and appreciation of who we are, not self-judgment or criticism.

If you are a particularly sensitive person, you may feel a little hesitant about allowing yourself to be more open, because it takes a willingness to be vulnerable. In the past you may have associated being vulnerable with being hurt, or at least that is what the world has taught you. However, when we are true to ourself, there is only Love.

As we become more self-aware it is common to experience periods of confusion and inner conflict. Knowing more compels us to be more discerning and decisive about our choices and the actions we take. Do we follow our heart and the calling of our Soul, or do we make a rapid retreat to what feels comfortable? Living with what we already know, despite the pain that keeps us there, is so often the choice of those who never come to experience the joy of self-love and acceptance. If you are able to let go of your fear and insecurities, and trust that God and the Universe is there to support you, you will in time learn that it is safe to be 'you', and there is nothing else that is required of you other than to be 'you'. As we grow in love and appreciation for ourself, slowly our heart opens, and as our heart opens, we demonstrate our readiness to see, experience, and learn.

It takes courage to go places we have not been or experienced before, even if in the recesses of our inner world. If we take the risk, the rewards of trust, love and compassion for ourself far outweigh the fears we imagine.

On my own journey to greater love I have felt fear and self-induced pain, and yet there has always been a deeper knowing that I am never on my own, even when I feel lonely. As much as possible I choose to follow my heart and the calling of my Soul, rather than stay in fear that drags me down. As I choose to live more from my authentic self and with love, I feel myself grow stronger and more grounded in who I am. When my heart is open, and my mind and body are relaxed, I learn more about myself and it is easier to live from my true spiritual essence. In this space my thoughts are clear, and my energy is lifted.

Gradually, I have realised I do not need to be perfect. As I stay on my true path, I am more inspired to move towards greater love. It is compelling, the more I focus on love, the more peace it brings to my Soul. The more I focus on my worries, concerns and fears, the more I drift away from love and self-empowerment. As human beings we complicate our life by expecting to have the answers to everything, and by trying to achieve all the time. Yet it is as simple as focusing our mind, heart and our intentions on living life with more Love. With a focus and intention of Love, we can experience greater awareness and wisdom that is available to us from our Higher Self and the Divine.

## From Fearful & Powerless, to Loving & Powerful

Coming to terms with choosing a new path in my life and learning to manage my thoughts and my energy was a big stretch for me. I wondered why it felt like I was taking one step forward and two or three steps back. My emotions were still taking me on a roller coaster ride and so my confidence was shaky. One moment I was on top of the world, grounded and feeling aligned with my soul-truth. Then, something would rock my boat and my unshakeable ground would shift, move and roll, throwing me overboard with little mercy.

It had not occurred to me that despite all the work I was doing to manage my energy, I was undoing all the good with my negative thinking and self-talk. I realised I was reverting to old patterns of behaviour, allowing myself to engage in negative conversation, negating my true feelings. I was de-valuing and disempowering myself each time I allowed my overactive mind to recite all the reasons why I could not succeed or see the goodness in being my authentic self.

Our words, which are an outward expression of our thoughts and beliefs, are incredibly powerful. They have the power to raise us up or tear us down in one sentence. With the help of some supportive friends, I began to pay more attention to what I was voicing and what I was telling myself. I realised that my language was self-defeating and negative. It reflected the fear that still plagued my thoughts and the doubts I had about being my real self. I constantly second-guessed my ability to make change that would effectively shift me from feeling fearful and powerless to powerful and loving.

Some of us may have been raised to 'be seen and not heard', and if we are female, we have likely been encouraged to tend to the needs of others before our own. Even in my parents' generation, men were given a greater status and it was expected that women would be there to support and meet their needs above their own. The trouble with this is that it had been taken to extremes, where lack of respect and value for one's own needs fostered the belief that someone else should be responsible for meeting our desires, such as the desire to feel happy, loved, good enough, approved etc. We may have also been conditioned to suppress how we feel, and as a result we shut down our voice in order to fit in with others. As women, we told ourselves that sharing how we feel or what we want, is selfish. It is therefore better to avoid having a voice. We have believed it is preferable to not make a fuss and allow someone else to feel happy, so we are accepted, and we can avoid the pain and shame of being rejected.

I have also witnessed this for men, where they too have lived for a long time, feeling disempowered and without the right to voice or express how they feel, or have the freedom to choose for themselves. This behaviour is a learned pattern of thinking and believing, originating from feelings of not being worthy or good enough as a child, and is now being played out in adulthood. Ultimately this way of thinking leads to not living as your authentic self and it can create deep feelings of resentment and rebellion.

Limiting beliefs and behaviour patterns are built on a spiritual untruth that we are not deserving of love and respect. Every person is equal in Divine truth, and whilst it is important to show compassion and generosity toward others, it should not be at the expense of your own well-being and happiness or limit your own value and self-worth. To act in a way that is disrespectful or harmful to yourself is an act of un-love. When we are not loving toward ourself, we are diminishing the value of who we are and limiting our spiritual growth and personal development.

In some cultures, it is acceptable for women to have a voice, and it is encouraged. In other cultures, it can be forbidden to voice what you want and how you feel. We live in a world of incredible diversity with different social and cultural rules and norms. Becoming our true self is to recognise that we are not defined by these rules, even if we are to live with them. Spiritually we are all the same. Our voice is one way of expressing the depths of our Soul, our heart and our mind.

Self-expression can take many forms, through creative pursuits such as writing, dance, art, making things with our hands, playing music, song writing, and singing. Or, it can be how we use our talents in our profession, our hobbies and interests. It may be how we express our love when we relate to our partner, friends, family, or our pets. Our voice is one way of expressing our desires to others, from the most basic of needs to our deepest thoughts and feelings.

Some of us may not have had much practice in voicing how we feel and what we are thinking, and so it can feel scary, unfamiliar and confronting. Perhaps it takes more courage or skill for some than it does for others. It's interesting when I examine and reflect on my own experiences. In some areas of my life I have no hesitation to express how I feel or my thoughts on a particular topic. Yet, there are other areas of my life that I have felt a definite hesitation and fear around expressing how I really feel. What about you? Are there areas of your life where you feel your throat close over, and your heart rate increase, or your body shrink when you try to speak or express how you feel? Do you shut-down, avoid or deny how you truly feel?

Different people and different situations may trigger us to close down our voice, causing our throat chakra (our energy centre for expressing our true self) to shrink and diminish. Suddenly we feel 'tongue tied', heavy in the chest, or croaky in the throat. The ease of expressing how we feel seems to rapidly retreat. These are the physical signs of our body responding to the emotional response of fear and the thoughts that run through our mind. What are we telling ourself in that moment when we feel ourself close down? When we choose not to voice or express our true self (whether it's the spoken or written word), we are responding to the fear that we are not good enough, and that we are not valuing our own needs, opinion, or desires.

In order to truly give love to others and live in a way that is genuinely kind, compassionate and generous toward others, we must first learn how to do this for ourself. It is so important that we nourish ourselves with the knowledge, experience and love we need so that we have more love to give others. To a live a life that is limited is to diminish our ability to shine and be truly connected to all others in a meaningful and positively influential way.

Expressing my true essence with my outer voice is at times challenging for me. However, my thoughts and feelings tend to flow when I put pen to paper, or fingers to the keyboard. We all have our own way of expressing our true authentic self. What's important is that we give ourself permission to do so. This is how we can live a more soul-filled life where we acknowledge our true self rather than suppress our soul's guidance and influence in our life.

I notice than when I struggle to express my true self, it's usually because I am afraid that I will not be accepted or understood. Can you relate to this experience? Sometimes it's preferable to hold our own counsel and choose to not share or express our thoughts and feelings. When we are in the company of negative people and naysayers, it's not always wise to share your dreams.

However, to choose to withdraw your inner voice and withhold your naturally loving expressive self will prevent you from being the real you, and this will lead to diminishing your self-worth. People who habitually learn to hide their true self (or restrain their inner voice) tend to develop physical ailments around their throat, lungs, upper chest and mouth area. Emotionally they can become repressed, depressed and suffer from a lack of self-esteem and poor relationships. They become accustomed to believing they are not good enough, and they are rarely self-compassionate or self-accepting. Others have a tendency to over-compensate by acting out or rebelling through more overt behaviours to hide their perceived lack of ability or true desires and feelings.

The relationship we have with ourself suffers when we retreat within and avoid opportunities to learn, grow and express our true nature. Spiritually we limit our ability to receive love and wisdom, and our natural intuition dulls so we can no longer sense the spiritual guidance that is available to us. Over time, if we continue to choose to be 'small' and not give expression to our true feelings, the light of our spirit dims. Divine love exists within us all, but if we choose to not access this and allow it to shine, we prevent ourself from living as our Divine nature intends. Essentially, we create our own inner prison, and this leads to feeling trapped, stuck, and powerless.

Next time you feel the urge to express your truth and you feel yourself hesitate, allow Love to be your guide. Ask yourself, 'What would Love do'? When you love and value who you are, others will come to love and value you with the same measure. We cannot control others, however the response we get is usually a reflection of how we see and treat ourself. People tend to say and respond to the cues we give them. That's what it means to 'relate' to others or be in 'relationship' with other people.

When we express our preferences to other people, it gives them a chance to know us more closely. This information helps them to know how they can respond and relate more appropriately. In this way we can live as our authentic self and improve the relationships we have with ourself and with others.

# Attachments and Illusions

*When our perceptions become illusions we are
being limited by our attachments.*

The path to self-love may not feel like an easy one if we have lived with years of limiting self-belief. Having the desire to love and be loved is wonderful, but to truly experience love we must understand the nature of unconditional love. Most of the time our humanness tends to lead us to loving others based on conditions that satisfy our needs or preferences. We have unwritten rules on how we prefer to give and receive love. Without being too conscious of our own behaviour we tend to compare ourself with others in how we look, how we perform in our job or in our familial role, and our own measure of recognition with our peers. We notice what others have and what we believe we do not have. When it comes to self-love we tend to be our biggest critic, tying ourselves up in knots with the illusion that we are not good enough or worthy of love, or there is not enough love within ourself.

Have you noticed how you use your self-judgment to determine whether you are worthy of love, or whether you will like or love someone else? Have you prejudged someone before getting to know them? Have you been distracted by how they present themselves, rather than what is beneath the surface? Have you already decided that you are not worthy of love until you have lost a few extra kilos, or completed that course of study or professional development, or achieved that amazing sales deal that will top your personal finances and career reputation? Perhaps you are waiting for your partner to 'get their act together' before you decide they are worthy of your love.

These are examples of 'conditional' love, where we have a set of rules or criteria for loving ourself or someone else. However, true Love that comes from the Divine, is not conditional or based on anything that you say or do, nor the way you look, how smart you are, how financially successful you are, or even how wise you become.

Unconditional love for yourself is the complete acceptance of who you are in this moment, with all your uglies and beauty, foibles and strengths.

You are made from the Divine and this is pure love so there is nothing that needs to be taken away or added to you to make you any more or less loved or lovable. We may choose to improve different aspects of ourself so that we are living more healthfully or growing towards our full potential, but this is not a measure of our worthiness of love or a reflection of our true Divine spiritual design. Unconditional love for yourself is to love and accept who you are as a person, regardless of the beliefs you have about yourself, what you have been told growing up, or any strengths and weaknesses you perceive yourself to have. Waiting for your idea of 'perfection' is futile, as you are already everything you need to be.

As human beings we live a physical life of dualities. Everything we perceive is usually according to our preferences of either 'black or white', 'right or wrong', 'this or that'. In this physical life our preferences can help us to make choices to understand our identity in some form. Through our identity we interact with the world so we can learn and grow. However, our personal preferences can also become our attachments which ultimately constrict and bind us, and eventually lead us away from experiencing unconditional love.

When we become so attached to our preferences, we tend to see ourself as a separate identity in this world, rather than spiritually connected with other human beings, nature and the spiritual realm. In truth we are all energetically and spiritually connected since we share the same spiritual origins of the Divine Source. However, most people forget their spiritual origins and we become largely influenced by our physical nature and our physical needs.

When we depend upon our preferences in order to be happy or to accept ourself or others, the experience of love becomes very conditional, or dependent upon external factors. For example, most people desire a loving relationship in order to feel love. However, experiencing love is not dependent upon having a loving relationship with someone else. It can be an easy habit to develop when we repeatedly make decisions based on what we believe will make us happy, comfortable or secure. When we live in a way that's highly dependent upon our environment and what others say or do, we can be easily disappointed since this is not something we can control nor is it guaranteed. When we don't get what we want, we leave ourself to the mercy of our emotions, and we become either distressed, frustrated, anxious, angry or sad.

Our sense of well-being and happiness is authentic and sustainable when it comes from an inner knowing that our sense of self-worth, love and joy originates from our own heart and soul. Most of us recognise from time to time that we seek love, approval and a sense of security from other people or from external factors. It's human to desire love and connection with another. However, when this desire to seek love and happiness from others becomes our primary drive, it is a sign that we are living our life conditionally, and with rules about how we expect to receive love and feel happy. Love and connection are available to everyone, when we are first able to experience complete acceptance and love for ourself.

### Life is all about our perspective

Our own reality and what we believe to be true in our mind is often very different to the reality of others. What our ego-mind will have us believe usually doesn't lead us down the path of True Love. Our ego is constantly looking for affirmation and reassurance because it is primarily existing from a place of fear in order to protect us. True joy in life comes from knowing that Divine Love dwells within. The practice is to tap into the love for ourself and know that this love is real and always there. Life is all about our perspective. If we choose to see life through eyes of fear, then our experience will be that of fear. If we see life and others through eyes of Divine Love, then our experience will be loving.

It's a common phenomenon for our patterns of thinking and behaviour to be conditioned by our childhood experiences. My pattern of dependency and my need for external reassurance began as a young child when I would frequently suffer from separation anxiety. As a child my parents were my primary source and experience of love. So anytime I felt I was being torn away from that source of love, it felt incredibly unsafe and it left me feeling alone and vulnerable. Unfortunately, I carried this pattern of belief and conditioning into my early adulthood and this led to feeling insecure. My low sense of self-worth and personal value affected many of my choices in life. I learned to seek security from outside of myself, in my circumstances and from others. I was at the mercy of people's mood, and their capacity and willingness to give love and tend to my emotional well-being. I became a 'people pleaser', believing that my measure of love and attention to others would be returned equally when I needed it. I set myself up with false expectations which led to continual disappointment, because of my lack of understanding that True Love is experienced when it first emanates from our spiritual being.

Between the ages of 0-7 years we form habits and conditioned ways of thinking, beliefs and behaviour that we carry over to our adult years. The meaning and interpretations we give to our experiences as young children can often become the criteria and foundation from which we decide to think, believe and act in our day-to-day life as adults. This is part of our development and the human physical condition. However, as we grow in self-awareness and consciousness, we can learn to become more adept at discerning more clearly what is no longer serving us as adults.

What are some of your habits that affect the way you think about yourself, and your own measure of self-love? Often our language, the way we talk about ourself and others, will give us a clear indication of what we truly believe about our self-worth. Are you in the habit of downplaying your skills, talents or abilities? Do you make jokes about your quirky behaviours, your looks, or your personality traits in a way that is negative or unfavourable? Sometimes we may find we avoid making friends or reaching out to other people because we believe they will not accept us or like us. Other times we may recognise that we tend to dismiss favourable opportunities because we believe we are not good enough or deserving of them. For others, feeling comfortable with their own insecurities is masked when they judge or criticize others for their inadequacies.

Do you notice that you restrict your own expression of love and acceptance toward others for fear of rejection? Or, do you find yourself clinging to friends or your partner for fear of being left alone or feeling unloved? Is it easy for you to find fault or flaws in other people? When we become focused on what other people are doing or not doing it's often a reflection of our own lack of self-worth and self-love. What's important is noticing some of the habits you may have developed that demonstrate your level of self-love and acceptance, rather than ways to criticize yourself.

Harsh criticism and judgment of others is often a neon-sign of how we think and feel about ourself. Take this opportunity to recognise the signs and chose to give yourself more love, more compassion and more acceptance for who you are. Initially it may take some practice and patience as you make the choice to love and accept yourself without rules or conditions. Gradually you will experience a deeper sense of inner peace and respect for the beautiful soul that you are. In time you will learn to replace your dependency on your self-made rules, and the conditions you set for other people's behaviour, with more love and a deeper respect for your own value and worth.

Happiness is not about self-perfection nor is it about having what we want or expecting life should always be smooth sailing without pain or disappointment. The attachments, dependencies and illusions we form constrict us in a way that lowers our energy, dims our inner light and closes our heart and soul.

## Soul Sandwich

Our thoughts and beliefs about ourself have a powerful impact on our sense of self-worth and our ability to love ourself.

## Pause. Ponder. Reflect

- What are some examples of the way you think about yourself that reflect self-judgment and a lack of love and self-acceptance?
- In what ways have you judged others or withheld your expression of love to others?
- In what ways can you see a similar pattern of withholding love and acceptance of yourself?

# 14

## Soul Connections and Spiritual Encounters

There were many times I felt despair and loneliness during those transformative years, however I knew I was never truly alone. In my darkest hours there were also moments of joy when I felt touched by the angels in Heaven. I developed a close connection firstly with Archangel Michael, who was with me from the very beginning. I felt his loving and protective energy guiding and comforting me every evening before I went to sleep and when I awoke each morning. It was always in the quiet moments and in the stillness that I would feel his presence and hear God's loving wisdom come through in whatever way I needed.

I remember one evening, early in my journey, I was feeling very sad and in need of the comfort of healing touch. I had drifted off to sleep, and sometime later I surfaced to a more wakeful state. My eyes were closed but I had the distinct experience of someone stroking my head, as if I was resting with my head in the lap of a loving entity. In that moment I recognised I was feeling the healing energy of an angel, giving me comfort and letting me know I was safe to rest and let go of my worries that were burdening my soul. It was a beautiful, Divine and soulful experience.

I have had many such encounters with angels, and every time, there has been no doubt about whether the experience was Divine or imagined. Angels are very direct, loving and compassionate. They are always clear and to the point in what they want to convey. For me their message is usually communicated through a transfer of their energy, which gives me an instant knowing of their presence and message.

As humans we are conditioned to think and interpret our experiences through words. We see, hear and feel something then we process that experience through the filters of our own thoughts, beliefs and previous experiences. We then use words to express that experience. Angels communicate with their energy and their vibration, which means they are more direct, giving clarity and certainty. As a result, their influence and impact is felt immediately. When we struggle to hear or understand their message it's usually because we get in the way. What I mean by that is, we tend to let our fears, doubts and lack of certainty block or cloud the message. Our mind gets in the way of Divine love and desire to assist us.

Do you remember having an experience where you know you should choose option A instead of option B, and you could feel it in your gut? You may have been receiving several clues or signals to indicate the better choice, however because you let fear cloud your decision, or you listened to someone else instead of your own intuition, you chose the other option. In the end you're kicking yourself because it turned out to be the least favourable option. This is a typical example when our angels give us the clues for the better way, but we are not tuned in or listening to their guidance.

*When we create stillness in our heart, mind and*
*body we become open and receptive conduits*
*for receiving messages and guidance from the Divine Source.*

When I was 16 years old, I was awakened to the energy of the spiritual realm and the presence of angels. I had a burning question inside of me. I wanted to understand how I will know I am in the Divine presence of God and the Angels, or whether I am experiencing the opposite energy? At this age I had a limited understanding of the expansiveness of God and the Divine loving presence, only the 'personified' being that religion provided me. In an unusual semi-conscious state, I was visited by an angelic being. The experience goes beyond what words can describe. It was extremely powerful, and it affected me throughout my whole being (physically, mentally, emotionally and spiritually). I received the most loving pure energy that appeared to surround and encompass me like the most brilliant white light. It was a spiritual experience and yet physically I felt as if I was dropping to my knees with the strength and power of the loving energy. The answer to my heart-felt question was the loving energy that washed over me. No words were needed, they were irrelevant. I was left with absolutely no doubt about how to recognise the pure Divine love of God.

Every thought, worry, concern and material reference in my physical life suddenly had no relevance. There was no sense of space or time, just loving energy. The experience was so intense that I had no concept of where I was or how long the experience lasted. From that moment on I knew for the rest of my days that I would forever know and be able to discern God's (Source) love. My psychic senses were enhanced so that I could see and know, without question, the Divine in all people, even when they could not see it themselves. Since then I have been able to discern the difference between my own thoughts and communication from the Divine. Whenever we are in doubt about anything, it is always because of our own thoughts, disbelief and our own fears.

For most of my life I have used journaling as a way of processing and expressing my thoughts and feelings. It has been the language of my Soul, and a communication channel from which I have received on-going spiritual guidance. This has been incredibly helpful as I've travelled the path of my soul's growth and transformation. When I feel doubt and confusion, and I am unable to see or hear the spiritual guidance I need in that moment, I write my thoughts and feelings down to clear and release from my over-active mind. This helps me to get in tune with my spirit guides and angels, and free myself to hear their loving messages. I've since learned I am strongly clairaudient and it is through writing that I am able to clear my mind and create space to receive the messages that flow through me onto the paper. During this time relevant guidance is revealed to me, and I experience clarity, a heightened awareness and a deeper knowing. I always feel grounded, with a deep sense of peace, much like my initial encounter with the angels. My concerns melt away.

When I over-think and over-analyse problems in search of solutions or clarity around issues that bother me, I find that writing enables me to surpass my ego and chatterbox mind, and the usual barriers I put up that confound me. I am able to enter a space of ease and flow to allow the inspiration and channelled messages from Spirit to flow through to the paper. As I dive deeper by letting go and allowing, I am able to surrender the need to figure everything out. In this state I am able to reach a closer vibration to the angels, so we can connect more easily.

When we are too busy in our thoughts, and pre-occupied with fixing things, forcing outcomes, or trying to convince, persuade, or manipulate people in order to feel better or get what we want, we create even more distance from our authentic self. Energetically we block our ability to receive, to see, think or feel other possibilities. We become numb and unreceptive to our own value, and as a result we don't see our true self. It has the same effect as snuffing out the light or turning down the dimmer on our Spirit. When we do this, we are not connecting with our Soul or living our Soul's purpose.

When we are in a state of stillness and calm, we make room to receive insights and we are able to expand our intuition. For me, uplifting and non-vocal music often helps to transport me to that place of stillness and receptivity. It also works when I focus on my breath rather than my thoughts, or when I expand my awareness of nature around me, such as the gentle breeze by the ocean and the rhythmic sound of the waves.

We all have our own unique and individual way of connecting with our inner being or soul. When I walk in nature or spend time journaling or meditating, I am able to raise my vibration, tune in to my Higher Self and hear messages from the angels and my spirit guides. The experience feels loving, expansive and what I refer to as spiritual abundance. If it is anything other than this, then you are still trapped within your own thoughts and fears, or you have entered a space that is non-Divine or not of God. When we connect with our Higher Self we are fully tapped into the Divine Source, and this is the spiritual realm of God and the Angels.

It's possible that many of us will remember experiencing a pivotal moment (or moments) in life, when we feel connected to our soul-purpose, or our reason for being, even if it's in a fleeting moment of recognition. It's an amazing feeling, when everything seems to be clear, unobstructed and you experience a deep connection in your heart and soul with something that resonates to the core of your being. Your passion for what you do takes on a new and uplifted energy that seems to flow and become your guiding light for the path ahead, as if nothing else matters. This is the experience of connecting with your soul-purpose, where you feel an inner guidance to serve and contribute in a way that is unique to you.

When we are in-tune with our Higher Self it is easier to sense the spiritual guidance available to us. However, we can miss the signs if we believe we are limited in any way. When we allow ourself to become distracted and influenced by our ego (our fears and doubts), this lowers our vibration and dulls our ability to hear the guidance of our Soul and of Divine Spirit and will lead us off course from our soul's purpose.

Everyone's primary soul-purpose in life is always to be our authentic self and to grow in Divine Love. Prior to our birth our soul reviews our spiritual growth and chooses a life path that will provide us with more opportunities to experience contrast so that we will freely choose the path towards True Love. The circumstances in which we are born into provide us with the landscape that is most suitable for our next stage of learning. However, our circumstances will not necessarily be comfortable or desired. It is here that we are offered the chance to repeat lessons not yet fully integrated or embrace new challenges that will assist us to rise up to the next level of love and wisdom. For some people, their life purpose becomes a very specific mission that involves a contribution to society on a grander scale, and for others the ripple effect of their seemingly insignificant life will touch the lives of many unknown souls. For all people, the lessons of self-love, compassion and mercy are not only self-serving, they are significantly serving all others at the same time through our connection with Spirit.

## Our Spiritual Nature

Many people mistakenly believe that only gifted people are intuitive or psychic, but the truth is, we are all born psychic. It is our natural way of communication and connection. It is only as we reach that human developmental stage of around 5 or 6 years of age that we begin to live by the rules and conditions imposed upon us and block our natural connection with Divine Love. We begin to perceive and believe in our limitations and separateness from God, which leads us away from our true Divine nature and our ability to listen and connect with Spirit and our soul.

Our core nature is spiritual. We may be living a physical and earthly experience however our very essence is of spirit. Life on earth provides us with fertile ground for learning about our true nature, which is both Divine and human. Our life lessons are personal challenges that offer us spiritual growth, or they may be lessons learned through the experiences of those around us. Experiencing challenges first hand does have a deeper impact, as it brings us in direct connection to our vulnerabilities, insecurities and our fears, all of which block our path toward True Love. There is no doubt that it is through the contrasts and discomfort of personal challenge that we are given the opportunity to choose between self-imposed imprisonment or spiritual freedom.

Either way, no true lessons are learned unless we first go through the experiences. In doing so, we get to see and feel what works and clearly what doesn't work. Some call these moments 'failures'. There are no failures. Every experience we encounter and every choice we make is teaching us about whether we are in alignment with our inner truth and soul-purpose or whether we have veered away from our soul-path and become distracted by the influence of others or our external circumstances. This is valuable feedback to help us to learn more about ourself and the path we are choosing in life. Our experiences and outcomes are a reflection of our internal focus and the beliefs and perceptions we have about ourself and others.

It's human nature to want to avoid discomfort in life. You may know many people who typically will choose the option of 'no-change' in their life (job, relationships, health, home life, finances) if the choice to change is difficult or challenging, or there is any perceived risk. As a result, many people live armchair lives - reading, watching and observing the lives of others vicariously through their experiences or even through the drama of their favourite TV shows. However, we all know this is not real life. We cannot experience true transformation, growth or wisdom through observation alone. The learning is only going to be at a mental level. When we are able to apply what we have learned through physical experiences, where we are faced with the contrasts of life and the consequences of our choices, we can then connect emotionally and spiritually with the experience.

Our intuition is a quality of our spiritual nature. Like anything in life, the more we practice or strengthen this skill and ability (or spiritual muscle), the more developed it becomes. When we use our intuition, we can listen more deeply to our soul and recognise that we are more than our personality that we present to the world. Our soul is the core and essence of who we, and it is through our soul we connect with our spiritual nature and our physical experiences.

When we don't tap into our intuition and we switch off from that deeper knowing, we can often experience a lack of flow in our life that shows up as the struggles in our relationships, issues in the workplace, repetitive dramas in our family life or continual financial problems. When we live unconsciously and disconnected from our spiritual nature it can cause us to believe we have few choices in life. However, there are always options to choose a better way, a path that leads to True Love. It's through the contrasts in life (the challenges we experience) that we are given the opportunity to choose our own reality, not the other way around. Many people live out the days of their life believing that their level of success or happiness is dependent upon the circumstances that present. In truth, our circumstances are a reflection of what we are thinking and believing. Our world within is what determines our world on the outside.

*The power to create is truly within our own capacity.*

Authors such as Barbara De Angelis, Wayne Dyer, Eckhart Tolle, Don Miguel Ruiz and Deepak Chopra, speak about how our energy and vibration attract the same or similar energy into our life. We may spend a lot of time wishing and wanting things, people or specific circumstances in our life and yet we wonder why we are not making any difference or manifesting what we desire. While we keep wishing and wanting, hoping that someday things will change, the Universe will just keep delivering the same energy that we put out there.

However, when we evolve to understand that our concept of 'what is' is merely an illusion, or whatever we imagine and believe, we then understand that there is enough of everything for everyone. The key is knowing that the energy and spiritual essence of our being is what brings whatever we desire to the forefront of our physical experience and reality.

When we connect with our spiritual essence we see and know that our physical reality is just one aspect of our being. As spiritual beings we are always connected. Our spiritual essence is not separated by a physical entity or barrier. Even though we are all unique, as spiritual beings we are energy that merges, transforms, moves, and is 'all' at the same time. The key to our universal connectedness is the power of Love. It is through the energy of Love that we are one and the same, as we share that Divine spark that unites us all. Our differences are our flavours and unique experiences. However, the Love that is Divine connects our spirits above and beyond our physical and mental experiences.

In the beginning of my journey, when I felt the calling to spread my wings, feeling as though I was like a bird trapped in a cage, I knew my Soul was calling me to come back home and reconnect with Spirit. It was a recognition of my spiritual essence and the desire to connect with my Higher Self and the spiritual realm. I needed to remember that

I was first and foremost spiritual in nature, and that I have lived many lifetimes, learning and growing in wisdom and understanding. Over many years I felt myself drifting away from my spiritual core, losing my memory of who I was in Spirit. When we forget our spiritual nature, we can become so focused on our physical experience and external circumstances. If this is all we notice as our reality, then it is bound to cause dissatisfaction and a lack of fulfilment which impedes our soul growth.

It took me quite a long while to understand what to do next. I had always been somewhat connected with my spirituality, but the landscape of my life began to decrease my awareness and receptivity. I was not living in a way that was allowing me to hear my Soul or give full attention to my life purpose. Deep down I knew I needed to step away from that landscape and take a different path in order to awaken what was lying dormant.

When you hear the calling of your Soul, don't ignore it. Your Higher Self will always guide you to greater love and increased wisdom. As human beings we are fearful of what we perceive to be painful or challenging, however when we understand that God only has the best plans for us, we can trust this and go with it. It may feel like a huge leap of faith. I struggled with trusting, listening to the inner guidance from God and the angels, and taking the next steps. I was full of fear, self-doubt, confusion, and a lack of self-confidence. I was more focused on my perceived inability rather than trusting in the Divine and in my inherent 'abilities'.

I feel as fallible as the next person however I have been rewarded with more growth, wisdom and love when I have acted with courage, despite my fears, and persisted even when I felt unsure. I have always kept Divine Love as the reason for being, and for what I do in my life. Responding to Divine spiritual guidance has helped me to discern the better path to take and prevented me from delaying my progress. Every step towards love (love for myself and for my life) opens my spiritual sight, and as a result my intuition and psychic senses expand.

Life is not always easy and smooth sailing. Now and then we can tell ourself that life is not fair. It certainly may seem unfair and challenging at times, but this is not the point. Our opportunity is the perspective we choose, and this is how we get to turn our life towards Love.

My journey in recent years has been very challenging, however the lessons I have learned have been worth it. The choice to leave my marriage, to live on my own for the first time, experiences of loneliness, relationships discovered and lost, financial loss, change in jobs, moving from home, a deep struggle with self-esteem, and having to develop incredible courage despite my fears, were the fires of my inner and outer transformation. The spiritual journey that many people encounter is the calling to grow to the next level of wisdom, understanding, compassion and love for oneself and for others.

It wasn't always clear to me how to dive deeper and connect with the core of my true being. All I knew was that I was driven to do this. I started by listening to my heart, asking myself how did I want to feel? What could I do that was different and what would bring me the most joy?

The answers that came to me were not profound, and at first my actions were tentative. I felt like I was waving my hands around in the dark, trying to find my way in a huge ocean. In time I realised that it made more sense to hang out with my own tribe or those people who shared similar interests. This helped me to feel less overwhelmed and it was a faster way to feel connection, a sense of belonging and a degree of safety and certainty in my life.

When we hit rock bottom it's essential to tend to our most basic needs to survive physically, mentally and emotionally. Whenever people go through big changes in life, the quickest way to lose your footing is to throw yourself out there into the big unknown with no safety net. That's just not smart! I knew that change was happening in my life, but I also realised it was necessary for me to not resist the change. The saying goes, 'whatever we resist will persist'!

I realised that any level of resistance toward change or growth would mean I would stay stuck in my despair and apathy, with no change in my circumstances. So, I gave myself permission to be curious and to explore. As silly as it sounds, I realised I didn't need anyone else's sign-off to do that, however it was more difficult to put into practice.

Everything felt strange, new and unfamiliar. A lot of the time I felt out of my depth, so going gently helped me to ease into unknown territory.

I see myself as typical of many women my age who are going through their own version of midlife change, even though life change can of course happen at any time. Most of the Australian women of my era have been raised and conditioned to see a woman's purpose (as wife and mother) to support the man (husband, father, partner) in his career and as head of the family, above the love and support of their own self. I know that people more senior than my age still hold this view, and certainly this belief supported them in the world and the landscape in which they lived most of their life. Love and support between two people is beautiful, especially if it is mutual and unconditional. I now see through a lens that gives me an expanded view of love that begins with love and full acceptance of oneself.

When I began to live my life more connected with Spirit, I began to see my own true value, and to love and accept myself, rather than compare myself to the perceived worth or value of others. For many years I had learned to unconsciously give away my own power and value. I had an underlying belief that men were more capable and more likely to succeed, after all that was their role in life. I had lived my life with the foundational belief that I would be supported by someone else who was smarter and more capable than myself. This was how my parents and their friends were raised, and it was the model on which we were raised as children. There was an acceptance that this was the status quo, and so I felt less driven to discover my own powerful potential and unique capabilities.

Awakening to my own true self was a slow unfolding, and it felt strange. At times I felt like a fake because I was daring to go into territory that was not permissible. Only the bold alpha women went there, and that was not me. It took a lot of mental gymnastics, going back and forth in my mind, trying to work out my place in the world. As I settled more into my own skin and I felt the benefits of quietening my mind, I was able to more comfortably tune into my Soul and listen more deeply. In time I began to realise that all of the pre-conditioning of my childhood and married life was no longer serving me. It began to fade into the background as I came to know myself at a deeper level, and this was bringing me closer to my spiritual core. It was a powerful awakening for me.

Initially I was angry and rebellious at the thought that I had been duped, and that my opportunity to live as my true self had been dampened, limited, and squelched. I had unconsciously grown a seed of resentment for many years, believing I was the victim of my circumstances. The realization that I did deserve to shine and live as my true self was confronting. I went into a silent blame game, which festered inside and made me feel very sad. It took me many years before I realised that I had created my own self-imprisonment, despite my conditioning, and that my current and future reality was really up to me. This was a huge 'wake-up' call.

As the dawn began to appear in my heart and soul, I vowed to be responsible for my previous choices and the beliefs I had held onto. I played the part during all those years, and sadly I was dismissive of my own value as a person and as a woman. It was never someone else's fault, because ultimately only I can control my thoughts and beliefs. However, when you have only ever seen yourself and your life through a certain lens, it takes quite some adjustment to see with different eyes.

When I could no longer resist the urging of my Soul to release from my own chains, I didn't really know where to start. After I established myself in my new home, a humble one-bedroom unit, I was faced with a blank slate and a new beginning. The new space was welcome. I knew I needed to be alone to breathe and rest while I figured out my next move. Leaving everything that I knew was frightening and liberating at the same time. I wanted to come to terms with the huge decision and the massive leap that drew me away from my comfort zone and the only world I had ever known. The inner work ahead of me would be very challenging and I knew it was going to involve diving deep, confronting my shadows, and discovering more about my true self. Over the next few years I did exactly that. The path was rocky, often scary, and yet there were moments that were exhilarating. Above all, it was a path that was leading me toward my soul healing, a path of self-discovery and a growing consciousness.

In the beginning I read many books on spirituality, the soul journey, the spiritual realm, and human behaviour. I attended courses to develop my spiritual knowledge, my psychic awareness, and the healing arts. I immersed myself in an environment that would nourish my soul growth. I knew that in time, all that I was learning would in some way help others to grow in their spiritual awareness and self-healing. My desire to understand our spiritual nature was seeded when I was a very young child, as far back as I can remember. My mother's influence and psychic awareness, and some significant spiritual experiences of my own, opened me to new possibilities and initially led me towards studies in psychology, counselling, pastoral ministry, and Christian spirituality.

During this time, I intuitively felt drawn toward my natural creativity. It wasn't just about getting out the art pencils, it was more about accessing multiple ways to more fully express myself, through writing, dancing, physical activity, socializing, meditating and learning the healing arts. I felt drawn to learning to 'be me' rather than the actually 'doing' of any activity. My creativity was helping me to connect my mind, my heart and my body. I had been so disconnected within myself for such a long time. Learning to freely express myself was a form of therapy and healing. Certainly, it helped me to listen to what made my heart sing and to reconnect with my heart space. I had previously given myself so many rules to live by, and it always revolved around the belief that I needed to take care of everyone else's needs first. There was little time left for me, and even then, I did not feel I was good enough at anything. I felt I was just blindly going along on a ride that was not *my* soul journey.

The more time I spent with myself I realised that learning to listen to my Higher Self was key to reconnecting with my true nature. I started with the basics, of becoming more aware of my body. I became more consciously aware of how I was feeling inside at any moment. I noticed whether my stomach was in a tight ball from anxiety, or if my shoulders were aching from the weight of worry, and whether my head was feeling foggy or clear. I started yoga classes to stretch and release, and to still my mind. I enjoyed many bush walks with my friend along Sydney's northern beaches. I spent time outside to feel the sun on my face, breathe the fresh air and feel the energy of the trees, the ocean, the animals and the birds. It was incredibly healing, and it helped me to 'feel' again, to awaken my spirit. I was experiencing a physical and emotional cleanse and benefiting from the high energy of nature all around me.

## The Prana of Life

*Prana – breath, life giving force, energy, life; also known as chi or qui. Universal energy which flows in currents in and around the body.*

I have always loved being in nature, and particularly being next to the beach. As an empath who is highly sensitive to energy, I find that the energy of nature rejuvenates my soul and restores my balance and sense of well-being. When I am in a very noisy and crowded environment, or when I have been indoors for several hours, my energy begins to drain.

It is the same if I have been eating low energy foods that are dense or processed, or if I have been eating too much dairy, this will also drain me and make me feel sluggish and unwell. High energy foods such as fruits, vegetables, legumes, seeds and nuts, are foods that remove toxins from my body, so I am no longer feeling bloated or tired. High energy foods are generally loaded with natural enzymes and help me to feel lighter and clearer. This is a definite plus for reducing anxiety and the habitual patterns of negative thinking and behaviour.

During the early discovery stages of stepping out, I knew it was important I connect with people who shared similar values and were consciously aware in their life. An important part of my support and growth was recognising the difference between people who are energy drainers (or energy vampires), and those whose energy is uplifting. My friends are very supportive, and their positive energy is my inspiration. I am not dependent upon them. Their love and the example of their own life encourages me as I walk into new territory.

When we first hear the call of our Soul, we can feel an inner urge to reach out to make other soul connections. We intuitively begin to gravitate towards other people who resonate with the same energy and vibration. Our Soul knows who is on the same spiritual journey and so we feel a desire to be closer to these people as we become spiritually conscious and open to new spiritual experiences.

When we feel a connection with another soul, it can feel as if you are 'speaking the same language'. There is often a sense of peace and ease, as you relate on the same energetic frequency. Often their soul is going through the same learning process or stage as yourself, and so you 'get each other', feeling like you are on the same wavelength in terms of your thoughts, feelings and intentions. We can also experience what feels like a soul-connection when we are with animals. Animals live in the present moment, and so they do not hold on to the past or concern themselves with the future. Their energy is unfiltered, and their love is unconditional.

Nature is extremely powerful and instrumental in assisting us to feel connected with the Universe. We can experience the same sense of connection at a soul level when we are outdoors, amongst the trees, by the seaside, or in the mountains. Nature's energy is clear and uplifting and helps us to cleanse of toxic physical and psychic energy that we store as stress and worry in our mind and body.

As a young child I grew up with a love of nature, since my parents were garden-lovers. Every weekend we were outdoors, weeding, re-shaping and tending to the flowers, shrubs and trees. My mum and dad loved creating something beautiful and enjoying the fruits of their labour. As children my sister and I would help with the weeding and clearing, as well as planting new seedlings and bulbs. After many hours of work, by the end of the weekend, we would sit back and enjoy what had been created. As a child I learned to appreciate how wonderful it felt to be surrounded by the energy and beauty of nature. When the garden was well looked after, it attracted more birds and wildlife and we felt content and relaxed to spend time in its colourful refinery.

When I spend time outdoors, all the cares of my world seem to melt away, as I reconnect with my true self. In this space I am able to feel more connected with Source, the creator of all that is. It's a wonderful reminder that we live in a beautiful, dynamic, ever-changing, and living universe. We are part of this universe. Our physical world provides evidence of life, and responds to what we give to it, and what we take from it. As we let go of what ties us up in knots during our day, nature helps us to get back in touch with what we sense, feel and intuit. The mind becomes still as we rest in the present moment and enjoy the natural abundance that surrounds us.

The energy of life ('chi' or 'prana') is the source of what helps us grow physically and spiritually. When we are in nature, we can breathe in the 'prana' of life that connects us with all that is living, helping us to feel at one with all that is. When we resonate at this vibrational level of peace and calm, we expand our level of conscious awareness, helping us to see, feel and experience Divine truth, bringing us closer and closer to pure love. A love that is wise, compassionate, understanding, accepting and giving at the same time.

Many years ago, I was given the opportunity to visit Central Australia with a group of students. An Aboriginal elder, who remembered the first time he saw 'white man' come to his land, generously shared his wisdom with us through story-telling. On the clearest of days, we sat in a dry river-bed that was surrounded by huge white ghost-gumtrees. We were a long way from civilization (about 500 km) in the APY lands on the border of South Australia and the Northern Territory, in the outback of Australia. With all the patience of a 90-year old elder, he sat with a large circle of young 16 year old boys, and slowly and purposefully shared a story that helped them to appreciate the gift of nature, and their journey as boys becoming young men. He spoke for a while, then paused, so we all had time to soak in the message and breathe the fresh air and powerful energy of the gumtrees that surrounded us. Then he would break into an earthy song, using his clapping sticks, as if to give thanks to Mother Earth for all that she provides us, in both its beauty, energy, wisdom, and resources. It helped everyone to feel at one with the red earth on which we sat, and to feel gratitude for the simple joy of connecting with nature.

The experience that followed seem to seal it for me. We were asked to sit under a tree and spend time being in the presence of these magnificent giants. When we felt ready, we were invited to lean in close to the trunk of the tree and place our ear against the tree. Our task was to not think or over-analyse our experience or have any expectations other than to be open and to listen. As expected, most of the boys were rather sceptical. There was a lot of banter about doing this 'tree hugging' thing. However, nothing ventured, nothing gained.

In the stillness of the beautiful morning I sat next to my chosen tree and stared up at huge blue sky through the thousands of leaves of this giant. I placed my ear against the trunk and breathed. I waited. After a few quiet moments I could hear a noise that was akin to running water. I gazed up to check if I was imagining it. There was no wind in the trees. I thought perhaps it was the sound of the leaves and branches moving, vibrating down the trunk of the tree. There was no wind. I listened again. This beautiful tree felt alive. There was energy coursing through the veins of the tree, and it felt amazing. I was not too sure what I was hearing, and whether it was actually water in the tree, but this didn't really matter. Beaming from ear to ear I raced up to the Elder and said to him 'I heard it', and he nodded and smiled. That was it. His part in this scene was complete. He wanted to give us the opportunity to connect with nature, and to experience life through these magnificent trees.

*The power of nature and its living energy never ceases to amaze me, heal me and transform me.*

## Meditation Exercise – Prana of Life

*Close your eyes and imagine yourself to be sitting comfortably somewhere in nature; by the sea, in the forest or bush, in your garden, the local park, or perhaps in the mountains. Feel the breeze on your skin and through your hair. The sun is shining and gently warming your body. You can hear birds close by, the rustle of leaves or the rhythm of the waves moving back and forth. You can smell the sweetness of the air and the warmth of your body on the inside.*

*Breathe slowly and purposefully, in for four counts, and out for six. Feel the breath coming in through your nostrils and gently exhale through your lips. After a few moments, when your mind has come to rest, and your focus is on your breath, imagine yourself to be a large tree, with deep roots that stretch down deep into the earth. Feel the warmth of the dark earth beneath you and remember all that has been in ages past. Draw this knowledge and life affirming energy up into your trunk, so that you feel grounded and strong in this present moment. You are here and now.*

*Visualize yourself as the tree and feel the strength of your core, the channel that allows the flow of prana and gives life to all parts of your physical being. You have seen much, weathered a multitude of storms, and provided sustenance to all who have gathered beneath the shelter of your branches. The thickness of your trunk is testimony to the wisdom of the years contained within the strength and resilience of your core. Breathe in, breathe out.*

*As you gaze skywards, slowly reach upward to feel the energy coursing through your large limbs, along the smaller branches, and all the way to the tips of every leaf. Feel your energy expand high and wide as you reach toward the heavens, to the spiritual realm. You are glowing with the warmth of your prana energy. You are connected to all that has been, all that is, and the Divine that gives life to all. Breathe in and feel the connection to nature, to Spirit, and know that this is Divine Love. We are one.*

*Stay for a moment as you experience the expansiveness of this universal connection that is both spiritual and physical. Feel the Love. Give thanks. You are loved.*

## 15
### True Love is Divine Love

When we speak of true love, it's common to expect most people to believe this is the ultimate love we crave to experience and receive from someone else, either from our partner, family, or friends. We associate true love as being that state of infatuation, bliss and perfection, when we finally have all of our needs met, especially when it's from the one true love and focus of our affection.

However, this is the myth that most of us have been led to believe. We are so conditioned in our life to expect and believe that love is found outside of ourself. It's in the messages we received from our parents and our community when we were children. It's prevalent in the role models presented in the media today, and it's the wide-spread belief society promotes, because it's a saleable commodity. Love can be bought, or so it seems. When we expect to find love in this world from someone or something else, our belief is that love cannot be found within, it must be attained from some other source. When we think we have finally found love, we hold onto it tightly so that it cannot be taken away or lost.

The truth is that *True Love* is Divine Love (or The truth of Love) which comes from Source and also resides within us. As spiritual beings, we are seeded with this love, and we are eternally connected to the Divine, the source of True Love. Divine love connects us to our soul, where Love resides. When we remove the shackles from around our heart, we can experience this Divine Love.

Heavy energy, depression, low motivation and inspiration prevent us from experiencing this love inside, and so we go seeking love from other people and in other ways to fill the void we feel in our heart, mind and body. When we have not recognised the love within ourself first, this mission to find love can lead to obsessions and addictions. The experience of lasting love, inspiration and fulfilment will continually elude us when we don't first recognise and develop the seed of love within ourself. As we surrender our attachments in life, we can journey within to connect with our Soul (our Higher Self) and allow the transformative process of growing in trust, compassion, self-acceptance and love for ourself to evolve.

When we live with the soul-power of Divine Love, we can feel truly content with the person we are, without the need to judge ourself. There's an inner peace and acceptance of all aspects of our being. The desire we once had to compare ourself to others, to be perfect or as intelligent, skilled, attractive and successful, is no longer driving our thoughts and actions or whittling away at our self-esteem. When we are inspired by Divine Love and we live with a heart of love, we feel a lightness within and we are enthused about who we are as a unique individual, excited at the possibilities to unlock our potential and become the best version of ourself.

Sometimes it can feel as though we are not there yet, or that we will never achieve this state of self-love and appreciation. We only see our flaws and our failures. At times life can feel as if we are on a treadmill when the same life experiences keep repeating over and over. We may feel as though we are not making any progress, and that life is never going to get any better. In these moments it's a temptation to focus on our pain, feelings of rejection, inadequacy and a lack of love. It's not unusual to experience periods of doubt and low energy, however dwelling in this state is only going to drag us down.

To live with true love and as an empowered soul-being, we must practice raising our vibration through actions that are loving. This means choosing healthy options in our life, speaking about ourself in a loving way, having compassion and gratitude for who we are and what is available to us in our ordinary everyday life. It's also about listening to our Higher Self for the guidance and support we need for our spiritual growth and transformation. When we're open and attentive to our soul-journey, we benefit from the accumulation of wisdom gained from soul lessons experienced over lifetimes. Living with Divine Love fully activated in our life is possible for everyone.

Longing for love, approval and acceptance from others is an indication we don't feel love for ourself. It's a reflection that somewhere inside we still feel wounded or not good enough. Secretly we long for someone to make us feel better, valued, whole, and complete. We want to feel and receive love, attention and approval in exactly the way we desire it and at the right time. We are always longing for someone else (perhaps our special person) to top up our cup so that we will feel good again. The problem with this, is not the desire to experience love – that's amazing. The problem is that we are constantly giving ourself and the Universe the message that we do not have love, that we do not love ourself, and that we are always in a state of being depleted and empty. Why else would we be constantly seeking love outside of ourself?

When we base our sense of value and happiness on what we long to receive externally, we will be disappointed. It is not possible, nor is it the responsibility for someone else to do this for us in a way that will sustain us eternally. We are each able to stand in our own soul-power and Divine beauty, and experience the Love that exists within our soul.

When we truly love and value ourself to the fullest extent, without the desire for perfection, then someone else's responses, what they think, say or do, will no longer have a negative impact. When we have love and respect for who we are, we will know there is no reason to compare ourself to others. To grow in spiritual wisdom and love for ourself, we must do the inner work. Only then can we truly know our value and see Divine love in ourself and in others. Our soul growth can then be enhanced, enriched by other loving soul-beings. It is true, when another soul says they love and appreciate us for who we are, this is a gift to treasure, however it does not add or take away from our value as a unique individual.

Loving yourself is what makes all the difference. This may be the way you take care of your daily needs and your health, enjoying your unique personality and talents, and acknowledging your achievements. True Love is loving and appreciating all of you, what you feel great about yourself, as well those shadow aspects that appear occasionally in those low moments. We develop self-love when we nourish our spirit, our mind, and our body. Even though others may demonstrate their love for us, it is not a measure of our worthiness of love or self-worth.

## Becoming Love

What does it mean to love oneself? If we are not familiar with the concept of what it means to love ourself or how to access those inner feelings of compassion, joy and appreciation, it may be difficult to know where to begin. I believe the first step is to *like* who we are as a person. If we cannot be our own best friend, then we will find it a challenge to go deeper and truly love ourself. Think of a friend in your life you appreciate, has similar interests to you but is not necessarily the same as you. He or she has different strengths, talents and abilities. You appreciate their kindness and support, especially when they are there for you through the ups and downs of life. They also accept you for who you are, without the need to change you. Is this how you relate to yourself? Do you accept who you are, without the need to be perfect in all ways? Can you appreciate your quirky individual ways, and value your unique self?

Looking back on your past and seeing only the areas where you feel you didn't achieve, or where you feel you didn't measure up, is not the way to grow in appreciation of yourself. Life experiences are what shape us, teach us and help us to grow in wisdom and self-love. When we reflect on our life choices and honestly acknowledge how we have made progress in our life, then we can truly appreciate our value.

When I observe the very old trees that have lived for decades or even centuries, I notice their gnarly bark, knotted trunks, and twisted branches that speak to me of their long lives in all sorts of weather and challenging conditions. They may not look like my idea of perfection in terms of beauty, and yet they have survived, and their magnificence speaks of years of developed resilience against the weather, as well as seasons of glorious days reaching for the sun and sinking their roots deeper into the earth. These trees have great wisdom and fortitude. They have no doubt provided much joy and benefit to those who have either sheltered beneath their branches, feasted on their fruits, or enjoyed the clean air they have filtered.

Progressing to a place of being able to love who you are may be a bit of a stretch, especially if you have been conditioned to believe you are not worthy. Some people may have been exposed to long-term ridicule from others, or years of negative self-talk and personal berating. Learning to love yourself is recognising that you're deserving of Love and it's not dependent upon your perceived value or self-worth. In Spirit, you were created by the Divine and therefore everything about you is already perfect. Without changing anything, you already have all you need in terms of Divine Love. All that's required is for you to see that Love in you. The seed and the makings of Love is within everyone. It takes some watering of that seed, self-compassion, and nourishing of your mind, body and soul to bring that Love into full bloom.

Creating a foundation for self-love to thrive begins with nourishing the body. With practice you can develop healthier choices in terms of what you eat and ensuring you get adequate sleep. Ensuring you have the right amount of physical activity, movement and ways of maintaining strength and flexibility is also essential for honouring your body and providing the best possible home for your mind, heart and soul to reside.

It's also necessary to learn to manage your mind, or your thinking, and to cease telling yourself what you believe you cannot do. To consistently tell yourself what you are 'not', is to stop the flow of Divine Love that gives life. You are condemning yourself every time you speak disparagingly about who you are. A negative mindset brings more pain and more obstacles into your life. True Love sees your full potential. As we learn to see what is beautiful and magnificent in life, the Divine light shines brighter so we can see more possibilities. This is you.

As we grow in self-love our vibrational energy rises to a new level. What we see, feel and experience is now through eyes of love and a heart of love. Our perspective is less about comparing what is and is not, and more about seeing the fullness of other people and all living things. It is an interesting phenomenon. You may notice on those days when you are feeling particularly centred and in tune with yourself that you attract the attention of others, particularly other like-minded souls. Your positive energy gives off a vibe of your self-assurance that comes from Love, and you will feel as if your day is in flow.

When we are more loving and accepting of ourself, our energy is calm and therefore it is much easier to step back from the drama of life and see things as they really are. In the same way, our ability to see the Divine in others becomes clearer. There is a shift away from seeing other people through a lens of expectation or judgment, to accepting where they are on their soul journey.

People often use the term 'I love you' very loosely, without understanding its true meaning. The word 'like' is to show a preference for that thing or person. When we 'love' there is a far deeper meaning, energy and intention. Love is energy, and as spiritual beings in human form, we live as this loving energy and we can share this energy with others when we are being our authentic self.

Love is dynamic, eternal, an action as well as an experience. It is an energy that is life-giving, forever expanding, and not restricted to time or space. When we say we have love for another, for ourself or for the world, we experience this expanding energy as gratitude, compassion, inclusivity, kindness, appreciation, passion, and purpose. It's powerful and more than words can describe. This loving energy dwells in our heart and soul and shines from the inside out. It fills our being with energy that raises our vibration so that we can see more clearly and *be* the essence and power of Divine Love.

When we choose to love ourself or another person unconditionally, we love without rules and expectations. To love unconditionally means we are not imposing conditions in order to satisfy our need to feel worthy of receiving, giving or being love. We freely choose to love, with no inhibitions or limitations. We experience this phenomenon of Divine Love from our heart because we are one with the Divine, already made from Love. We do not need to earn love or feel worthy enough to receive love. When we love who we are, we are being our true authentic self, knowing our Divine nature and our true value, and this needs no judgment.

Experiencing the power of soul-loving is living as our true self, with acceptance, compassion and gratitude. Through our spiritual nature we are all one, connected by the Divine, made of the Divine, and therefore perfect in the eyes of the Divine (God).

## Embracing our Truth

Learning to accept all of who we are, including how past mistakes, our painful experiences, and what we perceive to be our weaknesses, may feel too difficult, painful or perhaps not even possible. Many of us will assume that when we are asked to accept ourself, we must face and accept our shadows, the deep dark recesses of our soul for which we feel ashamed and do not want to reveal. It's a rather dim view of who we are as a soul-being if that is all we wish to see of ourself. Self-acceptance is loving all of our being without reducing ourself to an inadequate and limited version of our true self.

Self-acceptance is a deep love for our soul, knowing that our purpose in life is to live and learn, and this requires us to experience both the dark and the light so that we know the difference. It's through missing the mark as well as experiencing the joy and elation of when we are on the right path, that we can grow in wisdom and spiritual maturity. Self-acceptance is not to judge but to love. It's to see ourself as a loving soul, not defined by our past choices, but as a soul that is constantly evolving and experiencing life lessons to help us grow.

Personally, I have needed to go through many life lessons and growing pains to experience those essential 'aha' moments that bring me more clarity and understanding. We are all a work-in-progress for getting to know our true self and learning what it means to love ourselves without criticism or judgment. If we are open to learning, and we desire to understand, we will gain spiritual knowledge and insights, and increase our ability to raise our own vibration for experiencing love and happiness in our life. Self-acceptance is the route to mastering True Love, especially when we learn to be accountable for our own thoughts and emotions.

It took more than a few challenges for me to hear the voice of my heart and soul. When I kept experiencing the same drudgery, disappointment and heartache in my life, I used to feel great despair, and at times I wanted to give up. It was exasperating and exhausting. I was continually struggling with accepting myself and my circumstances following my separation. It was challenging for me to not feel desperate to have my need to feel love fulfilled by another person. It caused me a great deal of emotional pain and heartache. No matter what I did, I seemed to always come up short, feeling neglected, depleted and disappointed. The hunt for love was unsatisfying and lonely.

For a long time, I under-valued my own worth and this was regularly reflected in my work environment. Despite my education and skills, I chose jobs that were easy, and ultimately a reflection of my low opinion of my skills and value. This meant I didn't develop myself professionally or utilize my skills and experience to my fullest potential. I lived with a huge amount of fear as well as resentment. As a result I constantly felt undervalued, dissatisfied and as if my life was continuously dull and mediocre. I knew that I was not doing what I love the most, nor living as my true self.

I also found it difficult to accept that other people communicated differently to me, and when I did not receive the same effort or energy in return, I took it very personally. As an empath I have a more heightened psychic sensitivity which means I am very preceptive and communicative, and I enjoy connecting physically, mentally, emotionally and spiritually with others. Sometimes this made me feel lonely, especially when I realised that other people's energy was dark and heavy, or when others were not able to connect with me on the same level. The lesson for me was to release from having expectations of others and allow them to be who they need to be, in their own way and in their own timing. I longed to feel understood, to receive their acceptance, approval or at least their acknowledgment. I now realise there was a deeper unfulfilled need to feel good enough, and to feel love and a deeper connection with my soul-self. I was yet to learn the gift of self-love and self-acceptance.

For this period of time in my life it felt as though I was on a personal battle ground, feeling the pain and never healing from my self-inflicted wounds. When I look back and remember the thoughts, the depth of my feelings and my beliefs, I wonder how I managed to keep my head above water. At times my emotional tank felt so empty and I struggled to know how to fill it up. In the early days, I only knew how to respond by seeking comfort and security from outside of myself. I was grateful for any love and approval I could receive. I felt starved for love, and with this belief came a strong sense of desperation.

When you have conditioned yourself to believe you are not worthy, that you don't have enough or that you will never be enough, it is easy to fall into the trap of always seeing yourself and your world in a state of lack and therefore unsupportive of your needs. Holding onto these beliefs works against you. They colour your perception of yourself and other people, and they snuff out your natural ability to shine, to be content and fulfilled. When you see yourself as unworthy, you cannot live as your true and authentic self.

My world revolved around trying to manage my circumstances and other people so that I would not feel so poorly. I put a lot of energy into organizing my life, my family, my work colleagues and other significant people in my life so that they would feel happy and I could therefore feel worthy. Whilst people may have appreciated my generosity, which elicited in them feelings of ease and comfort, they also became used to me always being there to manage things for them. After a while, my efforts to consistently meet the needs of others, in an attempt to feel love and appreciation, backfired. I became exhausted and resentful. So much of my energy was about protecting myself from feeling vulnerable, unloved, hurt, and insecure. At the time I blamed others for not doing their part. In truth, my lack of love for myself was what influenced my thoughts and my actions, and this energy was reflected back to me with the same measure.

When we don't sustainably manage our own energy or understand how to nourish ourself in a way that brings inner peace, happiness and fulfilment, we are likely to burn the candle out at both ends so that we can no longer shine. We have nothing left to give. What's left is resentment. The truth is, we can't control external situations or other people. I regularly suffered the pain of rejection and I felt the experience of lack in my life because this was my belief about myself. It became the energy I was projecting to the world. It's not that other people in my life wish to cause me pain or choose deliberately not to show their love. What they do, or think is not really the point. It's more about what I believe, what I think, what I say and what I do that influences the experiences of my life.

When going through so much change I was especially grateful for my friends, *my earth angels,* who were there when I needed their support. It was a welcome blessing when even strangers seemed to be perfectly timed to cross my path and give me an unexpected smile, a wave, or a reassuring comment. No doubt my spiritual guides were giving me the encouragement I needed and a reminder that what I perceived to be my troubles today, would surely pass in time. Today I am so grateful that God and the angels regularly reminded me to stay on track and to listen to my heart and soul (my Higher Self).

What also helped me along the road was being determined to not give up on my dreams, and to adopt a spirit of acceptance and love of my whole self. There were many times I slipped back into self-pity and I cried a bucket load of tears. It was challenging. However, having had many instances of falling down and getting back up taught me resilience and courage. It strengthened me on the inside, and it helped me to believe in my capabilities and self-worth. I began to value myself more and feel self-love and a desire to care for my well-being.

The way to build resilience, is through self-love, and by exercising the muscle of inner strength, courage and determination. For myself, it was going through the tough soul lessons of feeling so low and then realising that I had a choice to either sink or swim, to give up or to pick myself up and find a benefit in my circumstances. It was by experiencing the challenges, despite my fear, that helped me to find my courage and build resilience. I learned to be curious and to ask different questions that were self-empowering. I practiced ways to shift my mental and physical energy as a way to support my new way of being. I focused on doing things that inspired me, and were good for my health and well-being, enabling me to let go of things that were toxic and draining in my life. Over time I developed faith and acceptance that it would take time for me to heal, and that I needed to do this in my own way, regardless of where I was on the continuum of my soul-growth. I learned to trust myself and I realised that I didn't need to follow the path of others, rather it was more important that I recognise what was true for me.

I realised that the Universe was not conspiring against me but working for me and with me. Each time I dropped to my knees with exhaustion and mental despair, I knew I had the spiritual support and the ability to get back up, and that I would be fine. My courage and resilience developed when I made the effort to improve my thinking and to take steps forward, even when I felt inept. I knew I needed to practice doing this every day, which meant thinking and doing things differently. We are in the *school of life* and soul lessons are learned through practice, practice, practice.

Everything that was happening in my life, the self-awareness, shedding my previous need to control my world, understanding more about relationships and the wisdom of letting go, and learning to see through a lens of compassion and self-love, were the experiences that were helping me to grow. Unfortunately, many of us develop the habit of complaining about our world, and we fall into the trap of believing we are victim to our circumstances, or that people are out to take advantage of us. This is disempowering. Our soul growth and fulfilment in life is a reflection and measure of our perspective and where we choose to focus.

The Universe is always working to bring opportunities for us to grow in wisdom and understanding. We are a part of Divine Creation so when we choose to cooperate with this energy, and work in synergy with nature and Divine Love, we can notice the opportunities for growth and abundance and benefit from this.

When I was focused on my sadness and the challenges I was experiencing, I became resistant to change, and this disempowered me. I drained myself of my energy and I snuffed out my light, and this made it difficult to see the path ahead. I felt like I was in a continual fog, and no matter how hard I tried to see the way forward or force things to happen in my life, the more I seemed to stay stuck. When we are in pain, it is human nature to return to the same pattern of thinking and behaving as we have always done in the past. It's a protective mechanism to ensure we are safe. Experience soon teaches us that doing the same thing, responding as we have always done for most of our life, gives us the same results over and over.

## Love Heals

When I first stepped away from my married life, I dived into the unknown, and this was like a massive jolt to my soul. It shook my world entirely. I felt like a child, somewhat helpless and ill-equipped, embarrassed by my ineptness, vulnerable and clumsy. I desperately tried to pull myself up to regain my composure and dignity after having experienced a massive fall that left me utterly bruised and rejected. There was pain, shock and humiliation. After a while I felt myself go numb and speechless, not knowing what to do, think or say. I wanted to be brave, but for a long time I didn't feel brave. I was scared and alone.

Initially I felt denial and shame about what had happened to my relationship. Friends offered comfort and well-intentioned advice, and though they meant well, I was confused and dazed for a long time. I was unable to process anything, and I found it so difficult to act on their advice. All I could do was cocoon myself from the reality of my circumstances and find ways to protect myself from feeling more pain. All I wanted to do was to close off from the outside world and limit conversations with those I perceived could hurt me even more.

Much later I realised how important it is to not force answers, solutions or explanations. Healing is an important part of our growth and transformation, and it takes everyone different amounts of time and energy to support this healing. Before we can expect change or progress, we must first heal, and the best medicine for healing our perceived brokenness and separation, is through love.

It took me a couple of years to learn to love and accept myself, despite my circumstances. I became emotionally closed off for fear of feeling more pain and losing control. The problem is, when we shut down, we resist experiencing love in our life, Divine love. Divine Love is available to everybody. When we choose to live in a way that honours our authentic self, we become open to experiencing Divine love within, rather than seeking love or validation from external sources. It's not until we desire to truly see and accept ourself in this way that we can begin the process of healing and growing.

## Connecting to Nature and the Universe

Connecting with nature has been food for my Soul. All my life, the experience of being outside, listening to the birds, breathing in the fresh air, or sitting under a tree, fills me instantly with life-giving energy and gratitude. Nature is creation and its essence has incredible power to facilitate our healing.

During my time of diving deep, my walks by the beach helped me to find peace within. I was able to release my mind from the mental torture of going around in circles, filling myself with doubt, worry, anger, pity and sorrow. Nature helped me to feel the living energy wash over me like a spiritual and physical cleansing. It was calming for my mind and body, and soothing to my soul. When we connect with nature for our healing, the wisdom and Divine love of God awakens us and brings into our experience exactly what we are ready to receive.

At first, I felt guilty for feeling negative and sad. I used to tell myself that I should be able to snap out of it. I wanted to know that even when I had bad days, I was still going to be okay. In time I realised those were the moments I could give myself permission to rest and recuperate, without judgment. Even when there were moments when I felt so low, I was grateful for having a roof over my head, and incredible friends who were supportive and reminded me that I was never really alone. Time in nature also reminded me that I was Divinely protected and guided. I was learning to let go and trust in the love that was surrounding me, I did not have to go looking for it.

For all of us, difficult days will come, but they also pass, just like the sun that rises and sets every day. Life continues to move and transform around us. Energy is always flowing and in motion. When we learn to see and feel this, it is much easier to be in flow too, rather than resist the tide. As we let go of struggle and move into peace, we re-enter the zone of being with Spirit and in flow with ourself and the Universe. When we connect from our inner being with the energy and flow of nature, we become open to the healing that is available to us all. As we return to peace and calm, healing does its magic within our soul and in our mind and body. Only then can the doors to happiness, success and liberation open for us naturally.

When we are in tune with our Higher Self, we are able to live a life as our true self, making choices that nourish all aspects of our being, loving what we do, and witnessing our heart sing.

## You Are Beautiful

For most of my life it has felt much easier to give love and support to other people. As a daughter, wife, mother, employee and friend, I gave a lot of myself, and more. This was partly due to my upbringing, when females were raised to not question authority, and to always give what time and energy was required to support others. It was a period of time where women felt the unspoken expectation that to consider one's own needs was considered selfish and unloving towards others.

Perhaps this influence was unhelpful, to live with the belief that other people were more important than myself. My generation was raised to believe only half the truth, failing to recognise that the greatest love is the love that we are willing to give to ourself - *Soul Love*. If we are not nurturing our own life and soul, then how can we possibly give love to others. If we have not experienced what it feels like to have deep love for ourself, then how can we give that kind of love and compassion to another? True Love for oneself is not narcissistic or self-inflating; it is self-compassion, respectful and kind. It is unconditional love that accepts others as they are and where they are on their soul-journey and it values the Divine presence within all of us.

Heart-felt love (soul love) and self-acceptance is perhaps one of life's most challenging aspects of our soul growth. Most people who are feeling out of alignment and disconnected from their true self are struggling to feel or give themselves love. The pain of self-doubt, and the belief that we are not good enough can be life crippling and can hold us back from being all we can be.

It's easy to spend time and a lot of money on worldly distractions, multiple personal development courses, reading hundreds of self-help books, visits to counsellors, psychologists, medical and health practitioners and spiritual guides, all in search of happiness or the solutions for our physical, emotional or spiritual dis-ease. The healers of this world are necessary, and they help us by lighting the path ahead as we travel on our own soul-journey. However, underneath all of our efforts to 'problem solve' our way through life in order to find peace and happiness, is a deep desire to feel loved and to feel good enough.

Without sounding like a broken record, the message about the path to True Love or *Soul Loving,* is still the same. Healing and forward progress comes when we learn to love and accept all of our being, warts and all. It is about truly valuing ourself as a person, unique and distinct from others, and at the same time knowing we are of equal worth to everyone else, despite our external circumstances. It's never about perfection or comparing our self-worth with other people's achievements or what they appear to possess. Material possessions and even our unique gifts, are not a measure of self-worth. We all share the same inherent spiritual nature and soul essence.

When we focus on our external world, other people and our circumstances, it is easy to feel separate and alone. However, feeling separate is an illusion. The landscape and context of our life may be different to that of other people, but we are all going through similar learning experiences and soul growth. On a spiritual level we are all connected. The difference between us is our level of awareness and what we choose to believe and focus on.

As we experience different phenomena in life, our soul is constantly and subtly speaking to us, to open us so that we can begin to see what we cannot see and feel what we have not felt before. Our soul is leading us to a deeper understanding and greater wisdom that will bring us the love and connection we desire. At our core is the desire to feel our full sense of value and worth, exactly as we were created by God. We want to matter, yet do we believe that we matter? Do we believe that we are loved, lovable and loving?

What we have not yet realised is that we are one with Source, all that 'is knowing' and all that 'is loving'. In each lifetime we have forgotten to see the true nature of our spiritual self and how magnificent we are, and so we return to a physical life to have more experiences to remind us and teach us what we have not yet integrated. The purpose of our life experiences is to awaken our soul, to stretch and grow our spiritual muscle so that we can understand the truth of Divine Love. The truth that matters is not our human concept of right and wrong, good or bad, it's about recognising that True Love comes from the Divine, and our opportunity is learn to live and love from the soul, which is eternally connected to the Divine.

What we decide to think and believe ultimately influences our decisions and the actions we take. One person's response to a situation may help them to feel loved and uplifted, whilst another person can quite easily decide that they are not worthy or good enough. Guess what? Whatever we decide is exactly what we attract into our life and this becomes a self-fulfilling prophecy. If we have adopted a negative outlook to a situation, we have lowered our vibration and we are likely to feel low as a result, attracting more disharmony in our life. However, when we choose to see the opportunities in a situation that may have turned out differently to our expectations, then we are likely to feel more uplifted and better able to refocus our energy.

To be practicing self-love we need to be vigilant at avoiding what disturbs our inner peace. This can be easier said than done. We can often be triggered by events, situations or people that will cause us to slip back into a negative mindset or an emotionally vulnerable state. This can happen when we feel hurt or disappointed and it can be difficult to shift from that lower vibration when we focus on a negative perception of the situation.

When the mind works to protect us, it can be a challenge to change our mental or emotional state. Altering our physiology is a great way to shift our mental focus. When we move our body and raise our physical energy our brain creates 'feel-good' chemicals (neurotransmitters) such as endorphins, serotonin (also created in the body), oxytocin and dopamine, which act as a natural analgesic that relaxes the body and creates calm, helping us to raise our energetic vibration.

Start with something simple, like going for a walk or a brief run, yoga, gardening or housework, or any activity that you enjoy. Regular exercise or movement will help you to naturally increase the levels of endorphins and neurotransmitters in your brain and body so that you are feeling more uplifted. As we raise our physical energy, we also increase our energy vibration, helping us to feel more self-aware and receptive, and we become a clearer conduit for giving and receiving love in our life. We are designed to live in flow and when we are not, our energy becomes stagnant. As a result, we can suffer from emotional disturbances, a sense of disconnect and mal-alignment with who we are. This can lead to dis-ease in our body, our mind and our soul.

Living a life with greater self-awareness will put us on the path to greater love. Our self-awareness increases when we are prepared to look honestly at who we are and how we choose to think, believe and behave. It is only through facing our personal truth that we can live authentically. It can be challenging to do this, particularly if we have been conditioned to use denial (the opposite of truth) as a way of protecting ourself from emotional pain. When we live in our personal truth, we can be open to accepting where we need to grow, and to unconditionally love who we are.

As we learn to manage our thoughts, live in a health way, and accept our personal truth, we create more peace within. It may feel at times that it's very difficult to be peaceful, as there are many things in life that can upset or distract us. It's easy to respond negatively when we believe there has been an injustice. However, we always have a choice as to how we respond.

When you feel challenged by your strong emotions, it's wise to pause, and then you have time to reflect and discern whether the matter is worth responding to and whether it is good for you, or good for others. Does a negative response help you or hinder you? Will pursuing an issue without compassion lead you towards your own soul growth and self-love?

Do you feel triggered when you hear about someone else's good fortune, their fabulous job, their latest clothes, car, furniture, holiday, and so on? Maybe they have more education than you, more confidence, more friends. Have you noticed that while you are so focused on what they have, you are also telling yourself about everything you believe you don't have? Remember, your perception becomes your reality. So, now you are living with a mindset of lack, poor self-esteem and low self-worth. You are so much better than that. There is no-one else in this world that can be you. *There is a reason for you being here, and you do matter!*

Today is a great day to honour and accept every part of you. All of your lumps and bumps, personality quirks, mess ups in life (aka learning experiences), as well as the achievements, progress and wisdom gained along the way, are what make you the magnificent person you are. Today is a great day when you decide that you are a Masterpiece. You are the embodiment of all that is complete and wonderful, and yet you have not seen it in yourself. We are masterpieces that are waiting to be unveiled by ourself.

The journey to self-love is not only about increasing our awareness or improving our physical and mental health and well-being. These things are important, however, progress is made only when you choose to spend time with yourself and you take steps to nurture your well-being. Only then will you be able to shift to a new belief that you *are* worthy of love and capable of loving yourself. This step is more than a mental process of hearing the words. Life and the feeling of love deepens through experience. Often, we will go through considerable pain to understand the depth of love, and love for our true self. This is especially true when we are learning what it means to shift from a love that's dependent upon another person or our circumstances, to a love that dwells and expands within.

*Perfection is an illusion. It's progress that counts.*

## Healing and Forgiveness

When we are in considerable pain, it's difficult to contemplate the idea of forgiveness. It may mean to forgive ourself, or to forgive another person. Either way it requires a willingness from our heart and action on our part. It is very human to want to protect ourself and withdraw when we have felt pain, no matter how long it has been. The pain we feel may have been there a long time and we may have become accustomed to denying its existence or burying it so that we don't feel it. Or, it may be recent pain from an experience, and it is still feeling very raw. When we are in a state of emotional pain, healing is needed before we can process the meaning of our experience. How we choose to heal may be different for each person, however the best starting point is to get out of our head.

When we experience pain in the first instance, our response may be to ignore it or we may choose to run for cover, to what is familiar, such as old ways of thinking, doing or being, as a means of protecting ourself. What is familiar and easy often feels safe and less risky. Another strategy may be to become overly focused on finding answers and reasoning as to why the painful experience occurred. It's our way of being able to process the experience and make sense of what has happened, so we can return to what feels safe and within our control. However, what the mind usually does is go around and around in circles to re-live the moment that occurred leading up to the event.

The best way to begin the process of healing is to still the over-active mind and work through the process rather than look for ways to 'zone out' as a means of distraction. This only serves to block unwanted thoughts. Through meditation and creating stillness in the mind, you are allowing space for the thoughts to come and go, and therefore be acknowledged and then released. In this way you are able to 'process' what comes up to be noticed, and then let it go. Healing can take place at a natural pace. *(refer to the Breathing Meditation, Chapter 13)*

With mindful awareness, you will be able to calm your mind so that you are not over thinking about how, what and why you are feeling emotional pain and grief. Allow yourself to be exactly where you are and take measures to nurture yourself. Practice your meditation and sit in silence and stillness, feeling your breath, and noticing whatever comes up. Surrender and release the thoughts, the emotions and the tension in your body. Give yourself time to accept how you feel, grieve and comfort yourself as the need arises. This is a different energy to dwelling on what has happened in the past. It's about giving yourself space to just 'be'.

I've experienced deep emotional pain many times in my life and when I give myself the time to go through the experience, it has greatly helped me to transform my energy from mental self-torture and heartache, to self-love and compassion. Healing requires our gentleness of spirit and compassion from our heart. Offer up your pain and sadness to God and the angels and ask for their assistance to heal the wounds. Without compassion for ourself, our pain and our over-active mind can easily lead us down the path to resentment, bitterness and retaliation.

After experiencing the first instance of emotional pain, I have sometimes found it difficult to let go. My body closes up, I can't breathe, my heart pounds and I can't sleep. This can last a day or several days. One of the best ways for me to release the pain is to have a really good cry. It releases all of the pent-up emotions, which have accumulated from past experiences, and it floods my body with endorphins to give a sedative effect. The result is I feel very calm afterwards. It's a cathartic experience of a powerful emotional and physical release. I have also found that Yin Yoga and relaxation massage are gentle ways to initiate that physical and emotional release before I can even cry. Other people may find that physical exercise or sport is an effective way of providing the same release that leads to an emotional and spiritual surrendering.

It's necessary to experience release before we are ready to emotionally move to a space of forgiveness. The timing and how this will happen is unique to everyone. There is no 'right' amount of time to go through this process. Whatever is good for you, is appropriate for you. Forgiveness comes from a place of self-compassion, and unless you have let go of the pain, anger, and the desire to attribute blame, it will be difficult to progress to feeling forgiveness from the heart.

The word or act of 'forgiveness' is an emotionally loaded word and often conjures up powerful feelings when we have been hurt or we have felt deep pain and sorrow. Sometimes our response to forgiving ourself or another can trigger feelings of defensiveness, as we tell ourself we have either nothing to forgive (assuming our pain is attributed to someone else's actions) or we are not worthy of forgiveness. If we feel triggered by the word, it may indicate more about our own wounds and how we feel about ourself. We can live in a reality that consists of judgment of ourself and others, or we can choose to accept what is, perfect or imperfect in our eyes.

Let's take a moment to reflect. If everything external to us is from our own perception of reality, then so too are the actions and words of others. We can choose to feel hurt by what others say or don't say, what they do or don't do. Some people may be able to brush off the judgments of others, and yet others will take the words and actions of others personally and deeply. In truth, what others say and do really is none of our business and it is out of our control. This can be very difficult to accept. Other people are living out their own version of reality, and their own soul journey. Their words and their actions are a reflection of their perceptions, their choices and their pathway of learning. Another person's soul journey is not your soul journey.

So, what is your reality? When you go within, how do you perceive yourself? Do you like what you see, or do you judge yourself as being too this or not enough of that? We are often our harshest critic. What other people say and do is of little consequence compared with how we judge ourself. Our thoughts and our beliefs have a profound influence on how we live our life and how we travel on our soul journey.

When we feel defensive and we don't recognise the need for forgiveness of self, this comes from a lack of self-love. Forgiveness is not a judgment it is an act of love and an acceptance for all that we are in this moment. We are not our past or our future. We are who we are today. We may perceive ourself as full of imperfections, and reminded of our past mistakes, however there are no mistakes. Everything that we do in our life will have a result of some kind. It's how we respond to our outcomes that matter. Do we get back up and practice what we didn't achieve or integrate the first time? It is helpful to reflect on the learning and adopt an alternative perspective to see how we can access other possibilities for going forward.

Defensiveness comes from the ego, which is the opposite of love and compassion. When we notice we are feeling defensive and unforgiving, our first response may be to feel victimized and angry, and we may want to attribute blame to others. Our feelings may be completely justified however we may have also attracted a situation into our experience because there has been some aspect of ourself we have denied or not healed. This is not to say anyone is deserving of being treated badly. The opportunity here is to recognise that our own energetic vibration (how we think, feel and believe) will attract a similar energy. A great approach is to be curious and ask yourself 'what can I learn about myself from this situation?'

For example, if you believe you have been the victim of betrayal or dishonesty, where have you been dishonest with yourself? Have you ignored your own intuition or not been honest about yourself or the situation? Did you choose to ignore the red flags because of your desire to hold onto something else? What negative energy have you been holding onto that has potentially attracted this into your experience? Are you addicted to a need you believe you must fulfil?

It can be difficult to confront our own shadow self. It's painful, embarrassing and humiliating. However, if we desire to live with integrity and Divine Love in our life, honesty and truth is the only way. There are no shortcuts to True Love. We must first look inside ourself and examine where we have chosen to ignore the red flags and walked the grey path, telling ourself that our actions are justified.

We all have our own version of what is true for ourself. We speak about living authentically and being true to our values. This truth is an important aspect of our character and the way we chose to live our life. Then, there is *The* Truth, that comes from the Divine. This truth is unquestionably founded in unconditional love, compassion, honesty and integrity. It is an undeniable and eternal truth that embraces all that is and is available to us all to receive into our mind, heart and soul. There are no compromises when it comes to *The* Truth.

Unconditional love is Divine Love, without judgment. It is a love that does not hold onto expectations, nor does it place conditions on how love is given or expressed. It is a love that is eternal, beyond time and circumstances, and sees the Divinity of our soul. Unfortunately, I have witnessed others mis-use and manipulate love. It is not True Love when someone expects you to accept being treated poorly and then call this unconditional love. Unconditional love begins with having love and respect for yourself. It's loving who you are without compromise and living according to your values, with integrity and honesty, and being truthful with yourself. When we love ourself unconditionally, we develop wisdom and discernment for our relationships, ensuring they are based on mutual respect and love for one another.

On our healing journey, forgiveness is an act of love, mercy and compassion toward ourself. It is not an admission of guilt or a lack in ourself. It is loving acceptance of who we are. It is not possible to live our life without experiencing challenges. When we do suffer, we can choose to pick ourself up and keep going. Sometimes we repeat the lesson until it becomes integrated into our learning, and that is how we grow. Despite our challenges, big or small, we are always an expression of the Divine, of True Love and of perfection made from God.

If we are unable to feel mercy and forgiveness for ourself, then we are unable to value ourself enough to see that we are deserving of love. Forgiveness and mercy toward ourself and others is the ability to love and accept a person's Divinity, beyond what we say or do. Our actions and our circumstances are not our 'identity' or what makes who we are as a soul-being.

## Pause, Ponder, Reflect

Love in Action: what does it mean to love yourself?

- Recall a time when you have judged yourself to be not good enough, then describe how that makes you feel.
- Describe a time when you have felt accepting of yourself, without feeling the need to be perfect.

Foundations for self-love – Nourishing the body

- List a few ways you can nourish your body as a way of showing love and appreciation for yourself.

Raising our energetic vibration increases self-awareness and self-appreciation.

- List a few ways you can raise your energetic vibration by doing something you love.

Self-forgiveness leads to healing and is an act of love

- Describe your favourite meditation practice (moments of stillness) that assists you to surrender and release negative thoughts, emotions and tension in your mind and body. (*refer to Chapter 13 for the Breathing Meditation*)

## 16
### Stepping into your Soul Power

When we love and accept who we are, there is a beautiful opening that occurs in our consciousness and in our Soul. The weight of our attachments to others and the need for validation from our partner, friends, family or work colleagues no longer has a hold on us and we are free to be our true self. Before we reach this level of awareness, we may feel very strongly influenced by our fears, and so we work to control our emotions and our environment to avoid feeling discomfort, hurt, and disappointment. Maybe we have set up personal rules and conditions for what we believe makes us feel happy, and yet at any given moment life can deliver what we don't expect. With so many rules we become bound and trapped by our own beliefs. It's easy to limit our view of the world and experience disappointment when our self-imposed conditions are not met.

There are two polar opposite energies in life we may frequently encounter – high vibrational energy which feels uplifting, inspiring and loving; and low vibrational energy that feels heavy and attracts conflict and confusion, often resonant with selfish and demanding behaviour. Our beliefs and our way of thinking generate a particular frequency and energetic vibration that attracts people and experiences vibrating in a similar way. The energy and situations we draw into our life, whether we want them or not, are often used by us to validate our beliefs. For example, a negative and self-defeating attitude is likely to attract more of this kind of energy. When life presents negative circumstances we use this to validate and reinforce our beliefs and our fears. As a result, we typically create a self-fulfilling prophecy of repeated negative experiences.

We can only experience real freedom when we transcend from our fears and the need to control and manipulate other people and our environment. Peace and clarity become a regular way of being as we let go of obsessive thoughts, anxious emotions and physical stress in our body.

Stepping into our soul-power is seeing the truth of who we are and lovingly embracing all parts of our being, including our unique gifts and talents. It's letting go of the fear and recognising our value and worth through the eyes of the Divine. When we stand firmly grounded in the knowledge that we are a beautiful soul beyond earthly measure, we can live as our true self, with the powerful essence of our soul-being.

## Soul Love

Stepping into our soul-power is living unapologetically as our authentic self. To do this well, it requires a willingness and a decision to truly love ourself from the perspective of our soul; to see ourself and the world through the eyes of Divine Love, without criticism and self-judgment. This means acknowledging our own truth, all that we are doing well, and those areas that still require inner work. We may have good reason to want to hide from our truth, but over time this refusal or denial leads to complications, heavy energy and fear-based living.

Acknowledging our truth is how we step into our soul-power and live a life that is abundant and free. This can feel challenging and overwhelming, especially when we know we are required to be open and vulnerable to acknowledge our truth. What is hidden in the shadows becomes revealed in the light.

If we are fearful of confronting our own truth, it can be easy to avoid or deny our truth. Or we may not yet be clear about what is true for ourself. As a result, we can become overly accepting of the views and opinions of others, or we may allow ourself to be distracted by the daily routines of our work or home life as a way of avoiding our inner truth. We may have been raised to believe that it is *right* and *unselfish* to attend to the needs of others at the expense of our well-being. Over time, not tending to our own need for self-love and acceptance can leave us feeling as if we have lost our personal identity and self-worth.

Today, men and women are encouraged to favour the world of their working environment as a way of expressing their identity and to feel more powerful. However, the distractions of our busy working life can often become a willing distraction to avoid addressing our deeper feelings and emotions, and even the call of our soul, for the sake of immediate physical and corporeal rewards. A lack of self-esteem and self-love may have also been influenced by the negative and manipulating energy of parents or partners who have misused love to exert their will and feed their own need for love and attention.

When we have not experienced self-love and we have been conditioned to believe that our own worth is less than the worthiness of others, or if we have been robbed of the opportunity to grow into a mature self-loving adult, we can easily lose sight of our unique talents and strengths. More importantly, we can become out of touch with our true soul essence that is beautiful and unique. We become blinded and unable to see our own Divine magnificence.

When we place so much focus on other people, ensuring they are happy and their needs are met, it is easy to forget to take care of ourself. We may be so used to using strategies to avoid tension and confrontation or we may believe we don't have the courage or skills to stand up for ourself. As a result, we lose our ability to attend to our needs in a healthy way, with clarity and self-awareness.

When we stop listening to the voice of our Soul, we lose sight of our soul-purpose, which is to *be* love and *give* love. If we don't feed our soul and listen to our intuition (our Higher Self) we can wander from our soul-path. The fire or spark within dwindles and life becomes mundane, without inspiration or enlightenment. Life becomes a treadmill of thinking, doing, and speaking about the same things, without heart or soul for our created reality.

Is this really living as your true self? We can certainly love and care for those people in our life, but if it is distracting us, or preventing us from growing, then we will be limited in becoming the best version of ourself. Stepping into our soul-power means to live in a way that is aligned with our values and brings the most joy in life. When we are doing what we most love, and live as our authentic self, we are fulfilling our soul-purpose.

Our friends, family and work colleagues usually show up in our life to support us on our soul journey, to show us what we need to learn and discover about ourself so we can grow and become spiritually mature adults. Sometimes we meet our soul mate and this person's role in our life is to be our mirror, and sometimes our lover or partner. They are not meant to be the same as ourself, but to lovingly reflect back the aspects of our being that need growing and maturing. They may challenge the shadow parts of ourself, but they are always there to bring out the soul lessons for the benefit of our growth towards Divine Love.

Noticing our emotional triggers is valuable as far as highlighting those aspects of ourself that we need to work on. We may need to work on our patience or our ability to release and let go of how things will unfold in our life. We may need to examine our measure of self-love or our ability to feel and experience our value and self-worth. Other people are there to champion us and encourage us to build our inner strength and spiritual awareness so we can become the best version of our true self.

Then there are those people and situations that distract us from our soul-purpose. These distractions may be more difficult to see personally because there is a gain when we allow ourself to be distracted. It's either because we are either enjoying the attention and satisfaction of the distraction, or the distraction may represent a place of safety, comfort, familiarity and a way of avoiding the truth and therefore transformational change. The truth may simply be our attempt to avoid noticing our behaviour patterns and coping strategies are not serving us. Or, the truth may be our choice to hide our own light and not recognise our own value and worth. When we allow distractions to dominate our choices, we tend to give our power away by devoting all of our time, energy and resources to others with little regard as to whether it is hurting us or pulling us away from our life purpose and soul journey.

When we stray from our soul's path, we will encounter conflict and challenges, and so our Higher Self will work to draw our focus back to our soul-purpose. A lack of peace, constant challenges, inner and outer chaos in our life, and recurring poor health are possible signs we have strayed from our soul's path. They are indicators that we are out of balance in our life. The upside is that the challenges we encounter can serve to strengthen us and provide greater clarity around what we value in ourself and in life. The contrasts we experience help to shine the light into the crevices and shadows we need to examine within, so we can continue on the path of soul growth, soul-loving and spiritual maturity.

When we are presented with circumstances that feel conflicting or uncomfortable it's a great opportunity to observe our feelings, our thoughts and our behaviour. We are so often unaware of our own perspective and how it may be keeping us in an unhealthy holding pattern, causing us to go around and around so we get the same result over and over, and then we wonder why. When we pause to reflect on what we are doing and what we are telling ourself, we have the opportunity to ask if it is working for us. Are we really where we want to be, or do we need to make a course adjustment? Is our life currently matching our values? Have our values and focus changed over the years? Have our choices placed us in a position that is in contrast to what resonates with our core essence and soul-being? Are we doing what we love? Are we learning, growing and becoming a more awesome version of our true self? If not, why not?

As individuals we may language our preferences in life differently to each other, however no matter how we choose to express our passion in life, our soul will naturally draw us towards the experience of Divine Love, our spiritual home. This is where we spiritually grow and we are our authentic self.

Times of conflict and turmoil usually create a lot of inner confusion. When we feel caught in the battle between the mind and our heart it can be difficult to discern the best choice or path to take. How often, in those moments of confusion, have you struggled to know what to do? Our mind can be screaming at us to make one choice (usually the safe one) when we feel the immediate pressure or discomfort of conflict. Our intuition will always nudge us to listen to our Soul and to step back away from the drama we create in our mind. When we rush into making a decision, based only on what our mind tells us and without considering our intuition, it can often lead to us being swayed by racing thoughts and powerful emotions, which ultimately produce heavy energy and a poor outcome.

The head and the heart (or soul) are equally strong internal forces. Engaging in a battle of the mind and soul only produces lots of busyness, wasted time, emotional torment and sometimes physical dis-ease. From my own experience I have found that a good way to discern the best way forward is to listen to my intuition, whilst maintaining a state of calm and readiness. I have learned from trial and error to always ensure I am peaceful before making any decision, especially if I know I have been triggered to experience very strong emotions. Often the best course of action is for me to 'sleep on something' or allow time to pass so that my emotions can subside to make way for reviewing possible alternative perspectives. In this way I am able to gain clarity around the situation and maintain a higher vibration for clear intuition. I know this is the best way to hear the wisdom of my Soul, God, the angels and my spirit guides. When I know I am struggling with my emotions and I'm in a state of confusion, I call in my spiritual "A team" to help me out.

Another way to recognise when we are straying from our soul-path is to notice when we are regularly feeling a lack of peace around what we are doing or whether the results we are getting are not aligned with our values. Ask yourself, where are you placing your time and energy? Is what you are doing feeling good, and are you achieving some level of progress? Do you have a sense of flow and ease with what you are doing or are you engaged in trying to push to make things happen? If you are consistently getting a lot of resistance and the results are not coming easily or there is no flow when it comes to manifesting what you want, it's time to reassess your perspective, your personal energy and your beliefs around the situation.

When we spend a lot of energy convincing ourself why we are doing something, presenting a logical argument and justification for our actions, we are in the zone of what I call 'push energy'. If we are actively trying to justify our reasons for our actions, rather than coming from a place of deep inner knowing and acceptance, then we are creating the energy of resistance to the outcome. It's likely we are out of sync with our soul-self if we feel the need to force a particular outcome or control a situation or people to obtain what we think we want. With this energy we are unlikely to achieve what serves us well.

The ego-self (that part of our being that prefers to choose what feels safe over what is best for us) is very selective. When we operate from this part of our being we tend to become de-sensitized to the responses of our body and physical well-being, and to our ability to be receptive to inspiration and spiritual guidance. In essence, we shut down our creativity and our ability to see alternative perspectives and options.

When we're out of sync and disconnected from our Soul, our body will show signs of mal-alignment by manifesting a lack of ease in the body. It may show up as recurring headaches every time we justify what we are doing, or an irritated stomach, or perhaps aches and pains in our muscles and joints. What's important is to notice what happens in our body each time we are in that 'push energy' zone. Anytime we feel disconnected from the guidance of our Soul, we can help ourself by becoming still within.

The key is to listen with our heart, from a place of openness and compassion. When we feel unsettled or we have the sense that something doesn't seem right, these are signs to for us to pay attention. When we become the Observer of our life, we are in a better position to see clearly and then do something about it in a way that promotes physical, emotional and mental well-being.

When logic suggests that a certain choice makes sense and yet you are not feeling at peace with a decision or situation, chances are your intuition is letting you know there is good reason to pause and re-assess how to respond or when to respond. If you listen, God will guide you towards your soul-path, which you will recognise as the path that feels most peaceful, inspired and in flow. It serves us well to trust Divine spiritual guidance, particularly when it is strong and unmistakable, and there are repeat messages that present themselves in the absence of all other information. To return to your soul-space, step away from what is contributing to the inner confusion and follow the path of peace.

Our spirit guides are with us throughout our life to give us the guidance we need through physical signs to which we can most relate. If you are partial to animals or birds, they will send you a sign through a visit or interaction with them. If you are a 'numbers' person they may use recurring number patterns to draw your attention to what you are thinking in that moment. Or, you may notice recurring visions or thoughts throughout the day or in our dreams, or consistent messages you hear in songs and multiple conversations. Spirit communicates in an infinite number of ways. The key is to be consciously aware and to develop your sensory acuity (your level of awareness) so that you notice the signs more often.

Discerning the best path for our life and our soul growth requires us to listen to our Soul, to notice how our body is responding, and to pay attention to the signs that Spirit is giving us. It's also about having the courage to face our truth as well as our fears, and to take appropriate action when we are prompted by Spirit. When we honour and accept our truth and all of who we are, we step into our soul-power, which means we can live our best life.

## Connecting with your Truth

Connecting with your truth and your soul essence is a choice. You can choose to live a life of half-truths and denying your shadow-self, or you can choose to have the courage to face all aspects of yourself. If you choose the path to True Love, it will require you to live a spiritually mature life of honesty and integrity. To experience true joy and happiness in your life means there is no room for bringing along the baggage of denial or living in a way that does not honour the real soul-essence of you.

Let's do a self-check here. Are you prepared to make yourself a priority and step into your soul- power? Do you love yourself enough to honour the real you? If not, then the truth is you are not yet ready to face your own shadow-self, those parts of you that you have been conveniently hiding, ignoring or justifying for the sake of another gain. How has this served you so far? Is your life flowing with ease or is there discontent and conflict still residing within you? Are you living with self-love and fulfilment in your life? Have your choices honoured the best of you or are you still hiding from your real truth?

### Pause, Ponder, Reflect

The questions below are for you to ponder and reflect upon. There are no right or wrong answers. It may be helpful to either journal your answers or talk through these with a trusted friend or confidante.

- Where are you focusing now in your life? What are you giving your attention to most of the time?

- Are you serving someone else's agenda and life purpose, or your own?

- Are you waking up each day doing what you love to do, or are you doing it because think you *should* be doing it? (What's your intention and your reason for what you are doing?)

- Who are you listening to? Your parents, your work colleagues, your friends? Are they people who will support you in a way that is positive, and uplifting?

- How are you prioritizing your life? Is it according to your own values or other people's rules, conditions, traditions, philosophies, and social expectations?
- Are you listening to your own heart and Soul?

If you are prepared to continue on the path to True Love, then now is the time to take stock of where you are in your life. You have come so far in your spiritual journey and soul transformation. Your awareness and willingness to learn and grow has ignited the spiritual flame within you to be open to all possibilities. Why stop now? There are so many more wonderful things about you to discover.

*You are the author and creator of your life. Wouldn't you rather be writing your own script and living in a way that lights your fire and brings you joy?*

When we do what we love we use our natural gifts, talents, knowledge and past experiences in ways that create and contribute to others. When we are creating and immersed in what we love, we are in tune with our Soul and with the Divine. Our energy flows with ease and radiates outwards with a ripple effect that benefits other people around us. We become the communication channel, sending light and love out to the universe through our energetic vibration.

When you are fulfilling your life purpose it will always bring you joy, and in some way, it will lift the energy of others and inspire them to be true to their life purpose as well. When we don't do what we love in life, we become an empty vessel, trying to give what we have not yet developed within. As a result, we end up living for other people, when in reality we can only live for ourself.

When we do not focus on loving ourself and developing our potential, we eventually run dry and we end up being unable to offer or share anything with others. Rather than become like a dry desert that is constantly leaking all of our love and resources, we can nurture our own needs first so that we become the lush garden that is thriving and not just surviving each day. Recognise your soul-power and utilize it in a way that expands and grows you so that you are shining and radiating in a way that brings healing, health, knowledge, and happiness to others. Embrace what you love to do, your talents and gifts, so that you can experience greater love and abundance to share with others.

*A flower that is not watered will eventually wilt and die.*

## Your Soul Power

When shifts happen in our life we are often reminded or confronted with all that we don't want in life, what we don't like about ourself, and what is no longer working for us. It may be the lack-lustre relationships, the toxic environment at work, the dwindling finances, or the lack of inspiration we feel in our life. All the stuff that has been frustrating us can become a bit like the bubbling molten lava beneath the surface waiting for release.

If our focus remains on what we are no longer happy with in our life, we can easily fall into the pattern of allowing negativity to pervade our thoughts, our self-talk and our conversation. As a result, we lower our energetic vibration and develop a pattern of resistance to ease and flow. This energy negates our ability to receive all that is available to us in our life. The discomfort that results can become all we notice and focus on every day. Eventually we are likely to reach a boiling point and it can be easy to make a rash decision to quickly regain a sense of comfort, or to draw conclusions that are not in our best interests.

Rather than wait until we are ready to explode, we can recognise the signs and do something about it, sooner rather than later, so we can return to our heart-space and inner truth. Self-inflicted emotional pain and discomfort are mostly avoidable in our life because we can choose what we want to focus on and how we want to feel. When that inner crisis moment comes, and we realise we are no longer prepared to give our power away and that we *do* matter, we are prepared to commit to restoring our mental, emotional and physical health and to make this a priority. This awakening moment often occurs when we feel we are at a breaking point, or on the edge of permanently sinking. We recognise we have a choice, to save ourself and commit to loving ourself first, or be prepared to continue to suffer.

To develop inner strength, fortitude and self-empowerment we need to understand *how* we have been disempowering ourself. Unfortunately, most of us have ingrained habits of thinking and being that drain our energy and lowers our self-awareness. Our mind is very powerful. We have the ability to either see only what frustrates us, or we can see opportunities to make changes that will bring us back to our path of authentic living. In every moment we have the opportunity to come from a place of self-love and acknowledge our inner soul power, our connection with the Divine. We can also become victims of our fearful mind (the ego) that seeks comfort and reassurance, and this will often lead us down a path that is shrouded with doubt and illusion.

When you are feeling disgruntled, notice where your thoughts are going. Are you caught up in blaming someone or something else for your circumstances or for the way you are feeling? Life can present obstacles and disappointments, but you can control your response to those situations and choose how you wish to feel and what you want to do about it.

When we become so focused on what we want, we tend to place very specific conditions around our desired outcome. We imagine how things should be, how we want to feel, and what others should be doing according to our own expectations. Sometimes laser focus is necessary to achieve our goals and outcomes, however this needs to be measured with discernment and allow for Divine timing. When we develop expectations of others in order to create our desired outcomes or our version of happiness, we are likely to be disappointed. Our power comes from what we choose to create in our life, not from what others may or may not do.

Can you recall your response to feeling disappointed over something that hasn't gone the way you hoped? I'm sure we can all remember moments of feeling really upset and indignantly complaining about what has not met our own expectations. The ego can have a field day if it's allowed, and emotional outbursts are a signal we have lost control and we no longer have a clear perspective. Our response to disappointment can be directed towards others, such as our loved ones or maybe our work colleague, or we may direct our disappointment inwards as self-criticism and judgment.

Sometimes, in the face of disappointment we may want to retreat to our cave or sink into our well to heal our wounds of disappointment (shame, guilt, sadness, grief, anger, rage, hopelessness). Retreating inwardly may be our way of protecting ourself from further pain. It can be the private place where we seek consolation, solitude and healing. It can also provide us with the opportunity for self-nurturing and time to re-evaluate our situation and our response.

What's difficult to come to terms with is recognising that disappointment is our own. It doesn't belong to someone else, God, or some other thing that we want to blame. Our disappointment is our response to the pain we are feeling or have felt for a very long time. As adults we can experience many situations that trigger childhood memories of feeling misunderstood, unloved, invisible, insignificant or not valued for the unique person we are. We can also be triggered by traumatic events during our life that involve loss, grief, separation, and emotional or physical distress.

There is nothing wrong with experiencing disappointment. What's valuable is to recognise that our feelings are a signal we are being emotionally triggered about unresolved feelings or situations in our life experience or soul journey. There are lessons still to be learned and the emotions we feel when we are disappointed can be helpful in highlighting where we can refocus our attention, so we can continue to learn and grow. The intensity of our response is also a clue as to how affected we are and how much we have invested our beliefs and energy into protecting ourself from pain or hurt.

Being consciously aware and choosing to face our inner truth is an opportunity to understand who we are at a deeper level. We can choose to pour more love and compassion onto any situation that feels confronting or challenging, and this will help to reconnect us with Divine wisdom and provide us more clarity for going forward. Or, we can choose to respond defensively to protect ourself from what we believe will give us more pain.

Even though I have experienced intense personal and spiritual growth, I still succumb to the occasional melt-down and feelings of disappointment. When we are all fired up with emotions, this is not the time to take action or listen to our mind that wants revenge for the pain we are feeling. There have been many times it has been a struggle to prevent myself from acting irrationally in the moment and releasing my pent-up anger upon others. I have learned from past experience that this never works out for the better. I have regretted phone calls, text messages or emails sent in the heat of the moment. I now pause and wait until I feel calm, and rational.

I now give myself the time and space to feel my emotions without judgment or guilt. I may release these feelings with a good sob in the shower, or I will cry into my pillow at night. I know this is one way I can release my emotions and give myself some love and comfort. It's not so much permission to wallow in self-pity, as it is to allow self-healing. It's a cathartic process of release and leaves me feeling nurtured and comforted. Sometimes I prefer to give myself time to process my emotions by writing my thoughts and feelings into a journal, until I feel I have expressed everything I have wanted to voice without self-judgment or imposed restrictions. Once I have acknowledged how I feel and I have released the energy of pent up emotions, I am able to reflect and review my situation and my choices with more clarity and honesty.

It's important to give ourself compassion and forgiveness, rather than direct the pain of disappointment harmfully on ourself or others. When we take responsibility for our own thoughts, feelings and actions, we are truly exercising our self-empowerment and the ability to love and heal our own soul. When we are in the midst of pain, it can be easy to lash out and blame others or behave in a way that disempowers us. Learning to manage our feelings in times of disappointment is how we develop self-love, resilience and our soul-power. Our reality and what we create in our life comes from what we choose to believe, and our ability to love and accept ourself in all situations.

*We are all living our own version of reality. It's our life experiences and soul lessons that form our unique soul-journey.*

Life can be disappointing sometimes, and people will not always behave honestly or with integrity. However, if we choose to make our happiness dependent upon someone else's behaviour, then we are likely to be continually disappointed. When we have expectations of others, or an attitude of entitlement, we will not be satisfied. It's not possible to have our needs met all of the time, especially when we base our happiness or sense of self-worth on external conditions, and what other people will or won't do. Why set ourself up for disappointment and resentment? It only serves to disempower and cause more pain. When we insist on judging ourself or others, we become the victim, and this creates mental havoc and physical illness, which drains life energy and can lead to depression. Living with this disempowering mindset will pull us from our soul-path and before we know it, we are losing our '*joie de vivre*'.

We don't get to control what other people think, say or do. It is far more effective to neutralize conflicting situations by not giving them any more power or energy. It will never serve us well when we are focused on comparing ourself to others. As adults we may think this is obvious, however in that moment of pain, disappointment or rejection, we often resort to those habits of thinking and responding which keep us dependent upon others for our happiness. It also isolates us when we form an internal belief that we are different, not good enough, and separated from everyone else.

With practice you can choose to bring your focus back to what you know you can do to feel good within yourself. It's wise to take time before you act, so that you can be more discerning about your choices and ensure your next steps are based on what's important to you and will nourish and nurture you. Our happiness and well-being are truly what we choose to create for ourself rather than what someone else decides to say or do.

**Pause, Ponder, Reflect**

What can you do to change how you feel? What's another way you can see the situation?

For example, if the relationship you are in is toxic, or not for your highest good, then stop and change direction. This may require you to see things from a different perspective or take a different approach to the situation.

If your work environment is making you feel sick every day (physically, mentally, emotionally), what can you do to change the way you feel about it, or improve your situation so you are supporting your well-being?

Make a list of possibilities or alternative approaches to the situation, then consider sharing this with a trusted friend or counsellor so you can develop a plan to take new action.

In the heat of the moment it can be difficult to know how to respond or what to do next. A great first step is to stop focusing on what is upsetting you, or what's no longer serving you in your life.

Doing a self-check on your thoughts, your beliefs, and what you are telling yourself is taking care of your well-being, in other words, it's an act of self-love. Often when we are feeling frustrated, we can deflect and blame others in an attempt to ease the pain or discomfort. Or, we can turn the blame on ourself and judge ourself for not getting the results we wanted.

How are you managing your thoughts, feelings and reactions? Are you letting your thoughts run away with you? Are you being kind to yourself or do you tell yourself that you have blown it again?

Your attitude and what you choose to believe and focus on is really up to you. You can give your attention to what frustrates you, or you can redirect your thoughts to noticing and feeling grateful for what is working well in your life. You can choose to see the good in someone and your situation or you can pull it apart and highlight all the negatives. If inner peace is what you want in life, then the better option is always to focus on what you can do differently to improve your experience in life.

It's not possible to live without the ups and downs of our challenges. When we adopt a Spirit of Acceptance and know that the challenges are there to teach us in some way, then we can reduce the charge of those negative experiences and our negative emotions. The more gratitude we express and feel in our life, the clearer we are able to see what is working well. When we do this, we open up our heart and our creativity to enter a space that lifts our vibration, which in turn brings new possibilities for thinking, feeling and being.

*Our measure of gratitude affects our attitude.*

## Respecting Yourself

Part of stepping into your soul-power is having respect for yourself. If you allow yourself to get frustrated and upset about your circumstances over and over again, you are giving your power away, which is a lack of respect for your well-being. Truly loving who you are is to respect your physical, emotional and spiritual health and well-being. If you are compromising your values, and not utilizing your time and energy in a way that is good for you, then you are not respecting your authentic self. What are you currently telling yourself or believing about who you are?

The experiences you are having will be a direct reflection of what you believe about your true value and worth. Are you in a job that is aligned with what you truly love to do? Are you spending the majority of your time doing what you value most? Are you living your life with purpose, or are you living to tick boxes? Are you giving your time, energy and talent away for nothing?

Contribution to your community is important, however it's not healthy if you believe that what you are doing is not valuing your time and talent. It's all about what you choose to believe about yourself, rather than the external situation.

The same applies for the relationships in your life. If you are not feeling you are respecting and honouring yourself in the relationship, then it's time to make better choices. Notice, that the focus is whether *you* are respecting *yourself*. There may be plenty of people in life who don't show you honour and respect, and that's not cool. However, it's not about what others say or do, as you cannot control other people. The more you choose to love and respect your authentic self, the more you will attract this into your life.

If the people around you are not behaving respectfully towards you, where are *you* not respecting yourself? What are *you* doing that is not honouring *your* truth and authenticity? Where are *you* compromising your values? How *you* treat yourself is what matters the most. Blaming someone for not respecting you is not taking responsibility for your own life. You can always choose to move away from those who don't match your values, or you can choose to live in a way that is aligned with your values, and live with love, no matter your circumstances. Your energy will either attract or repel others according to how *you* live your life and your measure of self-love. You can choose to love yourself so much that you are no longer willing to compromise. If you choose how you wish to feel in your life, you can also choose to make changes in yourself that honour that commitment.

What is within your power to change? It is not up to other people to change for you. You have the power to choose your response to any situation if you give yourself the time, space and energy to do so. When you respect yourself, then others who do not have the same values will fall away from your life, and those people who resonate with your values, interests and vibration will be attracted to you.

## The strategies we use to deny our soul power

As we learn to access our soul-power and develop self-respect, we better understand the strategies we use when we are not coming from a place of self-empowerment. Heatherash Amara speaks about the roles we may adopt when we are feeling disempowered. Most of the time we have a dominant role that we tend to fall back on, but we can at any time choose to wear other hats depending upon our personal triggers. People may choose to step into the Judge and Victim role, the Controller, the Isolator or the People Pleaser role. You may recognise any one of these roles and use them as a coping strategy when you are feeling disempowered.

Growing up I learned to be a 'People Pleaser'. I believed that doing my best to please other people, to support them and make room in my life for others was the right thing to do. It was a sign of my love for them. What I didn't realise was that every time I did my best to please others, I was also giving myself the unconscious message that I was not good enough or worthy enough to give to myself first. Underneath I believed that other people were more important, more intelligent and more worthy of help, assistance and support.

When this happens to you, don't berate yourself. Just notice when it happens and remind yourself that this is not who you are and that you choose to honour and respect your authentic being. Bring your focus back to you and ask yourself, "Is my thinking and what I am doing honouring my emotional, mental and physical well-being?'" Practice being more loving and compassionate toward yourself. Choose to accept who you are in this moment, without judgment, and know that your value as a person is unchanged, no less or more than anyone else.

If you are someone who adopts the persona of a 'people pleaser' then recognise that you are giving away your personal power in a way that is detrimental to your own well-being. It is the shadow-side of your authentic self that will dis-empower you and dis-associate you from the magnificence of your Divine being. When you don't honour your own value or give equal time to nurturing your growth and well-being, it is disrespecting yourself. It's important to be kind and generous to others, however not to the detriment of your well-being. It's also wise to have healthy personal boundaries, and to know how to draw the line in terms of honouring and respecting your soul and your personal needs. As you take care of you, you will attract more positive elements into your life that will support you and your soul growth.

Adopting the 'People Pleaser' role earlier in my life was the most harmful and unloving thing I could have done to myself. It drained my soul-essence and dulled my ability to hear my Higher Self and the truth of my soul-being. It also blocked my ability to receive spiritual guidance through my intuition. With little self-respect I constantly drained myself so that I felt I was running on empty. Over a long period of time I began to resent having to be generous and to give of my time and energy. Instead of my intentions coming from my heart-space, I was acting from a place where I felt I 'should' do this or that. My 'loving self' gave to others, but my self-critic and inner judge told me that I was not a good person if I did otherwise.

For most of my adult life I was unaware that I had been doing this. I would never have believed that I was disrespecting myself. I always felt that I behaved lovingly towards others, that I acted with integrity and that I applied myself 100% to whatever I was doing in my life. I didn't notice my focus had been mostly on serving the interests of others in order to be accepted, loved or approved. I didn't ask myself if what I was doing was good for me, or even if I enjoyed what I was doing. I became quite passive in terms of my own choices.

Slowly I disconnected from my desires to the point that I no longer knew what I wanted. I allowed other people whom I cared about to make the choices most of the time, which meant I was not valuing myself and I was compromising my own worth. Over a long period of time I felt resentful, neglected, invisible and unimportant. I felt my ability to have choice was dwindling away, and in the workplace I felt unacknowledged. I lost my self-confidence, the awareness of my own skills and abilities, and I became disconnected from what I believed to be my passion in life. I learned to discount my own feelings and allow the agenda of other people to be more important than my own. Over time I lost my voice, my ability to outwardly express my truth. I remember having very intense feelings, and for years I poured these into my journals. However, I found it immensely difficult to say how

I felt out loud. I was afraid that if I spoke my truth, I would not be understood, and I would be rejected.

After a while I became quite numb and I found myself consistently sitting on the fence and not taking leadership of my own life. I made choices that were more limiting and as a result I blocked my own 'sunshine' and this caused me to significantly delay my personal and spiritual development. There were times I blamed other people and circumstances for my lack of progress in my career and in my relationships. I now take full responsibility for the outcomes, only now I have a new love and respect for my soul-journey rather than self-criticism. We are where we are in our life as a result of our focus, what we believe about ourself, and what we have chosen to do or not do.

This is my soul-journey and all the lessons, the pain, the challenges, and the achievements, were there to teach me more about myself, and for that I am grateful. I now realise that any pain I feel is a result of my mind not getting what it wants. In truth, we create our own suffering, regardless of what other people do or not do. It is how we perceive ourself, our value, our worth and what we interpret from any situation.

When we make choices from our fearful mind, we unconsciously decide that a small compromise here and there is what you do to keep the status quo or to ensure your need for security is met. What I didn't realise is that over a longer period of time, the little compromises I made day-to-day compounded to make a huge difference in my life. It not only affected the relationship I had with myself, but it also affected the relationship with my husband, my children and my work colleagues. I became very unhappy, resentful and judgmental. This led me to feeling like a victim without any way of changing my circumstances.

There were many gains I received from putting others before myself and allowing them to lead the way. One of my drivers was to feel constant connection and companionship. This gave me security and comfort. As a child I suffered from separation anxiety, and so the security of being with others filled a void. It also meant that if I appeased other people and allowed them to have their needs met before my own, then they would be happy. I believed that if I gave my all they would approve of me, and they would have no reason to leave me or reject me.

The Pleaser invariably becomes the person who seeks to fix everyone's problems and maintain peace and harmony for all. I was the good wife, mother, daughter, and daughter-in-law. I was also the chief counsellor, problem-solver, organizer and facilitator. It's not that being a caring and compassionate person for others is bad or wrong, it is wonderful. However, it is unhealthy when we do not take care of ourself or honour ourself and our own boundaries.

Generosity and compassion are the qualities of a spiritually mature adult. This is how we aspire to be when we are working towards becoming the best version of ourself. I am not advocating that we become selfish and uncaring of others or disconnected from showing empathy for other people. However, if we constantly think, feel and act in ways that disrespect our own needs, desires and values, then we are negating our own value and worth. As a result, we become disconnected from, and out of alignment with, our personal soul-power and the true essence of our being.

Other roles we may adopt in our life when we are feeling hurt, challenged, or disempowered may be the Controller, the Isolator or the Judge & Victim. Depending upon our measure of pain, hurt or disappointment we may feel at any time, we can easily slip into the role of being the Judge & Victim. When we're feeling hurt it's a common human response to want to criticize or blame the person we believe has caused us pain. I've caught myself doing this, using my energy and my words to direct my anger toward someone who has done something I have found incredibly hurtful. Similarly, I have criticized myself for being hopeless or a loser when my plans have not worked out or my dreams were unfulfilled yet again.

When we allow our mind to take over with cascading thoughts of judgment and self-criticism, there is a tendency to replay the 'story' over and over in our head. We can fall into the pattern of thinking and believing we are hardly-done-by, and so we are a victim to life's cruel intentions. Have you heard yourself say that life is unfair and that you always get the bad end of a deal? Have you complained that things never work out for you? Or moaned that people are so selfish, uncaring, and unsympathetic to your needs and how you feel? The Judge & Victim role is totally disempowering. In this role you consistently give your power away to the other person or situation. You give up your responsibility for managing your own thoughts, feelings and happiness, and you step into the 'blame' zone.

The <u>Controller</u> is another role or strategy we play when we feel overwhelmed or out of control in our own life. The Controller seeks to gain control or reassert their position when they feel they have lost it. When we play this role, we often live by a firm set of rules and conditions about how our life should be, how others should behave, and the outcomes we expect from ourself, our family, friends and work colleagues. The Controller becomes so focused on the external world that they become driven by the need to have everything match perfectly to their idea of how things should be done, or how others should behave. Sadly, it limits all possibility for genuine creativity and for other opportunities in life to come forth. The happiness or sense of fulfilment eludes the person who seeks to consistently control their world as they are reliant upon their external circumstances to match their obsessive need to have things match their criteria for what is acceptable. With a *Spirit of Trust*, they could choose to be more open to other alternatives and perspectives and open the way to unlimited opportunities. As we let go of our need to control, we can experience greater inner peace.

The <u>Isolator</u> has a tendency to want to retreat from the world and from social contact more often than not. It's a distraction, just as being a Controller is a method of distracting ourself from facing our inner truth and learning to embrace our emotions and feelings. As we move closer to becoming an emotionally and spiritually mature adult, we become more willing to accept our feelings and take responsibility for them, rather than suppress them as we may have learned in our childhood. Our feelings are there to help us by highlighting where we are out of balance or that something needs to be resolved. They are wonderful indicators to get our attention so we can examine why we may be feeling what we feel. When we better understand our reactions and responses to changes in our life, we can make more positive and healthy changes.

When we choose to ignore our emotions and feelings, and our inner guidance, we resort to adopting unhealthy strategies to suppress or deny our feelings. Adopting the roles mentioned above takes an enormous amount of physical, mental and emotional energy to sustain on a continual basis. When we relax and accept the essence of who we are and honour our real feelings, we become aligned with our Higher Self. It's only then that we can recognise our true self, our inner calling and our soul-purpose.

## Living from your Soul-Power

When I was experiencing significant change, growth and transformation in my life, I struggled to manage my own emotions, and this caused me considerable pain and inner conflict. I had not learned how to love and respect myself, and I lived for other people. This became a huge distraction that allowed me to avoid taking personal responsibility for the outcomes in my life. I also avoided stepping up and making changes that that would allow me to be my authentic self.

I had courage to a degree, and a determination to learn and improve myself. This was reflected in my desire to attend various educational and personal development courses, and to seek ways to extend my roles and responsibilities in my jobs and parish community. However, at a deeper level, I was not claiming *all* of my truth. I was nervous and fearful about stepping out of the familiar comfort zone of my family life, social circle and work colleagues. My avoidance strategy kept me from facing my fears, which was to shine my own light and risk being different to what other people wanted or expected of me. I realised that pouring so much energy into making excuses and blaming others was just a waste of time. If I truly wanted to be happy and to live as my true self, then I needed to make real changes.

I had an intense fear of disappointing other people and not being accepted or loved. I wanted to live as my true self, and yet deep down I wanted to make changes so that I could feel free and live in a way that was aligned with my truth and my personal values. I had finally awakened to the truth that the choices I had made in my life, and the way I was thinking, had created my reality and my current circumstances. It was not because of other people, but what I chose to believe and do along the way.

Often, we can travel down the path of our life, making small decisions here and there, not realizing that each small decision will influence the next one, and the next one. Each step, each choice, builds upon the previous one and reinforces the path we choose to walk. We may not think at the time that a compromise here or there will have a big impact on the direction of our life, but over a long period of time it makes a huge difference. Jeff Olson, author of the "Slight Edge", provides wonderful examples of how the smallest of decisions on a regular basis, compound to make a big difference. If we are really committed to becoming our true self and follow our soul-purpose, then every choice we make will either lead us in the direction of being the best version of ourself and living a successful life, or it will lead us down the path of compromise, poor health and dis-satisfaction.

After years of not loving or respecting myself, I realised I needed to think and do things differently. I was responsible for what I was experiencing and yet it took me a while to connect what I knew, with my actions. That's why we can repeatedly make the same mistake over and over. The more we continue to act out the same patterns of thinking and doing, the more we believe we have no choice and our results become the evidence of what we believe.

Whilst I had gained some new clarity and awareness of myself and my choices, it took a long time and multiple experiences for me to make the necessary changes, to feel safe to unlock the chains to my heart and connect with my true feelings. Slowly I learned that the path to self-love was to develop compassion and forgiveness for myself and to not hide from my truth. Mentally beating myself up for my choices is not an act of self-love or respect. I could hear my angels say to me – *Breathe and take a moment to pause. This is the golden opportunity. You can change this, and it's not dependent upon anyone else.*

Self-respect is the highest form of self-love. It's simple. Don't do what is not good for you. Take stock of where you are putting your time and your energy. Ask yourself whether what you are doing is giving you great joy and fulfillment, or are you resenting what you are doing? What is the feedback you are getting in life? If there is any inner conflict, then take note of this. It is a signal that something is not quite right for you and you are possibly making compromises. It's so important to avoid slipping into denial. Be honest with yourself. If not, a willingness to deny your truth will later lead to even greater pain and suffering.

Taking care of our well-being and treating ourself with love and compassion, shows we are able to come from a place of healing and love. It's only then that we are able to give unconditionally, without attachments to other people, outcomes or reward. Unless we have done the work on ourself, and truly come to love all of our being, regularly practicing self-love, compassion and self-care, we cannot truly give unconditionally to others. When we are healed and centred in our heart and connected to our soul-purpose, we are able to emanate a loving energy that allows other people to grow in self-love and self-awareness. This is how we are able to honour and respect the well-being and happiness of others, without expecting them to give in return or behave in a certain way that meets our needs or expectations.

We may have been raised or conditioned to believe that being a martyr and giving at the expense of our own well-being is the 'right' thing to do. When we reflect on the lives of great spiritual masters, such as Jesus Christ, Buddha, Krishna, Paramahansa Yogananda, they all took time out to tend to their needs and to realign with their Soul and Divine purpose. They did not compromise their values or step away from their soul-purpose. They gave generously and compassionately, and yet they balanced this with respecting their time and energy, so they were living true to their soul's purpose. When we live by our values, then we can respond from a place of clarity and self-empowerment.

As sensitive spiritual beings, we are going to feel the highs of joy and the depths of sorrow. Our feelings and our emotions are interpretations of our own experiences and what we choose to believe about ourself in the process of our soul growth. Learning to embrace all of who and what you are is self-love and self-respect. The experiences you have are not there to harm you but to help you better understand yourself and the path towards True Love. As you become more aware you will be able to use what you see, hear, feel and know to assist you on your soul-journey, and recognise the ways you are holding yourself back from being the best version of yourself.

Time and energy wasted on regrets and feelings of resentment in life are a waste of time and opportunity that is there to bless you. See the light in the people and situations around you and notice that what appears to be a negative situation has actually presented itself to help you see what is not good for you.

Developing a habit of gratitude in your life is the path to self-love and self-respect. When you live with gratitude, you are able to see that the Universe is there to love you and show you infinite ways for you to grow and experience joy. The choice is actually yours. Remember, we are the creators of our life. How we treat ourself, the level of love, compassion and respect we have for our being, is the same energy we attract into our life and our experiences. Our reality is what we actually choose it to be.

Directing negative feelings of poor self-worth, anger, resentment and rejection back onto yourself is the worst form of self-abuse. In time it will eat away at you and destroy the life and the love within you. If you allow thoughts, beliefs and feelings that you are not worthy of love, or that you are not good enough to invest in your inner-being, then you will begin to shut down. Your world will feel like it is shrinking, because you lose sight of what is beautiful in you and those around you. The lens through which you see life becomes discoloured, blurring your vision so that all you see in others is what you feel about yourself. Your body will begin to withdraw and respond with ailments and dis-ease, and your relationships will feel less nurturing or inspiring, because you are snuffing out your own flame within. Remember, it's the little things that count. Every day those negative beliefs, the self-doubts, the simmering resentment, slowly builds beneath the surface, and you may not even be consciously aware of these thoughts. Until, one day, someone or something triggers your emotions and you have a response that reminds you that your heart is not healed in this place.

It is highly likely that in your life you will be disappointed over and over again. However, if you see all situations as yet another opportunity for you to strengthen the love within yourself (just like *the magical kitchen* that Don Miguel Ruiz describes in his book "The Master of Love"), then you will have enough love and resources within you to never be bothered by what happens outside of yourself. What other people think and do is actually their business, and a reflection of their own soul-journey, not yours. So, forgive them and allow them to get on with their journey, it is not yours.

Meanwhile, your focus is *your* life, and how you are experiencing love within yourself. The more you 'top up your cup' or nurture yourself, the easier it is for you to connect to your heart and personally know the experience of loving you. In time you will have so much love to give you will never feel starved or in deprivation. You will be like a light in the dark that will attract other people who see the light and love within you. As you focus on this in your life and you learn to see the beauty in you, you will have no need for destructive and self-deprecating thoughts.

The path to self-love is truly the path to living a life of joy and happiness. When we take good care of our well-being, then all other aspects of our life fall into place. When we have developed a love and appreciation of our body, we respect the body by making choices to eat nutritious food that raises our energy and helps us to function at our optimum. Our choices are matched with the love and respect we have for our true self.

The relationships we have in our life will also reflect our choices. When we have love for ourself we become more discerning about how we spend our time and with whom we spend it. When we truly love who we are, our uniqueness, what we have learned through our own life experiences, our gifts and talents, and how we interact with others, will be reflected back to us. As we value and love ourself, others will do the same; and if they don't, then they will fall away from our focus and our life.

Travelling the path of our soul-journey leads us to that beautiful realization that we are all connected, and we are each gifted in a way to serve a particular purpose. As we become increasingly conscious and aware of our spiritual essence, it awakens our desire to learn and grow. However, it can be easy to become absorbed and overly focused on consuming everything that is new. It's exciting to learn and grow, especially as we see transformation in our life bringing new opportunities. However, we need to be in flow in life so that we can balance what we are receiving, with how we can contribute or give to others.

As we receive in our life it's important to recognise that things, people, and places are there for either a reason, a season or a lifetime. What we receive is not necessarily there for us to keep or hold on to. Being a good steward in life is about being grateful for what is given to us, what we have drawn into our experience and life, and to use these opportunities and blessings wisely. When we have benefitted from the blessings given to us, it's important we pass on these blessings to others, or release them when the time or purpose is complete. This can be applied to things we possess, our job, relationships in our life or particular circumstances that present for a period of time.

## Self-Love for Empowerment

Everything we experience in life is a result of the way we see our reality and what we choose to believe is there or not there. If we truly love ourself then we can choose to see life through a lens of love, forgiveness and acceptance, without a need or desire to control others or our circumstances. When we have love for ourself, we are able to develop an abundance of love for others, regardless of our circumstances, how other people behave or what they say. To be empowered is to truly see all of our worth and to believe that abundance is everywhere if we choose to see it. It is never out of our reach.

When we appreciate our value and self-worth, we actively choose to empower ourself to create what we want to manifest in our life. It's a conscious choice to see the possibilities and opportunities, and then act upon these choices by taking steps to bring our dreams to fruition.

To do this we must recognise that we have the ability and the resources to do whatever we set our intention to do and who we want to be. Empowering ourself is not just a thought or a decision, it requires love and belief in ourself. Without self-love we are unlikely to be committed to achieving our very best in life.

John Holland, in his book "Power of the Soul", reminds us of our inner power and our ability to create our own inner sanctuary. Our inner sanctuary is a place where we can retreat within to give ourself the rest and nourishment we need. It's the place we love to be, and how we love to feel. It has all of the qualities that make us feel happy, joyful, peaceful, inspired, rested and spiritually fulfilled. It looks, feels, smells, and sounds exactly as we may imagine the most delightful place that our soul longs to experience.

What we believe we are experiencing has the same effect as if we are actually physically experiencing it in our body. Our hormonal response to our imagined world is as powerful as the physical reality. If this is the case, then it demonstrates the power of our intentions, the combination of our mind and the psychic energy we generate by what we feel, sense and believe.

Visualising love and abundance in your experience of your reality is therefore possible. You can choose to feel empowered, or you can choose to feel forever in a state of lack, ineffective in your own life and without the ability to choose how to think, feel and respond to your life. Rather than give energy and focus to feeling hurt, angry, resentful, hopeless or disempowered in any way, you can decide to see, feel and experience love instead. Love yourself. Love the person you are. Decide to see your world and others in it as beings of light and love. You can imagine, visualize, and create the way you want to experience your life. Put colour into your life.

*"Be your greatest version" (Ralph Smart)*

We forget we are powerful creators. If you don't want to wake up every morning feeling lifeless, then choose differently. Rather than adopt the attitude or self-talk that you are 'surviving' each day, notice what there is to be grateful for, even in the smallest of things. Who wants to live as if life is a drudgery every day? Do you want to be just surviving? Why not thriving? The way you decide to feel each day is exactly the experience you are going to have.

So how do you want to feel when you wake up? Do you want to feel happy to be in your own skin? Do you want to feel loving toward yourself and see each day as another opportunity to feel gratitude in your life? Our attitude and what we tell ourself the moment we wake makes all the difference to how we embrace our day and the experiences we will have. For quite some time I struggled with the early morning blues, so I made the decision to get up and get moving. My joy elixir is going for an early morning walk by the beach. What can you do to inspire, nurture and love yourself in those waking moments of your day? When we start the day with a good attitude and we are mindful of our well-being, we set ourself up for success by being open to possibilities.

> *Love, compassion and gratitude are what build the*
> *foundation for living an empowered life.*

Build the habit of seeing the mini-miracles in your life each day. Stop waiting to win the lottery, or for that man in shining armour to whisk you off your feet and take care of you, or for perfectly harmonious relations in your family or at work. Miracles do happen. Sometimes they are big and incredible, but mostly we are surrounded by mini-miracles every day. What are you noticing?

If we expect to feel pain, to feel the drudgery of a treadmill going to work each day, or to feel lethargic and unmotivated by the same routine, then that's exactly the experience we are create for ourself. Check your inner voice. What are you telling yourself every day? Your life and your reality is not what someone else creates for you. Your life is not the result of what 'happens to you'. There will always be external circumstances beyond our control, however we can choose our response to these circumstances, and therefore choose our experience of how we live our life. Our beliefs, interpretations, perceptions and our choices are what create our reality.

We are not victims of our circumstances or other people's bad moods or beliefs. That is *their* reality. Life is happening 'for' you, not 'to' you. We are created from the same Divine essence, and yet we each have our own 'flavour'. Get to know who you are and love *your* flavour. You can't be anyone else, so you may as well love who *you* are. Empower yourself by loving who you are and begin with visualizing and creating the reality you wish to live every day. Start with being mindful over small things, such as choosing how you want to feel, and then choose what you do with that. Know that the Universe is there to support you, not drain you or remove you from existence.

*Life is happening 'for' you, not 'to' you.*

To live an empowered life, it's important you don't spend time living someone else's life instead of your own. Rather than be in 'their' world, live and be in 'your' world. Abraham Hicks says - *be tuned in, tapped on and turned on, so that the whole of you is having the experience in your life.* Your empowerment, your ability to live well and contribute in life is happening 'now'. It is not in the past, nor is it in the future. Everything is only 'now'. Take a step back and ask yourself, How am I *being* now?

Notice what are you observing and taking in. What are you thinking and believing about yourself? What are you choosing to feel? When we are mindful of our choices, we increase our sense of awareness of ourself, our surroundings and the opportunities available to us. To be empowered in your life is to recognise you have choice in every moment. If you fill your life with worry, it will influence your perspective on life so that you tend to see only obstacles and limitations. If you fill your being with love, and choose to see the possibilities in life, you empower yourself with powerful manifesting energy, and you become a beacon for others. What you think, believe and do creates more of this in your reality.

To reconnect with your soul-being and your sense of self, use this loving meditation to raise your spiritual vibration and your self-awareness. It will assist you to connect to the Divine love within you, the centre and source of soul-loving and self-empowerment.

## A Loving Meditation:

*Close your eyes for a moment and feel your breath flow in and out of your nostrils.*

*Imagine all the love and lightness that you can visualize as sparkling stars above your head, moving and twinkling. Then see and feel this loving light and energy enter your auric field from the top of your head (your crown) and slowly flow down into your body, your arms and hands, through your heart, chest, abdomen and down through your legs, feet and toes. Feel it fill your whole body.*

*As it expands within you, feel the light seep into every corner of your body, pushing out the darkness, the toxins, and any discomfort. Feel the warmth of the love expand within.*

*Breathe slowly and observe the nourishment and the life source that is raising your vibration. Allow the energy to flow through every cell in your body. Feel its healing presence and notice it washing away your troubles and worries. Observe the peace within that lifts your vibration.*

*When you are ready, wriggle your toes and fingers and slowly open your eyes.*

*Know that you are a being of love and light and filled with the Divine energy of Source (God).*

# 17
## Tending to your Soul Garden

Your soul-being, your body and your mind is a Divine garden. What you plant in it determines what you will eventually harvest. The nutrients you feed into the soil, is the loving energy and intentions you give to your soul garden. The way you tend to your garden will be reflected in the quality of what you produce or manifest in your life. Treat your garden with love and care. Ask yourself, what do you want your garden to look like, feel like, smell like and produce? How do you want to feel in the garden of your body, mind and soul? What do you want to do with the fruits of your garden?

Your garden is forever changing with the seasons and requires your love and attention. At times it will need weeding of what has finished its purpose, or what is draining the goodness from the soil. The soil of your garden is the foundation of your mental, emotional, and physical health. What your garden contributes to others will reflect your spiritual well-being.

Other times your garden will need preparation, nutrients, watering and time to rest, as the seeds you have planted take time to settle and germinate. The seeds of your garden are your thoughts, beliefs, and the energy you put into your spiritual development. Over time these seeds will develop a deeper knowing and connection with Divine Love and wisdom that infiltrates your being. Greatness does not come from a garden of weeds and neglect. It comes from loving intentions, conscious action and the desire to share its produce with others.

## When True Love eludes us

Sometimes it may seem that True Love (*Divinely inspired love*) is constantly eluding us. The soul-journey is all about the ups and downs, the twists and turns along the path to understanding ourself and learning how to experience True Love. Yet, we can often feel a lack of progress for all of our effort, as if we are spinning our wheels and going nowhere.

Often, in our search for true love, we expend a lot of energy seeking this outside of ourself, such as from our partners, family and friends, from the rewards of our career, or from the projects in which we heavily invest our time and energy. We can create an intense focus on what we want to manifest in terms of love, and as a result we often face disappointment and a lack of fulfilment instead. Our measure of love and fulfilment cannot be found in our external environment. When we expect to be fulfilled by the results of our efforts, what people will give us, or how our job or projects will satisfy our need for self-worth and financial success, we will not find true love that is sustainable, or the kind of deep soul fulfilment we are seeking.

True love, self-empowerment, and a deep acceptance of our soul-being, comes from within and not from our circumstances. If we are fortunate to reap the rewards of our efforts in life, this is a gift and a blessing. However, without self-love and a respect for who we are, sustainable and lasting love and fulfilment will always elude us. When the storms of life come, our circumstances will change. Without strong roots, a foundation of love and respect for who we are, we cannot withstand the changes we are likely to experience in life.

A strong foundation comes from the seeds we plant, in terms of our beliefs, how we to choose to think, and our willingness to come from a perspective of Divine Love. It can take time to cultivate True Love and compassion for one self. In tending to the garden of our heart and soul, we must prepare the soil by removing the weeds of untruths and the false perceptions. If we attempt to grow love from within, without removing the illusions, the fears, and the limiting beliefs about ourself, we cannot expect to manifest a life of love and abundance. It takes time to do the inner work, however it's necessary. Unless we see ourself worthy of the effort, and unless we have compassion for ourself to allow healing to take place, we will not be able to tap into the Divine love that exists within.

Tending to the garden of our heart and soul is not easy or a frivolous exercise, as if you can apply a formula and suddenly expect instant results. Soul-work requires acknowledging the weeds in our mind and in our heart, accepting they need to be removed, and making the committed effort to do the work. It may take time, as well as some set-backs, however it's possible to replace these weeds with new ways of thinking and believing, and new behaviours that demonstrate love and compassion for oneself. These are our soul-lessons and how we help ourself through the transformation of our soul, as we move towards greater love, Divine Love.

Until we are able to cultivate love for our Soul and our unique self, we are unable to share this with others. Relationships are necessary for many reasons. They can help us to grow and learn more about ourself and enable us to love and value our uniqueness. This can happen through the contrasts we experience with another person, as well as the deep caring and unconditional love and sharing that happens in a partnership. However, often we fall into the habit of expecting love to be given to us, without first learning how to generate that love within ourself. Knowing how to tend to our own needs for love and nurturing, without attachment to another person, is a sign of real love for oneself.

So, it is equally necessary to give time for True Love and spiritual maturity to be cultivated outside of a relationship with another.

## Barriers to experiencing True Love

Dependency upon another is perhaps one of the biggest blocks to experiencing True Love for one self. In our early soul-journey we can be tempted to measure self-love and self-worth according to the amount and frequency of love, attention and approval we receive from others. When we are living from our ego mind and not from our heart and soul, it can be easy to see love as an object we need to attain, control and hold on to, rather than seeing it as a natural resource within our being.

We may have lived many years in dependent relationships where our sense of worthiness, safety and emotional security has been based on the love we have expected to receive from others. At first it can be difficult to recognise this, especially when we have conditioned ourself to live, think and behave in a certain way when we are in relationship with someone else. When we see love in this way, we are often not consciously aware that we have developed our sense of worth based on our need and desire for love and approval from others. Our past relationships or life experiences may not have assisted our understanding of what it means to live with love for one self. So, the idea of what True Love is and what we want to experience in life, may have been limited or based on poor examples.

The need to control is another barrier to True Love. The ego-self seeks to control and attain love by holding on to it for fear of losing love. When we live in fear, we can spend so much focus and energy on aligning ourself with the opinions of others, seeking their approval of who we are, and what we say and do. The ego constantly seeks the experience of love through what we believe we can gain from others or from material things. When we focus all of our attention on what we believe we must obtain outside of ourself, we stand to lose the same. Desiring to manipulate or control others in order to have love, will drive away the true love and fulfilment we want to experience. When we believe we lack love in our life, this becomes our daily reality. Our focus on what we believe we do not have, gives more power and energy to what we believe is missing in our life.

True Love emanates from our heart, rather than from what we believe we gain from outside of ourself. The ego works by controlling our thoughts, which then affects our feelings, our choices and our behaviour. When we are able to master our thoughts (what we choose to tell ourself is true) we can release from the controlling ego-mind and focus our energy on sensing, feeling and communicating from our heart.

*The ego mind seeks to control through fear, which*
*is always a barrier to True Love.*

Pride is another barrier to experiencing True Love. When we become full of pride and our own self-importance, we fill our mind with the belief that we don't need anyone else. This leads to a desire to be separate and independent of others and causes selfish behaviour. It is when we become predominantly focussed on serving our own needs without consideration of the needs of others. The self-focus is only shifted when there is a perceived opportunity to receive from another without equal exchange. This self-focus is not self-love. The pride that comes from a desire for significance at the expense of others, drives away love, and leads us away from the path to True Love (Divine Love). Divine Love is not self-serving, it is life-giving and respects the connectedness of all beings.

Self-love aims to love and nourish oneself with the intention of being better able to love others through acts of compassion, kindness and contribution. Acts of pride and self-importance closes the heart and fills the mind with competitive and comparative thoughts in order to gain ahead of others. It does not leave room for expansion of the heart or spiritual growth and understanding. The focus becomes more about *'what can I get'* rather than *'what can I give'*, even when the giving is to love oneself and all of our parts.

*Be the Love you want to experience*

Real love is not something we possess, it is life-giving energy that is expressed through our actions, either toward ourself or another person. When we are experiencing True Love, it is expressed from our heart and soul as a desire to more deeply connect with our Divine nature. This soul-love is a heart-based intention, not only a decision from our mind, that leads to *love in action*. The starting point is a willingness to be open and emotionally vulnerable in order to feel and experience the wholeness of what is soul-love. Love is not selfish, nor is it a measure of what we can take or consume for our own benefit. Love is an act of giving and receiving from our heart and our soul.

In the Christian bible we are reminded of what True Love is: <u>1 Corinthians 13:4-8 (NIV)</u>

> *"⁴Love is patient, love is kind. It does not envy, it does not boast, it is not proud. ⁵ It does not dishonour others, it is not self-seeking, it is not easily angered, it keeps no record of wrongs. ⁶ Love does not delight in evil but rejoices with the truth. ⁷ It always protects, always trusts, always hopes, always perseveres. ⁸ Love never fails."*

We come to learn what True Love is when we put love into action. It's about living the experience of love, since love is not something that is static or something that we claim to own or have. It's a way of being and living. In Christian teachings the Latin word 'Magis' refers to 'more' or 'better' in relation to love. It's about living with more love, doing more for love, feeling more love and giving more love, for ourself, for others and for God (Jesus Christ, Source, Universe, Holy Spirit).

In Buddhism, love is referred to as the path to spiritual freedom. Both Christianity and Buddhism (and many other spiritual practices) share a common understanding of what love is and is not. Love that involves clinging, lust, confusion, neediness, fear, or grasping to self is seen as expressions of attachments and limitations. True Love is expressed and lived as kindness, compassion, appreciative joy, and through equanimity, or calmness and composure in difficult situations.

## *Love is timeless, inclusive, universal and life-giving*

It is possible for all people to develop their capacity to love; it's a matter of finding the key to unlock the door to our heart and be willing to practice even the smallest measure of love each day. Living a life full of love is like developing a muscle to be strong, constant and dependable. It is strengthened with practice over time. Each act, thought, intention and step towards living with more love adds more essence to our Soul so we are feeling more fulfilled with more love to share with others. To experience real freedom through love is to be able to develop the practice of living with more love in all aspects of our life, even in the more challenging moments, and to be loving with all people we encounter.

Sometimes it can feel difficult to maintain a measure of self-love on a consistent basis. When life is flowing well, and we experience a sense of ease, there can be a temptation to be less conscious of practicing self-love and demonstrating our love and gratitude for others. When we experience chaos and conflict which often results from allowing thoughts of self-doubt, fear and comparison to infiltrate our being, we dull our conscious awareness, and this can dilute our essence of love. The seed of separation that comes from our ego mind seeks to compare our self-worth and value with other people. When we focus on who is right and who is wrong, who is better, more skilled, more intelligent, more financial, more successful, more beautiful, more powerful, then we are not living the experience of True Love.

When we measure our experience of love in terms of what we believe we are worth or what we have achieved in our life, we create a perceived void of separation. If you are always thinking of yourself and others in this way you will consistently fall short of experiencing love for yourself. Every thought and act that separates us from others and from Source, is not an act of True Love. If we allow our mind to distract us, it will lead us away from the path to True Love and from our connection to Source. True Love is to fully appreciate all of who you are, and to see value and worth in your soul-being. Love is unifying, strengthening, and liberating.

Understanding our uniqueness is different to believing we are separate. It is true we are all born with unique gifts and talents, and during the course of our life we learn skills and acquire certain knowledge to help us grow. Our background and life experiences are lessons for our soul's growth, so we can develop in wisdom and in our capacity to love more deeply. As we grow in love and wisdom, we actually grow closer to our connection to the Source of Love, which is God. When we truly love all of our soul-being, we bridge the gap of our perceived discrepancies, and we become 'one' in the experience of Love.

The way we express love for our being is often through the power of the 'word', firstly through our thoughts and our beliefs. Words are very powerful, and when used inappropriately they can become a barrier to our ability to experience self-love. If words are an expression of our thoughts, we need to be aware of what we tell ourself out loud and in the privacy of our mind. We each carry a library of words, coloured by our life experiences and the personal meaning we give to these words.

Words have the power to lovingly uplift or to dis-empower us in a moment. When we express our thoughts through words, we are invoking a mental, emotional and physical response within our being based on the meaning we give these words. The words we use can be a hindrance to the way we see our self-worth, and the measure of love and care we have for our own being. The way we speak about ourself, in our mind or out loud, *does* matter. Our thoughts and our words create our energy and our reality, what we believe about ourself and the way we see others and our world.

How many times a day have you noticed that you berate your own self-worth or ability, even if in your own mind? We are often our own worst critic, even before we have voiced our thoughts to others. One of the keys to experiencing more peace and more love in life is to stop complaining. Every time we utter words of complaint and dissatisfaction, even over the smallest of things, or even when we feel justified (and we usually do), we create holes in our energy bubble and in our heart, which causes leaks that drain our love energy from our soul-being. Whether it's a complaint in our thoughts or through our speech, every time we engage in negative talk we move away from the experience of love, peace and happiness in our Soul and in our life.

*Our words can either uplift and empower us,*
*or they can be a barrier to our self-worth and self-love.*

Self-deprecation and a lack of appreciation of your worth can block your ability to love all of who you are and to see your true potential. Developing a spirit or attitude of love, kindness and compassion for yourself may not be something familiar to you. Be careful of what you think and what you say. Your thoughts and words reflect your true beliefs about yourself. They are powerful, and they will direct what you choose to do and how you behave. Speaking of yourself in ways that undermines your value blocks your ability to see options before you and how you can grow and attract more abundance in your relationships, career, finances, and for your health.

Our learned responses to different ways of thinking and behaving may have been influenced by our upbringing, the model of our parents or teachers, our cultural or religious background, or what we have been consistently told and therefore believed about ourself. Whatever your personal history and the path you have travelled to bring you to this point in your life, it is possible to alter your previous patterns of thinking and what you choose to believe about yourself. Remember, it is your life and you get to decide how you want to experience it.

Be the Love you want to experience, and the calm you want to feel. Give yourself the kindness and compassion you deserve and be patient with yourself. It may take some time for you to develop a new way of thinking, feeling and being. When we have lived for years with certain beliefs about ourself, it can take a while to change those super 'neural' highways in our brain and therefore think and do things differently. With practice in being mindful of what you tell yourself, you can eventually begin to grow and strengthen new neural pathways in your brain that reflect healthy and affirming ways of thinking. The path to True Love is not through denigrating your value and self-worth. It is paved through love, kindness, compassion, and forgiveness, as well as developing courage to release the bonds of previous negative self-talk and limiting beliefs. Remember, it takes practice, so you need to consciously decide to be mindful about how you talk about yourself. Change does not happen by doing the same thing over and over again.

Sometimes we may need to step away from the noise of our own mind and our regular routine to see ourself and our circumstances more clearly. Let me ask you…*are you feeling the way you want to feel about yourself? Are you getting the outcomes in your life that inspire you and bring you joy?* There will be times in your life where you will benefit from reflecting and re-assessing your direction and what is important to you. Making a slight change to your routine will give you the opportunity to see your life and yourself from a different perspective. It's a bit like taking a holiday, which provides a different atmosphere and environment to help alter your energy and shift your focus. Small changes can be all that's needed to see things differently. It could be a walk outside in nature, or catching up on a hobby that you love, meeting with friends, practicing yoga, getting outside in the sun or helping a neighbour. Take a moment to pause and *observe* what feels different.

## Pause. Ponder. Reflect

Be curious about what changes you can make and explore how you feel when you make these changes. When you feel the energy shift inside, ask yourself –

- What feels different?
- What are you now telling yourself that is different to before?
- Are you kinder and less judgmental of yourself?
- Are you more curious and open to exploring other options?
- What do you love doing that you forgot about when you were on the treadmill of your job and life in general?

- What do you now see, feel and appreciate about yourself?

- Who do you need to be, and what do you need to do differently to nurture your soul-being?

Give yourself some time to consider what you can do differently in your life that is more loving of yourself. Examine how it makes you feel when you make even small changes. You may find writing your answers in a journal helpful for reflection and gaining clarity around what feels new in your life as you grow in love for your true self.

A change in routine can bring about a new perspective that provides the opportunity to see things more clearly and help us to reconnect with our true self. When we are under pressure or feeling stressed and drained by our routine, it can lead to developing a low estimation of ourself and cause us to make impulsive decisions that generate unwanted outcomes that don't reflect our soul- purpose, which is to move towards living with greater love.

Time away from the normal routine can enhance our appreciation of our own self-worth, the gratitude we feel for other people and the circumstances in our life. What's showing up in our life is usually there to mirror back what needs our attention and action. When we give ourself time to pause and listen to our Higher Self, we can assess more clearly what we can do to create a shift in our life that is more loving and empowers us to live in a way that is more authentic to our true soul-being.

Begin with recording your ideas for changes that you would like to make either on paper, on your computer, in a voice memo or even in a video. Be sure you do this with purpose, loving intention and without judgment. Remember, the purpose of creating change is to live your life with more love, so that you can open yourself to the possibilities in life, rather than diminish your growth and your happiness. Changes do not need to be big, even the smallest of adjustments to your usual way of thinking and doing things will make a difference to the way you feel about yourself. The benefit is that when you articulate what you notice needs your attention and the positive changes you would like to make, you are committing to making a change for the better, by thinking and doing things differently.

As you make adjustments, it's okay to notice what you don't like or what hasn't been working. Avoid slipping into self-criticism, blame or even denial as you begin to face what has been in the past. See your previous experiences as valuable feedback and recognise that you are now well-informed so that you can choose more wisely going forward.

Rather than spend too much time and energy reflecting on the past, shift your focus to what you can do differently, and what is a better match for how you want to feel and what you want to experience more of in your life now. If you have not recognised your unique skills, talents, and gifts, then spend some time doing this. Acknowledge the real you and accept the magnificent soul-being that you are. This is not a 'compare and judge' yourself session, nor is it time to make a mental list about what you believe is not good enough about yourself. Every person is made from the Divine and is therefore inherently magnificent. Your Soul and Higher Self knows the beauty of *all* of you.

*There is only one you. You are special, you are loved, and you matter. You are in this world for a reason and a purpose. It is time to notice this and tune in to your Soul.*

Our ego is a large barrier to True Love. The ego is the part of ourself that is driven by doubt and fear and leads us down a path away from our true self. The ego expresses itself through the chattering mind that tends to over-think and over-analyse the details and seeks to find the discrepancies in ourself, others, and our circumstances. The ego is all about survival and so rather than seeing the Divine Love and the true potential within, it focuses on what it needs to get in order to survive. This kind of focus generates a victim mentality and a belief that you are not good enough, and that the world does not have enough to meet your needs. It's a mindset of lack and restricts our thinking to the limits of what we believe about ourself in that moment. This is not the path to self-acceptance or appreciation of your true value and soul essence.

*If you are focused on what you believe you lack,*
*then how can you truly love and value your soul-being?*

Living in fear is not a measure of True Love. When we live in this way, we close our heart and our Soul to our true potential. We no longer see the Divine light within ourself, nor do we see it in others. We tend to become so focused on the negatives and the discrepancies that we quickly learn to judge ourself or make negative assumptions about others. When we become so focused on the 'dark' it creates a cloud and a barrier to our innate goodness and soul-potential. Our mental focus dampens the way we feel energetically and restricts our connection with our Soul. It eventually affects the way we interact with our world, and what we believe about others. Rather than seeing the possibilities, we take on a more sceptical and narrow perspective of our own capabilities. In essence, our energy becomes a repellent to living, being and attracting love into our reality.

Have you ever felt this way? Do you recall feeling mentally caught up with what's not working in your life? I call this being in a 'funk'. It lowers our energy and creates a mental, spiritual and physical fog. In time it can become a struggle to see the opportunities in life and so we only ever see and speak about the obstacles. We spend more time and energy highlighting what we perceive as flaws in ourself and in our life, instead of noticing the golden gems that lie within.

Earl Nightingale, a renowned expert in the field of personal development, reminds us to first notice the diamonds beneath our feet (in our life and in our being). He retells the true story of a farmer in Africa who did not take the time and effort to see the riches in the land on which he lived. He went seeking those 'diamonds' everywhere else but at home, for the rest of his life. In a state of despair, he eventually threw himself into a river and drowned. Not long after he passed, another farmer discovered that his land was full of the richest diamonds in the world, in their rough and raw state, at the bottom of the river on his property. Whether the story is true or not, it demonstrates that when we are driven by fear and the belief we are not enough, or that we do not have enough love, happiness, or abundance in our life, we are often blinded to the gifts we already have within. We become so obsessed with seeking the answers and riches outside of ourself that we do not recognise that everything we need is within ourself already; if only we take the time to explore and discover the gifts of our true self.

Spend some time remembering the great things that have happened in your life as a result of the choices that you have made. Even if you are out of practice doing this, give yourself time to recall the moments when you have felt excited, elated or mildly buzzed about what you have achieved on your own merit. Enjoy remembering these moments, the big and small ones, they are the foundation of your Soul's growth and have assisted you in being the person you are today. Your life (and previous lives) have provided you with multiple opportunities to learn, all of which have added to your knowledge and your Soul's wisdom, for the purpose of helping you to remember your true Divine and loving self.

When you live a conscious life, and openly love and accept your whole self, you are better able to honour your Soul (or your Higher Self) and live your authentic truth. Being in alignment with your true self creates inner peace and flow. It is much easier to connect or resonate with your life-purpose when your thoughts, feelings and actions are aligned with your Soul. In this space your energy is vibrating more closely with Divine love, enabling you to spiritually grow and connect universally with others.

The barriers to living with True Love are entirely imposed by ourself. When we understand that we create our own reality, which is the summation of our thoughts, feelings and experiences, it is easier to stay on the path towards True Love. Awareness is key, however taking specific action to redirect our energy, attention and intention is the secret to creating more experiences of love, peace and fulfillment in our life. Feelings of self-worth and empowerment come from within. The definition of insanity is doing the same thing over and over again, expecting, wishing and hoping things will turn out differently.

I remember beating myself up mentally, and crying many tears into my pillow, pleading for clarity and wondering why I could not see what I needed to see, or understand what actions I needed to take to alter my circumstances. I could not figure out why things were not turning out for me, given I believed I was putting so much effort into improving myself and pushing for what I believed I wanted and deserved. It did not make sense to me, after all that effort, that I was getting the same results, with no change or improvement, and more of the same feelings of despair and hopelessness. I became exhausted physically and emotionally, and deeply sad, to the point where all the fight and resistance in my mind and my body was used up. And there lay the key!

I was pushing, fighting, and resisting. I had expectations rather than an energy of love and acceptance. My energy was repelling the very things that I wanted to attract into my life. My vibrational essence was a mismatch for what I wanted. Instead of being at peace and trusting that the Universe was there to support me, love me, and provide for me, I was pushing from a place of desperation and a lack of trust. The lack of trust within me was so deep and I could not see this. The result was a strong wall of defence and resistance that was the very thing that was preventing me from creating change or improvement in my life.

The Law of Attraction states that whatever level or frequency of energy we are vibrating in our life (which is a reflection of our focus and our beliefs), will be the same energy that returns to us. Whenever my energy was resistant, I realised that I experienced a lot of resistance and a lack of ease and flow in my life. The lack of trust I had in myself and the belief that my life would be a continual struggle, was reflected back to me with more experiences that felt isolating, difficult, and challenging. The evidence showed up in my relationships, my finances, my job, and in my health. Life became a perpetual cycle of struggle and disappointment. It was all to do with my focus, and where I was placing my attention and intentions.

If we direct our attention to what we fear or what we don't want in our life, then this is all we are going to see and experience. Fear is a lower energy that attracts the same energetic frequency. As our mind becomes filled with fear and doubt, our thoughts create beliefs to justify our thoughts. These beliefs affect the way our body responds to fear, flooding it with stress hormones that eventually impact our physical, mental and emotional well-being. In time our soul becomes dull and blocked, unable to respond to the light and guidance of Spirit. We become engaged in a cycle of fear that affects our mind, our body and our soul.

The moment we shift our attention to notice the light shining between the cracks of the darkness, we can see light pouring through, completely changing what we previously noticed. As we look closer, we begin to see a difference, a contrast that helps us to discern between what feels heavy and what inspires us to lift our focus and our energy to a healthier level. It takes practice to raise our awareness so that we are more conscious of what we are focusing on in our life. Like all things in life, we improve as we consciously practice, practice, practice.

The Law of Attraction is non-negotiable and works from the principle of energetic vibrations. If we want more love in our life, our energetic vibration needs to be one that is loving. If we want more abundance in our life, we must practice generosity of the heart, mind and body. Are we living with more self-compassion? Are we living in a way that is healthy for our mind and body? The energy of allowing creates ease and flow and therefore the energetic vibration that is returned is the same, bringing what you focus on into your present moments.

When I was not receiving the results in my life that I wanted, I felt even more determined to apply more effort. If that didn't work, I would reflect on what I could possibly change and re-apply myself in another way. Sometimes I would achieve my objective, but often the long-term fulfilment I was hoping for eluded me. The reason was due to my efforts not being aligned with what I believed in my mind. We tend to believe that 'effort' should be rewarded. This is not always the case. It's more to do with our energy and what we believe. Even though I was learning valuable lessons, my beliefs and expectations still remained the same as before. I believed that love and abundance would always elude me, and that I was not good enough to have this in my life.

We all have the power to change our own thinking, how we feel about something, and what we choose to do in response, however we don't have the power to change people or circumstances. They are beyond our control. No matter how clever we think we are at influencing others, ultimately everyone has their own free will and they will choose what they believe is best for themselves, regardless of what we want or believe.

My determination to keep pushing or fighting for what I wanted created a wall of resistance to what was really happening in the present moment. I was so focused on attaining what I thought I did not have, and I believed that I needed to keep working harder to get it. My resistant energy was repelling the outcomes I longed for. In other words, my energy and beliefs became a self-fulfilling prophecy. I was keeping myself in a holding pattern, experiencing the same results over and over.

One moment I thought I was moving towards achieving my desired outcomes, and then the next it would slip away from my grip. The constant cycle of push-pull was exhausting me and creating a great deal of anguish and anxiety inside of me. It was frustrating not understanding why things were not working out. I had not yet appreciated that peace would come to me when I let go of the need to control and to understand everything, and instead trust in the love and guidance of the Divine.

Having goals in life is necessary to achieve a degree of progress, and so we must be able to focus our attention and energy on the steps to take to achieve those goals. However, our efforts must be aligned with what we truly believe in our heart, mind and soul. Once we set our intentions, and we take the appropriate actions, we then need to balance this with trusting that the Universe will provide for us (or match our intention and vibration). When we trust that all is working out for us, our part in the equation is to take our foot off the accelerator and stop speeding down the highway in the hope of reaching our destination so fast. It is wise to put ourself on 'cruise control', to allow for Divine timing. Keep your eye on the road ahead, focus on what you want and where you want to go, and *allow* the Universe to be your engine to get you there. Trust the Universe to lovingly provide for you.

Enjoy the journey instead of being in a blistering hurry to have what you want. That need for speed and for instant gratification comes from a lack of trust that all will work out in perfect timing. The Universe will provide what is in alignment with our best interests and our soul-purpose. Everything is already in existence, and what is perfectly matched for you is within your reach. When we attack our life with the energy of desperation, we are reinforcing our belief that we don't already have what we want.

As energetic beings, living in a world of energy, all things are within our field of experience. It is up to us to ask for it to come forth and manifest. Energy does not evaporate, it transforms, moving from one form to another. Everything about our existence is 'energy' and so it's important to not become fixated on 'how' our desire manifests or 'what' it will look like in the physical. We often become despondent and fall into a lack of trust because what we 'see' is not matching what we imagined. However, when we release the resistance the Universe can deliver. Often it will appear in a different way to what we imagined in our visual and physical reality and yet still match our intention and our energetic frequency.

Now is the time to move from 'believing' what you desire will manifest, to 'knowing' it will be so. To 'know' something is true is more powerful than to merely state that you 'believe' something to be true. When you 'know' something, this comes from deep within your Soul. When we learn to live from a place of 'knowing' what is true, we are then resonating at the same vibrational frequency of what is. We are living from our 'soul' that is tapped into the universal consciousness.

## Soul Living

To be in alignment with your soul and to live from the perspective and energy of your soul may require you to change the way you are perceiving your situation. How can you adopt a different view or appreciation of yourself, other people or your situation? What can you believe instead of what you have always believed about yourself? What can you do differently? How does that change the way you feel? Do you notice a change in your energy levels and focus?

Following one of my emotional meltdowns, where I felt like I had hit the brick wall again and not really understood why things were not working out for me, I devised a game for myself. I used my imagination to visualise a different outcome. Instead of re-living, in my mind, an upsetting event and causing myself more pain, anxiety and resentment, I imagined how I could think differently about what happened. I visualized myself responding with more trust and love. Instead of imagining a negative scenario, I asked myself questions that created lighter energy around the situation and a more positive favourable outcome. I imagined myself feeling empowered, peaceful, and accepting of what I could not control, rather than worrying or fretting over what I believed to be a negative outcome. I re-played the situation in my mind and I wrote down alternative ways of thinking and responding. The key was to embrace the process without expectations of myself or others.

At first it felt awkward and I felt a bit like a phoney. I was still recalling the memories and the strong emotions associated with the event. It was difficult to re-live the experience, and to imagine it to be any different. I had developed strong feelings and repetitive negative thoughts that were reinforcing my beliefs. However, I re-scripted the story in a way that enabled me to alter my interpretations and responses at the time. As I continued, I focused on adopting a spirit of curiosity and acceptance. After about 15-20 minutes I felt a distinct change in my emotions and how I was feeling about the original event. I realised how powerful the mind can be in determining our perspective and the reality we create for ourself. I was astonished how I was able to change my response to what had happened. It was not about changing the reality of what took place, it was more about re-examining the meaning I was giving to the situation that unfolded. It became a process of forgiveness and letting go of what had happened.

Sometimes things don't always work out the way we expect, and we won't always understand the reason for this. The best course of action is to let go of that 'dragon' inside that wants to know and understand everything. Within a short space of time I began to feel peace and calm and a new appreciation that everything that happened was less dramatic than I first imagined.

Adopting a more loving and forgiving perspective of myself and the other person helped me to come from a place of trust. This time I felt trust in my own sense of self-worth, and as I grew this feeling inside, I was able to let go of the need to have my own expectations met. I released my fears and realised I did not need to take personally what I could not control outside of myself. I practiced seeing the other person through eyes of love rather than judgment, and this changed everything. There is no need to be 'right' or to prove the other person 'wrong'. It's not about making a point, ignoring the reality of the circumstances or trying to change other people. We are responsible for our own soul journey.

When we live aligned with our Soul we are in-tune with the energetic vibration of Divine Love. From this place we are better able to accept what is, without judgment. It also allows us to see our own truth and love within. As we embrace our own uniqueness it is far easier to have love for oneself and to value our true self. Emotional maturity is when we can be comfortable in our own skin, accepting of all of ourself, feeling grounded and connected with who we are, rather than constantly focusing on our perceived imperfections. Life will offer up storms on a regular basis, but the degree to which we are grounded will reflect our emotional growth and our ability to have trust and belief in ourself. Being able to bend and flex when we feel our sense of self-worth is being challenged means we are on the road toward True Love.

## Intuition versus The Thinking Mind

Our soul is our spiritual core that encompasses all that we feel and spiritually know, from where wisdom resides and love flows. The soul is where Divine love dwells, and from where our dreams and inspiration flow. It is our connection to Spirit. If we are to live a soul-filled life, then we need to learn to listen to our Soul's wisdom. We do this by tuning into our intuition (our Higher Self), or what some refer to as their inner voice or their gut feelings.

Sometimes it's difficult to know the difference between our intuition and the thoughts that occupy our mind. In our busy lives it's common to be preoccupied by our thoughts, as we either focus on our mental list of 'to-dos', or the next problem to solve, or perhaps we may be busy pondering over some 'what-if' scenarios in our mind.

Our mind is where we think and rationalize our experiences. It's where we process, analyse and categorize our version of reality in order to make sense of it. It's how we make necessary decisions that help us to take action and move forward. In any given day we are capable of having an average of 60,000 thoughts per day. Our mind is where we store recurring thoughts that make up our belief system about who we are, other people and our world. Our belief system is what drives our behaviour and influences our choices and decisions that ultimately create our reality.

Our mind helps us to think, plan and decide what action to take that will lead us toward our goals and dreams. The power of the mind is so great that it can enable us to dream big, take risks and achieve incredible heights. However, it also has the power to dis-able us and create a reality that will have us believe we are limited and that our world is one in which we must survive in order to live. When we let the mind control our very being, we are not operating to our full potential.

However, when we become more consciously aware and in-tune with our intuition, we can communicate with our Soul or Higher Self. Our Soul speaks to us through our intuition, synchronicities, and Divine signs in order to remind us of the wisdom we have attained over this lifetime and from previous lives. It's this wisdom that helps us to be better informed, so our decisions can more appropriately guide us toward the path of spiritual truth and Divine Love. The contrasts we experience from our physical life and the limitations of our physical being create a tangible canvas from which our Soul can deliver the truth as we need to hear it, for the purpose of our spiritual growth and happiness.

To begin, we need to firstly connect with our body. It is not possible for our body, mind, and spirit to be separated, even though we often behave as if this is true. Our mind is very busy being 'busy', processing, interpreting and problem solving. Its influence is powerful enough to affect our emotions to induce peace or anxiety, to which our body responds by producing chemicals and hormones in our body. The mind is that aspect of our brain that receives information from our external world and then gives meaning to what we perceive based on this information and past experiences.

Our intuition however is the *knowing* we have that is given to us by Spirit, facilitated by all of our senses, and informed by our Higher Self or our Soul. The combination of all three aspects of our being (spirit, mind and body), creates our energetic vibration, or our energetic body. This is the energy that emanates from our beliefs, our focus and our souls' intentions.

We are all made of pure energy. Our body is the container and a vehicle where energy flows, enabling us to connect our mind with our emotional body and spiritual essence. Our body is necessary for us to learn. It enables us to experience spiritual communication and soul lessons through our physical senses and the physical experience of pain and sadness and as well as pleasure and joy.

In the body, our chakras, or system of energy centres, are focal points of swirling energy that flow from the base of our spine (Root Chakra) to the top of our head (Crown Chakra). Each chakra is connected to our emotional body and has a specific function, indicating our state of physical, mental and emotional well-being. If the energy in each chakra is flowing well, we are likely to be feeling healthy and stable in our mind and emotions. However, when we are experiencing physical, mental or emotional challenges, our energy centres may not be flowing well, indicating dis-ease in the body or mind. *(see chapter 7)*.

In order to tune in to our intuition it's important to integrate all aspects of our being (mind, body, spirit).

### An Exercise for tuning into your mind, body and spirit:

- We begin by stilling the *mind* with quiet meditation and some relaxed deep breathing.
- Next, relax the *body*, by closing your eyes and tune in to your Solar Plexus (the third main chakra) that is located over the stomach area. If it helps, place your hand over your stomach. This is your power centre, where we often associate feelings of inner strength and courage, or feelings of powerlessness and anxiety, like the feeling of butterflies in the stomach.

- Notice what you feel or sense in your Solar Plexus. Does the energy feel relaxed or does it feel jittery and unstable? Sit with it for a moment until you can recognise the feeling.
- Ask your body what it would like to tell you.
- You can do the same by connecting to your heart. Place your hand on your heart to help make the physical connection, close your eyes, and ask yourself - What does my heart want to tell me?

If there was no mind to get in your way, no 'ifs', 'shoulds' or 'maybes', what would your heart say to you? Tune in to what your body is telling you about your emotions. Your feelings will point to what your Soul is whispering to you.

- Still the mind and become the Observer. Listen from your heart, which is the physical connection to your soul-being.

The mind is helpful and can provide us with facts we have learned, however it will not be able to assist you with accessing higher wisdom, the guidance we receive from Source (God) for when we cannot humanly know or predict outcomes. Our Soul has the benefit of being able to connect to a universal knowledge that is always there to help and guide us along the path that is most beneficial to our well-being.

I've often been asked, 'How do I know if it's my mind or my soul speaking to me?' Well, with practice you do learn the difference. Our intuition is easy to recognise as that inner voice, sense or knowing that gives you a deep feeling within that is unmistakable, even when you don't have all the facts. You will know what you are feeling is true when you have a sense of peace about the message you are receiving. That is, there is no confusion or doubt, the message is clear. I also find that my body will give me very accurate feedback. If there is tension or general dis-ease in my body, I know that I'm not listening to my intuition or Higher Self.

When we are still developing the skill of tuning into our intuition, we may doubt what we are sensing. It takes practice, and then more practice. It is good to trust what you are sensing. There is no need to fear you are getting it wrong. As we pay more attention to our inner voice, we become better at hitting the mark. When you tune in to your intuition, go with that first 'knowing' or 'gut instinct'. When we engage the enquiring mind, our ego tends to get in the way, and that's when we experience doubts, which then trigger our emotions, causing us to pull away from our first 'knowing' and move towards what the ego desires - the 'shiny silver balls' that we want in life - the safety, the security, the preferences the mind develops. We can recognise this as the difference between what we know is in our best interests, and what we just 'want' to have or feel right now.

When we operate only from our mind we tend to over-think or analyse what we are perceiving. Usually our mind will begin to question what we are sensing (feeling, seeing, hearing) and then our ego comes into play. The purpose of the ego is to selfishly protect us and ensure our survival. What that means is, it will lower our vibration to that of a 'survival mentality'. Our choices then become more focused on what we think we need in that moment (food, water, money, sex, material things, power, control etc). As a result, we may lean towards justifying what we want in order to satisfy the mind, rather than listen to and trust our intuition.

When we choose to only listen to our mind, our ego will take us down a path that distracts us from hearing our Soul, and the messages, lessons and opportunities that are placed before us for our soul growth. When your thoughts become more about your survival, or comparison with others, it leads to feelings of isolation and separation. Very soon you are feeling confused, doubtful and unsettled. If you find you are looping in your thoughts, or oscillating between two sides of the fence, then this is your mind speaking to you. Remember, the ego-mind focuses on your survival and can only provide you with the information it has already received, and what you perceive is your reality. Your intuition is the communication channel you have with your Higher Self that enables you to access your inner wisdom gained from past life lessons and the insights and guidance that come from God, Source, the Universe and the Divine angels in the present moment.

When you become more accustomed to tuning in to your intuition, it will assist you to make more informed decisions, and create more peace and certainty in your life, bringing you outcomes that will better serve you. The best way to live a 'soul-life' is to learn to do this every time you make a choice or decision. Be in the habit of pausing and reflecting, even momentarily, to listen to your body and your Higher Self before you take action. Ask yourself, 'how do I feel about this?' Step out of your mind for a moment and check in with how you are feeling and what you are sensing. You can also check-in with your spirit guides for guidance on anything.

Do you recall those moments in your life when you have a niggling feeling about something, but because you have really wanted to do something different you have ignored that recurring thought or inner nudge? Later, you realise you should have listened to your inner voice, as it was guiding you towards the better outcome and you would not have wasted your time or energy with a poor choice. We have all done it countless times. Remember, if you are feeling the need to hide, ignore the signs, or if there is any element of confusion around your decision to move forward, it's usually a good idea to pay attention and reassess your course of action.

They key is to learn to trust and listen to your intuition and know that it is there to help you. You know what they say, the more you exercise the muscle, the stronger you become. The more you develop the habit and learn to trust your intuition the more often you will make wise decisions easily, bringing outcomes that will best serve you.

When we live a 'soul-life' we can expect to experience a heightened sense of awareness because we are living a more conscious life, tapped into the Divine Source (the Holy Spirit) and our Higher Self that is there to guide us toward the path of True Love and wisdom every day. When we are connected to Spirit, we are able to expand our awareness and our ability to discern True Love. You may have experienced this during your life when you have felt like everything is in 'flow' and that all things, situations, people and opportunities appear to be synchronizing perfectly for your benefit. This is when we are tuned into Source and the collective soul wisdom.

When we experience a lot of conflict, confusion and lack of clarity, it's a sure sign we are not in flow and we have let our mind take over. As a result, it drowns out our inner voice and connection to Spirit. Conflict and confusion that reigns in our reality means we are out of sync with ourself and we're not living according to our values, what we know to be true, and what is in our best interest.

When you choose to live from your Soul, you are making a conscious choice to live a life that is from the experience and guidance of your Higher Self. When we are tuned into the living and creative Source we can expect to live a life that is more peaceful, a life that is designed to help us grow in a way where we can experience great joy and abundance.

## Dancing in the Garden of your Soul

If you are living a soul-life, then you are planting seeds and tapping into your creativity to produce something amazing. That 'something' is what you love to do. That's why you are here, to live your soul-purpose. To do what lights you up and inspires you. It doesn't matter what it is, so long as it is something that you feel passionate about. Just the thought of spending time doing your favourite thing is enough to switch on your energy and focus to what gives you joy.

When we are doing what we love, other people notice and sense this, because our energy and vibration is lifted up and we become an attractive light. Have you noticed that when you are absorbed in your favourite hobby or activity, or when you are sharing this with your friends and colleagues, others see you glowing and radiating? You may even receive comments about how well you look. Why is this? When we are happy and living from our soul-purpose, this energy becomes healing and extraordinarily powerful. It affects our health, our relationships, and our ability to perform well.

In the search for peace and happiness, many people get caught up believing that happiness will come when we have enough money, or when we have the loving relationship we desire, or when our health improves, and so on. Come on, admit it. How many times have you said to yourself, life will be so much better when the bank account is full, or when you have someone in your life to love and who loves you?

It is true, having money to live on so we are feeling comfortable and not in deprivation certainly goes towards helping us feel safe, secure and happy. Having the companionship of someone who loves us is also wonderful. However, we are unlikely to attract these things into our life if we are not already loving who we are and living a soul-filled life.

We are energetic beings and so whatever level of energetic frequency we are vibrating into the Universe, is what we will attract toward us. So, if we are feeling in a state of need or lack, and our self-esteem is low, then our energetic vibration will also be low. We are not likely to attract abundance or a loving healthy relationship into our reality. Nor are we in the frame of mind to look for the love and fulfilment within. The moment we are focused on what we don't have we become externally focused, expecting the world to fulfil our need for love, happiness, and security.

So, the key is to: *Love who you are and create your own state of joy and happiness.* In every moment of your life, live it in a way where you are connected to Source, to all that is vibrating the loving energy that you wish to experience in your life. It is as simple as pausing to notice what you are grateful for in your life. It takes practice, however it's in the small every day moments that count. Say and do only what feels loving, joyful and life-affirming. Appreciate your uniqueness, your gifts, and your talents. Live a life where you notice the blessings around you as much as possible. Live with thanks and gratitude in your heart, and then you will have little or no room left for self-pity, bitterness or anger.

Have you reminded yourself today how wonderful you are? You don't have to wait for someone else to tell you. You can speak loving words to yourself and do loving things that uplift your spirit and make you feel good. You are deserving of love, so why not give it to yourself? As you love yourself you raise your vibration and life begins to mirror back to you the same loving energy.

Living a soul-life is living in your authentic truth, and with Divine Truth as your soul-guide. It's living openly, passionately and honestly, as your true self and not the self you have become accustomed to presenting to the rest of the world. Are you constantly in fear of not measuring up, not looking well presented, or failing at the next task at hand? Do you spend too long worrying about whether your efforts are good enough compared to the next person, or whether you have worn the right clothes, or if you appear to fit the criteria for belonging in the team or crowd? Just be yourself and you will discover that people will see the real you and be attracted to your authenticity. Be your unique individual self and love who you are. Why not? You can't be anyone else, so enjoy who you are.

When we 'try too hard' to be or do something that is not really who we are at our core, we come across as inauthentic, and it's not attractive or attracting. We develop a 'push' energy that seeks to convince others, or to obtain what we believe we do not have. This is a low vibrational energy that has the effect of repelling others and whatever is available to come into our experience. As a result, we push away the very things we would like to experience in our life because we are not being our true self. This is something to rejoice about, because you don't have to work hard at being, doing or saying anything in order to live a life of joy and abundance. How great is that?

*You just need to be you.*

Life is precious and so rather than waste time trying to be someone you are not, pour more love and acceptance into enjoying being you. Dance in the garden of your Soul and enjoy what is wonderful right now. To believe you must chase your dreams means you are constantly giving the Universe and yourself the message that there is never enough, and that *you* are not enough. Relax. We only ever have this 'now' moment. When we understand the rich depth of appreciating what is occurring in our life at this moment, we realise that our experiences are everything we need right now. Raising your vibration through love for yourself and others is the only way to attract more abundance into your life. So, dance in the garden of your Soul, and enjoy what is there for you to experience today.

## *Dance in the garden of your Soul*

Celebrate who you are. Enjoy the gifts that you were born with, and if anything, spend more time and energy developing these so that you are living the greatest version of your true self. Why would you want to work so hard in your life at something that does not give you pleasure, all for the illusion that someday it will bring you love and happiness?

Why not ask yourself - *What* do I want to do? *Why* do I want to do that? What will it give me? It may help you better understand who you are and what you want in life. When we answer these questions, we usually express what is unique to ourself, our skills, interests, and values. If we keep following that line of thought most people come to the realization that ultimately they want to experience joy, peace and love in their life, which comes from a sense of fulfilment when we are doing what inspires us the most.

To live a soul-life it is helpful to go within and get to know yourself more intimately. Seek to know more clearly your preferences in life, what drives you, what excites you, and what you desire to achieve. Free yourself from the expectation that there is something huge you must achieve in life. What you desire may simply be to love being you every day and to enjoy the simple things in life, as your true authentic self. The more you allow yourself to reflect from your heart-space, without judgment, you will come to see, feel and know more clearly what resonates with you, and what you know you are here to learn in this life-time.

Reflecting on your soul-journey and what you are here to learn may not necessarily be at the forefront of your thinking. We have a tendency to get caught up in the day-to-day busyness of our life, of short-term thinking and problem solving. The treadmill of life keeps us going around and around with little reflection on where we are going or what we are doing, or even why we are doing it. Whether we are racing through our days or trudging along, we often avoid any kind of deeper reflection upon our choices until we are confronted by a significant change or disruption. It could be the loss of a job, a relationship breakdown, an illness, financial loss, or the death of someone close. Our initial response to significant change is likely to be a physical one that is directed toward our physical survival. However, it's common to stop there and miss the opportunity for a deeper insight into how we are living our life and why we are making the same choices.

Contrasting situations usually present themselves when we have something to learn. When we look into the waters to see our reflection, what do we see? Pain and suffering, self-absorption, a lack of love for ourself? Or do we see someone who is smiling back and enjoying the fullness of our being – the shining light as well as our shadows. When we realise we are more than our physical life, that we are spiritual-beings having physical experiences, we can see that our life is a landscape on which we learn and grow. The focus of our soul-journey then becomes more meaningful and relevant to the way we live.

Why would you want to waste precious time in your life doing things that are not aligned with who you are, or are not moving you in the direction of your soul's growth? To grow the garden of your soul, plant excellent seeds and nurture what will benefit your soul's growth in love, wisdom and spiritual abundance. Would you plant tomato seeds and expect to reap zucchinis? Would you plant an apple tree and expect it to give you mangos? Or would you plant daisies and expect to grow beautiful roses? With everything we do to nurture and grow the garden of our spiritual life, we will benefit from and reap a harvest in our physical life. As you take care of and nurture your physical, emotional and mental well-being, you are growing in spiritual maturity, love and wisdom.

If you have not spent much time in your life understanding what it is you truly love, now is the time to start. Take that time to pause, reflect and tune in to your Soul. Listen to your inner voice – it's not that far away. Practice by becoming more mindful and observant in your life. Hop off the fast-paced runway that we are told is the only way to get ahead and succeed. It's causing you to become numb to your Soul.

The faster we run in our life the more disconnected we become from our true self and our soul-purpose.

Do you feel caught up in the drama of other people's lives? Have you been giving your power away too often to the demands of work and other people? When was the last time you took time out to 'chill', go for a walk, or sit in a park and notice all that is happening in the world around you and within you?

One of the best ways to begin to reconnect with your true self is to spend time in nature. For those who spend most of their working week in the office or indoors, it can be easy to forget how healing and uplifting it is to be in nature. Nature is where we can return to the Source of Divine energy. Being outdoors with a bit of sunshine, fresh air and exposure to trees, the sea, mountain air or being close to birds and animals will rapidly restore your energy and sense of well-being. It can help to clear the cobwebs of our busy mind and relieve us of the build-up of toxic energy of stress and the pressure that we tend to hold within our body. As you feel the tension melt away, nature's energy will assist you to raise your vibration and replenish your body and soul.

The next step is to take time to do nothing other than soak in all that goodness and the living prana (chi or uplifting energy). Sit or walk mindfully, breathe and release. What do you notice around you? What are you feeling within you? Don't think too much, just be observant and then let the thoughts come and go. In time you will notice that your senses become heightened or more sensitized. Your sense of smell, sight, hearing and touch will become more alert.

When we are in nature it reminds us that we are also of the same energy, and that we are connected to all that is living. Spend as much time as you can to feel this and soak it into your being. If you have just 20 minutes in the morning before work, go sit in the garden or go for a slow walk. Or, take some time to move from your desk at lunch and enjoy the fresh air outside. Whatever you choose, do it mindfully, and preferably on your own so that you are not distracted. Enjoy the benefits of being still in your mind. As we slow down our physical body, we also slow down our mental activity and open ourselves to being more consciously aware.

If you want to live a soul-life you need to value your well-being and take the time to 'be' with yourself. You are important. If you are constantly trying to cram everything into your day and your life, you are missing opportunities to be present. When we are addicted to being busy, or in constant communication with other people, we are living in a way where we have the volume up so loud that we can't hear anything else. Our mind becomes so full that we suffer from becoming over stimulated energetically or completely numb. Our bodies respond by going into shock or paralysis, and then our health begins to deteriorate. That's why we end up with health problems after being in a state of hyper-drive for so long. We become conditioned (or addicted) to the fast-paced life that we don't even notice how fast we are going or the effect it is having on us physically, mentally and emotionally. Left unchecked it results in dis-ease in our mind and our body.

Living a soul-life requires us to listen to our Soul, and to love and value who we are. This may mean we need to make some changes and adjustments in our life so that we are living happier and healthier lives. How well do you know yourself? If you are feeling disconnected and out of sync with the real you, don't worry, we have all done this - some of us for long periods of time, others perhaps at various stages in life. It's easy to get caught up with our "to-do's" and our responsibilities. Sometimes we can become so conditioned to living unconsciously and responding only to our "daily to-do list" and the agendas of other people, that we forget who we are and what we really want to experience and achieve in our own life.

When those niggling feelings of dis-ease start to show up, this is a sign you need to stop and reflect. Ask yourself if what you are doing is serving you well? Is it helping you to achieve what you truly love? Is it reflective of what you value in life or are you making compromises for the sake of other people? Is it taking you toward happiness and your soul-purpose in this life? Living more consciously aware of our choices helps us to feel connected with Spirit and with our Soul, so we can enjoy the benefits of living a life of purpose, growing in wisdom and making a difference to the lives of others.

We are all teachers through the example of our own life and our soul lessons become a source of wisdom and knowledge we can share with others. Even when we miss the mark in our life, this is helpful to our soul's growth, the collective wisdom and the soul-growth of others. As we apply what we learn through our words, our actions and our energy, it develops our spiritual maturity and it also has a ripple effect for others, even when we are not aware of it.

When we know what makes our heart sing and truly inspires us, this can be the fuel to living our soul-purpose and feeling the most fulfilled in our life. One day I was watching my daughter in her Salsa dance class. She had been taking lessons for about six months and was very fluid and adept on the dance floor. It was my first time seeing her dance, and it was inspiring. It reminded me how much I love to move and dance as well. For my daughter, I could see that dancing was her way of expressing the essence of her soul-being.

At first it took Sasha and her dance partner a while to get into the groove of the music and allow it to flow through them. They were stuck in their heads, over-analysing the steps and the sequence of the dance routine. They made mistakes with their steps, their timing was out of sync, and it was looking and feeling a bit awkward. However, as they began to surrender and feel their way with the rhythm of the music, they began to move in synchronicity with each other. Before long they were in-tune with each other's body, and the flow and energy of the music. Their body language and the expressions on their face said it all. They were experiencing synchronicity and harmony as they freely expressed themselves and moved effortlessly across the dance floor.

This is what it feels like when we are doing what we love and when we are in-tune with our Soul and our life-purpose. There is no thinking required when we are tapping into the Universal energy of creation and Divine Love. It's all about 'being' in flow.

# 18
## Making a Difference

A personal awakening and a reconnection with our Soul is like coming back home to our authentic self. It's the recognition of our true nature and feeling at one with ourself. When I have experienced that inner contentment, and the feeling of being spiritually at home, I experience intense joy in my Soul. I feel in harmony with the Universe. When I have lovingly tended to the garden of my soul, I have nurtured and cared for my mental and physical health, my need for social connection, and my desire to express my creativity. I have a loving acceptance and appreciation of who I am, and I know how to return to feeling at peace within the core of my being, regardless of external challenges, frustrations, moments of stress, fear or doubt.

Living a soulful life is not necessarily staying in a state of constant bliss. It is knowing how to live authentically, and with unconditional love for ourself and others, despite the ups and downs of life. As we spiritually mature, we become more adept at stepping back from the drama in the lives of others, and the need to fix other people, or to rescue the world. We now have more clarity and wisdom as to who we are individually and collectively. There is a deep inner knowing of our spiritual connection with the Divine and our Soul's greater purpose.

Regardless of our background, qualifications, and life experiences, we all desire to experience greater love. As we develop more love for ourself, it becomes like a seed that grows, an expanding energy that radiates from our being, creating a fullness in our soul that is ready to be shared with others. A desire to serve becomes an extension of our Soul's purpose, which is to live with unconditional Divine Love.

If we choose to do nothing other than live our life as our true authentic self, with unconditional love for ourself and others, our energetic vibration would be enough to make a massive difference in this lifetime and in this world. The conscious and unconscious ripple effect of the power of love, lived unconditionally, is more powerful than words or deeds.

As we grow in real love there is an in-spir-ation (in-spirit-action) that expands from within us. Spirit inspires us to expand and by the nature of Divine Love, we experience the inner desire to share and grow in soul-love. When we grow in love, knowledge and wisdom, it is impossible to sleep through our existence. Love is always a choice, and when we say 'yes', we allow love to expand by nurturing our soul-being. We can then use our talents and gifts to help others along the path of their soul-journey.

Travelling the path of our soul-journey is about learning the art of mindful loving, and this requires us to be stretched and uncomfortable at times, so that we can experience the joys of love that follow. As we reach great heights of self-awareness and universal consciousness, we can at first feel overwhelmed and out of our depth in terms of what to think, feel or do next. Feeling dissatisfaction or being out-of-sync is actually a good sign, as it provides clarity for what is not working and points the way toward our soul's path. It's a helpful reminder to re-adjust our thoughts and re-language our self-talk so we can elicit more uplifting emotions and raise our energetic vibration. In this way we can be assured we are moving towards greater love.

The opposite of mindful loving is being driven by our ego. Our ego desires certainty and security and is driven by fear and doubt when this is threatened. We feel the egoic tendencies arise in us when we have the insatiable urge to have explicit instructions on how and what to do next, and exactly how to achieve happiness, success and love. We maintain expectations of ourself and others according to the rules and conditions we hold in order to satisfy our ego's desire for certainty. However, the way towards True Love is only through humility, compassion, listening to our heart and trusting the guidance of God and our Higher Self.

When left unchecked, our ego will cause us to suffer from what Buddhism calls the 'Six Poisons':

1. Pride 2. Envy 3. Desire 4. Greed 5. Ignorance and 6. Aggression

However, if we practice the art of humility, joy, satisfaction, generosity, the will and commitment to learn, and compassion for ourself and others, we can move closer to being mindfully loving. When we learn to let go the habits of the ego - fear, holding on, censure, control, and attachment to the outcome, we can free ourself of suffering, and stop causing the suffering of others.

*The ego is defensive and aims to interfere*
*with our attempt at being present.*

A life that is not fulfilling its soul-purpose is a life that has no point or value, it is simply existing. Why wait for the day when it's time to transition from the physical to the spiritual and return home before you ask yourself, 'What has been the point of it all?' The purpose of our physical life is to learn and grow in wisdom and love. More specifically, despite our self-focus and our personal challenges, our goal is to *be* the experience of love, and this in turn becomes our loving service to others.

Love within grows when we choose to fill the space inside with gratitude, appreciation and compassion for ourself. As we become more mindful of how we think and what we choose to say, we begin to radiate more love and a genuine positivity that is noticed firstly by our energy and what others sense when they are in our presence. This is our most powerful way of being effective through love. As we grow in love this naturally leads to a desire to share through the active service of being, giving and receiving Love. Love cannot exist on its own, in isolation.

## Heart and Soul Giving

When you are living, doing and being your natural and authentic self and loving all of who you are, you are at your most potent and empowered state of being. There is a reason for this. You are now in a state of being the most effective teacher and vibrational being to be of service to others who are also experiencing their own version of their soul's journey.

When we tune in to living a life that is aligned with our true nature and authentic way of being, we gravitate towards doing what we really love. This is what we are designed to do in this life, as a means of not only expanding our own growth, but as a resource to help others along the way. We each find our niche by exploring our strengths, talents and skills, and utilize these in our careers, jobs, business, family-life, in our relationships and in our hobbies. Deep down, when we listen to our heart, we know what we love doing, and if you are not doing what you love, then you know it's time to reassess so that you don't veer from your life's purpose.

When we are doing what we love, we are in the best state to serve others and contribute to the soul growth of fellow human beings. To serve other people is never about giving away something to the detriment of your well-being. This can only occur if your perspective is one of separation and your belief is that you must protect and hold on to what you perceive to be yours.

Giving from the heart is about valuing the gift that you offer and knowing that love and service flows freely through equanimity, or equal exchange. It's not that we give only to receive. When we genuinely give for the purpose of sharing and being of service, the Universe rewards by providing something of equal value to us in return. If our focus on giving is anything other than genuine love, then our gift of service becomes a transactional currency. Real service is sharing through the gift of what you know and do with ease, passion and dedication. It's about unconditional love.

Giving with a spirit that fears we will deplete our own reserves or that we will miss out on something of value, is to give conditionally. If we find ourself caught up with this mentality, we are likely to cause ourself unnecessary suffering. What we constantly focus on is what we will end up attracting more of into our life. If we 'give' to others with the concern about the cost to ourself, then we are not coming from a spirit of unconditional love and service. This applies to anything of monetary value, our time, personal resources and our energy. Giving with fear not only nullifies the gift, it creates a deficit in our being - mentally, physically, emotionally and spiritually.

If we give in order to control someone so that they become dependent upon us, or feel indebted to us, this is a form of emotional blackmail or manipulation. Have you experienced this in your life? Perhaps you have been on the receiving end of this kind of giving from a family member or work colleague. It can create feelings of guilt because we swing between feeling grateful for the gift but resentful for the attempted control or manipulation from the other person. In other words, the gift (of time, money, energy, or resources) is given with conditions. This form of giving can develop into abusive relating that is often difficult at first to discern, especially when you are unable to clearly define your own boundaries and personal value. Conditional giving soon results in feelings of resentment or entitlement by those who are on the receiving end.

Sometimes we can fall into this pattern of conditional giving, and not realise that our giving has become a form of control of someone we care about. When we are not fulfilled, or we have not yet developed independence and stability in our own life, we can seek to gain the support of others, or have our needs met by giving conditionally. We may give in order to receive recognition, attention, affection, or appreciation. Have you given your time or energy to someone and then expected they return the favour in a particular way or in a certain timeframe? This is conditional giving and it is a form of control. When we fall into this trap, we are not giving freely, nor are we respecting another person's time, space or personal preferences. True Love is allowing others to receive by choice, in their own time and in their own way without expectation for anything in return. This can be difficult to learn because human nature is so often driven by our ego when left unchecked. Our ego is demanding and wants what it wants, when it wants it, with little regard for other people.

We have all done this, and possibly we are daily perpetrators of giving in expectation of return. Have you noticed your own attitude or what you have complained about when your own expectations have not been met? Have you willingly given of your time and energy but felt frustrated when you have not been thanked, or received compensation of some kind?

Sometimes we can slip into the mindset of entitlement, telling ourself that we deserve this or that for our time and service. Have you caught yourself complaining to a friend that you are incensed that you did not receive a phone call, invitation, or gift of time or resources of equal value in return for your effort or service? Have you heard yourself justify your expectation of receiving because of your commitment to others, your job position or status? Our attitude in the art of giving and being of service is what makes the difference between giving from the heart and giving in order to gain.

When we live in flow in our life, loving and giving without conditions, then we create an equal exchange of energy for giving and receiving. Knowing we are all connected reminds us that there is never a loss in our life, only an exchange of energy in the form of knowledge, love, and wisdom. The vehicle of that exchange is what we do in life, through our business, career, and our interactions with others. When we focus on a life of service, it is not about competition (which seeks to separate, divide and over-power), it's about collaborating with others and giving through these interactions and interrelations with others. We always have the choice and opportunity to show love and be more loving. In so doing, we are teaching, leading and guiding by our own example.

Living a life of service is about making a difference, in a way that brings growth and guides others down the path to greater love, wisdom and understanding. We may debate that the purpose to life is about growing our skills, knowledge, intelligence, wealth, position or power. All of these things are outcomes from what we do and focus on. However, they are also the vehicles for us to make a difference in this world. They become the attributes of our landscape from which we operate to demonstrate love and soul growth. As human beings we are vibrant, energetic, complex and varied. This is what helps us to live in our physical reality and to thereby grow spiritually.

In all that we are doing, and in all that we are being, we are consciously (or unconsciously) desiring to move and expand towards greater love. We express this through what we enjoy in life, through the satisfaction and fulfilment of our business, the relationships with our family, friends or partner, through our creative pursuits, and our contribution to the lives of others. Most of all, we are making a difference when we are being our own version of ourself, not some other model or concept that someone else has desired. When we are being our unique and authentic self, that's when we shine the most. There is no perfect or right way of being, regardless of how our friends may wish to influence us or what business protocol demands from us. If we are trying to fit ourself into someone else's mould, idea or agenda, then we will fail at being our true self.

When we live life from our 'whole' self, rather than from what we perceive to be our fragmented parts of what we like or dislike, then we are loving ourself unconditionally. It's essential to recognise that there is only one 'you' and when you are being the best version of you, living to your personal truth, you are naturally drawn to appreciate all aspects of your being, and doing more of what you love in life. We are more powerful and effective when we live in this way. When we love and accept all of our being we are most effective in making a difference in our own life and in the lives of others simply through being ourself. The power is in our loving and authentic energy that is felt by others.

Did you know our energy and our silent intentions are received by others before we even open our mouth? Whilst what we do in life goes a long way towards making a difference in this world, and our words are powerful and effective for sharing knowledge and wisdom, it is our energetic vibration that is more influential and ultimately has the greatest effect when making a difference. We are energetic vibrational beings and so whether our energy or vibration is low or high, it is always felt and noticed first before our words or our actions have an effect. Have you noticed how animals sense your energy? They know if you are friendly or if you are a potential threat, even before you have said anything or motioned to engage with them? They will sense whether you feel calm, friendly, hesitant or nervous. Babies and children are the same, in that they can sense when their parents are relaxed, or when they are stressed. They will respond to the energy they feel around them.

Our ability to sense the energy of others is an essential part of being human since there are obvious benefits for our safety, whether it is our physical or emotional safety. Managing our own energy becomes a powerful way to live intentionally and to communicate with others.

When we seek to make a difference in life, it's important to focus on our own life first. This may sound a little selfish, and it some ways it is, but it's not with the intention to take away from others. When we learn to be responsible in our own life and develop the awareness and skills for managing our own energy, we are better stewards of Divine Love and service for others. To adopt an attitude of being a 'caped crusader' on a mission to serve and save the world, or to become a martyr for the sake of others is somewhat naïve. In our enthusiasm to be loving we can easily lose sight of the importance of firstly managing our own life.

Your focus and intention for your life creates an energy that is radiated and communicated outwards to the Universe, which responds to your vibration. This is how we manifest or attract what we truly love into our life. When we do what we love and focus on being in tune with our soul, we raise our vibration. Our physical and emotional body responds with producing 'feel-good' hormones, and our mental focus is lifted. Recognising we are physical, mental, emotional and spiritual beings is the way to live life fully and in a way that will attract more of what we want in life. When we are living our life with a little 'spice' then we are the most effective for living our soul-purpose, and more effective and influential for assisting others on their soul-journey.

As spiritual beings living a physical existence, we are given many life-times so that we have opportunities to grow more deeply in love, for this is our Divine nature and design. The duality and contrasts of our physical life is the landscape, the canvas and the vehicle from which we experience the joys and sorrows, the challenges and achievements. All of which are ways for our soul to be stretched, strengthened, opened and expanded for the purpose of love.

With every side step I make, when I've drifted back into old patterns, I become more adept at course correcting and finding my way back onto the path toward unconditional love more easily. My awareness has increased, and so has compassion for myself. It is not possible to go through life without challenges and without faltering, but that's how I know I'm making progress and growing in love and wisdom. I am more grateful these days, and with a deeper level of contentment, acceptance and openness, rather than feeling fearful and uncertain about everything.

I recognise that my ability to be less attached to people or specific outcomes means I have moved closer to feeling love and being love. When we know we are less affected by what other people say or do, or how situations turn out, it means we are living life on our terms, managing our thoughts and our emotions, rather than believing our happiness and sense of fulfillment must come from others. As I focus more on seeing the love in others, and the light of their soul, I realise that maintaining a perspective that is loving rather than judgmental means I encounter my world with curiosity and compassion.

As we grow in love and compassion so does our vibration and this in turn increases our energetic field and our ability to recognise our soul-connection with others. Love attracts more love. When our vibration lifts and our heart expands, our soul reaches out far and wide like a warm breeze or the rays of the sun. We become a magnet for more love, attracting positive and uplifting vibrations, increased abundance and creativity into our experience.

*Love always makes a difference.*

Love withheld however, cannot be shared or be a blessing to ourself or to others. A beautiful bird in a cage can be admired for the colour of its feathers and its uplifting song. However, its beauty can only be seen and heard by a few within its radius. Birds that are free to fly in the sky and make homes in the trees can be enjoyed by many. Their song and their beauty are felt by all those who choose to notice. Their perspective is limitless, their freedom unbound.

Set yourself free from the cage you imprison yourself within. Be all that you can be and enjoy the liberation that is yours to experience. Your freedom emanates first from your Soul and is possible only with a heart and mind of love. Your body is the gift you have been given to fully experience the wonders of love, and a life that is lived from a soul perspective. Embrace all of you my friend and know that this moment is yours - to dream, to create, to learn, to grow and to be you in all of your magnificence.

*Go with love*
*as your soul journey continues*

Namaste

Printed in the United States
By Bookmasters

Printed in the United States
By Bookmasters